MW01268797

The
WINDBLOWN
GIRL

The Windblown Girl is bold and brave, revealing risks (even rewards) of "forbidden love." The author is an effective storyteller because she is authentic and compelling in relating her experience. Highly recommend!

Carolyn Curtis, Author/Editor
Women and C.S. Lewis: What His Life and Literature Reveal for Today's Culture

When your life is such a mess that you think you'll never straighten it out, there's hope. As you read Patti Townley-Covert's *The Windblown Girl*, you'll see how so much of her story reflects your own. And, as she finds Truth, Love, and Peace, so will you.

Colleen Myers, Rave Mom
Co-founder of PLUR Life Ministries

Jesus changes lives—but not every part in an instant. *The Windblown Girl*, Patti Townley-Covert's riveting memoir, chronicles the struggles of love and sex and relationship challenges experienced by a woman growing into her new identity. I couldn't put it down.

Sandra Glahn, award-winning author

The Windblown Girl is a love story within a love story within a love story. Patti shares deeply personal experiences about romance, intrigue, temptation, and heartbreak—some of it so surprising that most of us could only imagine being in her shoes—and yet she is telling MY story, and yours. It is a story about redemption and healing, about faith and hope, with a happy ending that every single one of us can choose for ourselves. This is no vapid, sensational tell-all. Instead, Patti bravely tells her story to expose the lies we are fed about sexuality, marriage, womanhood, and especially God, the lover of our souls.

Ann-Margret Hovsepian, author of *Restore My Soul*

The Windblown Girl is a painful, raw, and honest examination of well-articulated moments and memories that remind us that the road to heartache is also the road to redemption. This poignant memoir cuts deep and asks the reader to witness personal and spirit-led transformation in its most cutting form.

Christopher Lucey, Founder/Managing Partner
General Advisors

A beautifully written love story. Patti is vulnerable, raw and authentic as she shares with her readers the heartache that can come along with the choices we make in life. She sheds a beautiful light on discovering herself, as she learns to lean in on her faith, her inner voice and her ability to live honestly and be true to herself. A must read for any woman who is feeling the inner nudge to take a big leap into self-discovery.

Rachel Keith, PT, DPT, ATC Doctor of Physical Therapy

The Windblown Girl is a testament of how God can change your life amazingly, far from what you are dreaming and aiming. I highly recommend this book to everyone especially to those who are confused and struggling in life, love, and career.

Kaye Est, 29-year-old entrepreneur
Manila, Philippines

I have enjoyed the honor of knowing Patti Townley-Covert and reading her writing for several years. I have listened to our conversations and heard her wisdom, creativity, and care. I have learned through her words and appreciated those same qualities of wisdom, creativity, and care. Her latest book *The Windblown Girl: A Memoir about Self, Sexuality, and Social Issues* offers those traits to a larger audience. Each reader can notice Patti's authenticity through this memoir. We need that these days. Life is often difficult. News is frequently sad. Is there any hope through our struggles, our pain, our hurts? Patti believes there is. *The Windblown Girl* can help others believe that also.

Chris Maxwell, Author, Pastor, Poet
www.chrismaxwell.me

The Windblown Girl is a powerful literary work by Patti Townley-Covert who courageously dares to tell her story. She invites you in as a friend and allows you to behold a life of transformation. Jesus shows up for her in real, mighty, and healing ways. I can't wait for you to read this important book that is vulnerable, transparent, and hopeful.

Lisa Toney, Author, Speaker,
Pastor Podcast & YouTube: Faith Habits For Success

PATTI TOWNLEY-COVERT

The WINDBLOWN GIRL

A Memoir about Self, Sexuality, and Social Issues

pTc Publications

Copyright © 2021 Patti Townley-Covert

All rights reserved. No part of this publication may be reproduced, distributed, or transmitted in any form or by any means, including photocopying, recording, or other electronic or mechanical methods, without the prior written permission of the publisher, except in the case of brief quotations embodied in critical reviews and certain other noncommercial uses permitted by copyright law. For permission requests, write to the publisher at the address below.

Unless otherwise marked Scripture quotations taken from the (NASB®) New American Standard Bible®, Copyright © 1960, 1971, 1977, 1995 by The Lockman Foundation. Used by permission. All rights reserved. www.lockman.org

Scriptures marked TLB are taken from the THE LIVING BIBLE (TLB): Scripture taken from THE LIVING BIBLE, Copyright © 1971. Used by permission of Tyndale House Publishers, Inc., Carol Stream, Illinois 60188. All rights reserved.

ISBN: 978-1-7379712-0-7 (Paperback)
ISBN: 978-1-7379712-1-4 (eBook)
Library of Congress Control Number: 2021919901

This book is a memoir. It reflects the author's present recollections of experiences over time. Some names have been changed to protect the privacy of individuals.

Cover design by Jonathan Price
Cover Lladro figurine photography by Mark Ritter
Cover image courtesy of Depositphotos/Andrejs Pidjass
Lladro figurine used with permission

First printing edition 2021

pTc Publications
739 W. Fifth Street
Ontario, CA 91762

www.ptcovert.com

Contents

Dedicated to

The one who loves me most

"Every man's life is a fairy tale, written by God's fingers."

Hans Christian Andersen

PART I

Escaping the Pain

May he kiss me with the kisses of his mouth!
For your love is better than wine.

Song of Solomon 1:2

Chapter 1

In Pursuit of Pleasure

"Too bad Svein won't be there." My mom dumped her little bottle of Smirnoff vodka into the plastic cup, which was already partially filled with orange juice over ice. "You should have an affair."

"I'm *not* going to have an affair," I said keeping my voice low. I leaned the airline seat back wanting to sleep, but that didn't stop her.

"How did you get to be such a prude?"

My mother's words stung, reminding me how my husband had called me frigid. Still, I wasn't going to discuss my problems with her. With two failed marriages of her own, she certainly couldn't help mine. As children Valerie, Janet, and I had been devastated when she decided to divorce our dad. There was no way I wanted my son to grow up without his father. "Maybe I want to keep my family together."

She ignored me. I suspected she'd be thrilled to see my marriage end. My dad would have probably told me to have an affair too. That's what he did when my mom didn't measure up.

However, that didn't change the fact that after five-and-a-half years, I could barely stand for my husband to touch me. Unbidden images crept into my mind—Jeff coming in the front door, grinning. He carried the new Kirby vacuum cleaner he'd just stolen, looking like he'd won a prize. He didn't even try to hide the fact that he'd taken it, but proudly announced how when the owner went to the back of the shop, he just picked it up and left. Not knowing what to do, I did nothing.

The first year of our marriage, he'd taken me to an adult club in San Francisco where naked women twirled their tassels as they danced for men—and me. Maybe he was right, and I wasn't sexy enough. Regardless, I was determined to make my marriage work. More than anything, I wanted my little boy to have a family, his own family—no stepparents, who could do damage like my stepfather.

Thankfully my mom decided not to pursue our conversation and picked up her Danielle Steel novel. It was late, so I propped the airline's small pillow against the window and closed my eyes. With any luck, I'd sleep the rest of the way on the Los Angeles "red eye" to Miami.

But my mind wouldn't shut off. As I did most nights, I started wondering if my dad was being tortured in some Vietnam prison camp. He'd been missing since December 26, 1971—almost three-and-a-half years. Was he still alive?

He'd gone off to Vientiane, Laos, to fight in a war that, according to our government, didn't exist. During the "conflict," President Nixon kept insisting *"we have no men in Laos."* Politicians also claimed no association with my dad's employer. Air America gave my dad two IDs. While chatting one night at my sister Diane's house, he'd told me that one instilled the rights of an American. The other listed no country. That's what he carried on the missions he flew.

The CIA was rumored to be involved with his company, but my family didn't really know for sure. All we knew was that when my dad climbed into the cockpit of his plane, he became a man without a country. He warned my four sisters and me from the beginning—if the enemy captured him, they'd consider him a spy and put him in front of a firing squad. That might be if he was lucky. Images from the descriptions of POWs being tortured danced in my head.

Still, I was proud of my dad. Nearly 50, he'd needed the job. But he also believed in freedom and, despite the danger, wanted to make a difference. My dad performed feats beyond the capability of regular guys and took risks ordinary mortals didn't take. The C-123 he flew looked like a giant fish with a belly large enough to hold cargo, everything from refugees to white phosphorous. For a couple of years, Daddy wrote home about the bullets that riddled his plane. After landing, he counted their number—51 on one mission, 52 on another. I could almost hear my dad's chuckle as he described one that came within an inch of the fuselage. His life ridiculed death's threat. He was invincible, immortal, untouchable—until he wasn't.

Troubled Times

Ever since I graduated high school in 1968, nothing made much sense. Bobby Kennedy's assassination, then Martin Luther King's. Vietnam, napalm, Kent State, burning bras, and free love.

After Valerie married, my mom often took Janet and me to Corona del Mar for spring break, but in 1969 during my freshman year of college, the beach became so sewage-polluted that no one could go swimming. So, she insisted on taking us to Palm Springs instead. On Friday night, somehow, I convinced her to let me take my 14-year-old sister to the Sunair Drive-In theatre for the Palm Springs Pop Festival.

Several thousand young people shoved and pushed their way in to see The Doors, Ike and Tina Turner, Canned Heat, Eric Burdon and the Animals, and a multitude of others perform. With tickets in hand, we walked through the open gate as a bare-chested guy next to us jumped up on the chain-link fence. Climbing to the top, he waved his arms while shouting profanities—so high on LSD that his friends screamed at him to come down before he killed himself. Once inside, we found space to sit on the grass, next to some college students. When they offered Janet some pot, we moved, yet we couldn't escape the acrid sweet fumes of incense and Mexican marijuana.

A couple of my high-school friends had died from drug overdoses, so despite Ike and Tina's phenomenal performance and getting to see the Animals perform "House of the Rising Sun," I was uncomfortable exposing Janet to the raucous crowd. The increasing chaos scared me. For once I was grateful my mom had insisted, we get back early. The next night a 16-year-old boy was shot and killed by a gas station owner trying to prevent vandalism. Considered self-defense, he wasn't prosecuted. A 20-year-old girl was also shot, but she survived.

Woodstock followed in August. More than 50,000 hippies had descended onto a dairy farm in Bethel, New York, many consummating "free love" with virtual strangers. Superficial "love" without commitment. I'd always believed sex belonged in marriage. For some reason I didn't really understand, even though I hadn't found wedded bliss, I was still convinced making love should be special.

Times were changing. In the midst of so much uncertainty, all I wanted was the stability of a family. Now that ideology made me out of step with the rest of the world—even my mother. All I'd ever wanted was a man who would never leave me and children to raise in a loving two-parent home.

My thoughts shifted from the turmoil of the 60's back to the drone of the plane's engines and my problems. Before getting married, I'd thought my husband loved me more than I did him. But after the wedding, nothing I did was ever good enough. He told me how to cook, how to clean, how to dress, and how to wear my hair.

Concerns about leaving my son with my sister also kept me awake. It wasn't because I doubted her ability to care for him. My mom was right; Valerie was better with kids than I was. But Josh was so little. "He'll be fine," my mother had insisted. Yet she would have said anything to convince me to go with her on another cruise.

Our first cruise, I'd been pregnant. Last year, Josh had only been six months old, so I wasn't too concerned. But two weeks for a toddler might seem like forever. It would to me. Still being away from Jeff was a huge relief, too much of a temptation to resist.

A Life-Changing Trip

Nothing could ever be the same after that first voyage on Royal Caribbean's Nordic Prince in 1973. My 45-year-old mom had originally booked it with Janet. If my sister hadn't gotten a new job, I never would have gone, but when my mom asked Jeff's permission, he couldn't wait to get rid of me.

At least being pregnant, I'd carried my baby within me. Though my mother admonished me to keep my impending motherhood a secret, I was far too thrilled to remain silent.

At my mom's request, the maître d' had assigned us seats for the duration of the cruise at the chief officer senior's table. During dinner, it was natural to mention my pregnancy, especially when Svein said he had a newborn at home. That common bond made us instant friends. Though my mother flirted and teased him about his mistress, the sea, he and I shared respect for marriage and for our families. This time, he'd be on leave. Although I'd miss his gallant attention, as well as my son, being away from my husband would breathe fresh air into my soul.

The Second Time Around

As they often did, visions of dinners and dancing with Svein shifted my thoughts to the second cruise. After receiving my letter telling him we were coming again in 1974, Svein arranged our placement at his table with me on his right, my mother on his left. He'd surprised me our first night out by coming to the lounge before we even sailed to welcome me on board.

Most nights after dinner, we adjourned to the nightclub, along with my mom and her Danish friend, the ship's doctor.

Late the second night out, while dancing, Svein invited me to go out to dinner with him, Dr. Madsen, and my mother while we were in San Juan. The three of them had already made plans for the next evening. "Your mother said you should go," Svein told me, so I agreed.

Replaying that dramatic scene in my mind often interrupted my nightmares taking me instead to the place of sweet dreams.

As Svein opened the door of the taxi, El Convento's crystal chandeliers glowed a warm welcome through the old Carmelite convent's arched windows. He described how in years gone by the Hollywood elite like Rita Hayworth, Ethel Merman, Robert Montgomery, and George Hamilton had frequented this Spanish gem. Enthralled by exquisite antiques and old-world wrought iron as we entered, tonight I felt like a distinguished guest.

A long blue-and-maroon paisley print halter dress, made by my mother, flowed soft against my skin.

While perusing large red leather-bound menus, Svein said, "Order whatever you like, but we must all have the black bean soup." In such a hot climate, I couldn't imagine wanting soup, but even now I could almost taste those thick, spicy black beans with zesty chopped raw onions on top.

My knife had sliced through the perfectly pink-centered filet mignon as though it were butter. With béarnaise sauce dripping down its sides, the steak tantalized every taste bud melting into perfection. Dinner conversation and laughter flowed as freely as the robust Cabernet Sauvignon Svein ordered. Afterward, as Kahlua and coffee were served, the lights dimmed.

Center stage, a spotlight illuminated a lone musician who slowly began to strum his flamenco guitar. Picking up speed, he started slapping the instrument with his open palm keeping time with the complex melody. On the next song, another musician playing a cajón joined him. Soon, a bailaor appeared wearing skin-hugging black high-waisted pants and a short black jacket over a blood-red shirt open at the neck. At first, he danced solo, his intricate footwork intensifying from one tap to the next, faster and faster until his black boots studded with nails beat a staccato on the floor.

As the music slowed several bailaoras appeared, taking over the stage. Their graceful arm movements showed off black shawls embroidered with bright hues as their feet accompanied the simple rhythms of the guitar and cajón. Then, one woman became the focus as the others faded offstage. Her scarlet gown—a bata de cola—fit snug over her ample bust and hips, then flared toward the bottom into a long-ruffled train.

The bailaor returned and the pair danced with backs to each other, appearing indifferent. With a rigid body, he moved slow. One stomp. Then another. Looking over his shoulder at her. Yet, she remained aloof. Strong and noble, chin tilted high, her long black hair was pulled straight back from her face in a severe twist. She stepped out her own rhythm coiling the train like a snake, then whipping it behind her. Eventually their bodies began moving closer and closer. The music and hand clapping intensified, picking up speed. Sensuous movements became increasingly intertwined as their stomps built to a fiery crescendo that took my breath away and left my heart pounding.

As the lights came back up and regular dance music began to play, I sighed and lit a cigarette. My mom and the doctor moved out onto the dance floor. Svein turned, watching me for a moment, then asked me to dance. Instead of extinguishing my cigarette, for some foolish reason, I set it in the crystal ash tray.

The flamenco dancers' stunning performance lingered with such a wild fierceness that I soon changed my mind about dancing, and we returned to the table. As Svein pulled out my chair, there, next to the ash tray, lay my cigarette on that white linen tablecloth—blackened by a scorch mark bigger than my hand. Unable to speak, I just looked at Svein.

My words came, haltingly: "I, I can't believe—I, I did something so stupid." Thoughts of what my mother would say paralyzed me. Svein quickly picked up the cigarette, stubbing it out in the ashtray.

"Sit," he commanded. Then he gently took my hands in his and looked me in the eye. "Patti, this was not your fault. It was mine. I should never have asked a lady to dance while she was smoking a cigarette." His fault? The very idea brought a timid smile. "I don't think so," I said quietly. In my mind, my husband's voice berated me.

"Yes. It was," Svein insisted. "And, here," he added with a twinkle in his eye. "I can fix this." He picked up a charger plate that had been left on the table and centered it over the burn. "There. The others will never know."

A mischievous look on his usually serious face made me laugh. As my mom and the doctor returned, they asked what was so funny. Svein easily brushed aside the question, and the warm smile in his brown eyes spoke kindness. My horrid faux pas hadn't diminished me; our secret merely deepened our friendship. Before we left the restaurant, I saw him discretely speak to the maître d', then pulling out some bills, he pressed them into the man's outstretched hand. Both were smiling. . . . Svein must have suspected

I couldn't even offer to pay him back. I had no money. The only reason I went on cruises was because my mother needed a traveling companion. She paid for everything.

The balmy night air was soothing as we went outside, and I was happy to hear Svein ask if we'd mind walking back to the ship. On the way he'd had to sit in front with the cab driver, and he said it made him feel like a little kid. However, he was concerned because my mom and I wore high-platform shoes. Walking on the uneven cobblestone street was a bit treacherous, especially considering that my weak ankles sometimes sent me sprawling. Having suffered enough humiliation for one night, I asked Svein if I might take hold of his arm. Graciously he extended his elbow.

With my hand in the crook of his arm, I again apologized for my clumsiness. "It is forgotten, Patti. Why must it be so hard for you to let it go? It was an accident."

"My husband would have thought me stupid."

"You deserve better." I glanced sideways and, by the set of his jaw, saw that he meant it. Sighing I looked out past an old fort to the moonlit path illuminated on the sea. Svein's tenderness revealed the inner strength of a true gentleman. His kindness made him a hero to me. Soon, he became one to the rest of the ship's passengers.

A Daring Rescue

It was a lazy day at sea, the kind I treasured. Lounging poolside while breathing fresh ocean air with the ship moving slowly through the water, I relaxed—the coconut rum taste of a frosty pina colada still sweet on my tongue. Steel drums beat their tinny hollow melodic rhythm into my soul. My mom had gone below to get her hair done for the Captain's Gala, so I reveled in the peace of no expectations. Glaring sun bathed me in warmth as late nights and early mornings nudged my eyes closed. The sweet fragrance of Sea and Ski emanated from the sunscreen I'd slathered all over my body. My thoughts wandered over the past week—El Convento, Svein's kindness, pirate hideouts in San Juan, the rain forest, and a romance novel all intertwined. For a moment, I drifted with them at least until harsh blasts from the ship's horn jolted me out of my reverie.

Captain Andreasson's thick Norwegian accent blared over the loud-speaker. He'd already given his usual daily update. Now, his voice sounded more intense. "Your attention, please. Ladies and gentlemen, your attention if you please." He spoke slowly enunciating each word carefully.

"Moments ago, the bridge received a distress call. A seaman on board a Liberian freighter has been seriously injured. Because we are closest ship with doctor, we must rush to his aid. By increasing speed to 19 knots, we'll reach them in approximately 30 minutes. My apologies for not-so-smooth motion, but this man's life depends on our soon arrival."

"As Captain, I must stay with the ship," he continued. "Chief Officer Senior Svein Pettersen will lead rescue effort. His team will include our ship's doctor, Dr. Madsen. They will take lifeboat to bring sailor back to Nordic Prince, where he can receive necessary treatment. A rescue such as this is rare occurrence, so you may want to watch. But please stand back as the crew readies the lifeboat. Our primary concern is for this man's survival, so some comfort must be sacrificed. Time is essential. Thank you for your cooperation."

As passengers started rushing to their staterooms for their cameras, I climbed the steps to the Sun Walk on the Compass Deck. Crowds no doubt would form one deck below, closer to the action. Yet the lifeboats lining the deck obstructed that view. With high seas, the rescue operation posed great challenges, and I wanted to see as much as possible. The ship's photographer would capture photos far better than any I could take.

Propelled by loud engines, our ship picked up speed crashing through the whitecaps. From my vantage point, I could see blue-shirted crew members gathered around an open lifeboat on the deck below. Nearing the Liberian ship, these seamen wasted no time loading then lowering the open lifeboat containing four officers and three sailors. Roiling waves slapped the sides of that small boat as it rocked back and forth, then slowly got underway toward the old rusty freighter. Once there, the lifeboat was hoisted on board.

Wishing for a pair of binoculars, I watched and finally saw what looked like a toy boat being lowered. Progress was slow as the rescuers battled choppy 10-foot swells that blasted the sides of their vessel. As it approached, I could see a huge black-skinned man lying bare-chested on a flat piece of plywood placed across the seats. Dr. Madsen appeared to be trying to stanch the bleeding from the man's upper torso. Even from several stories up, I could see the deep-red blood. However, the officers' caps made it impossible to determine whether Svein was beside the doctor or at the helm. Regardless, wherever he was, he'd be issuing orders, expecting instant compliance. He'd once told me how lonely it got onboard the ship where the only friends he could have were the doctor and chief engineer. Now crew members scrambled to attach the thick steel cables that steadied the small craft, then began lifting it back into place.

Quickly I made my way down the stairs to get closer, hoping Svein might stop to explain what was happening. Despite the crowd of passengers, he caught my eye and came over to say that the man had been stabbed in a knife fight. He had a punctured lung and might not survive. Then Svein rushed after the doctor, saying he might be needed to assist in surgery.

Hours later, Svein and Dr. Madsen appeared in the doorway of the nightclub. The band stopped playing as passengers stood and cheered, applauding their entrance. We'd already heard the captain's report that the man's life had been spared. My heart beat faster when they spotted my mom and me and walked over to join us.

Looking Forward

Nothing could ever top that second cruise and the kind attention of a gentleman. Relaxing now, I wrapped the airline blanket a little tighter around me and shifted in my seat to get more comfortable. Though Svein wouldn't be on this cruise, I still anticipated two weeks of hot sunny days, shopping in ports like St. Thomas and Old San Juan, and laying by the pool. If that's all there was, I'd be happy.

Not long after that second cruise, my mom had convinced me to have her Beverly Hills plastic surgeon "fix" my nose, even though I'd never realized it was a problem. She urged me to "do" my chin, too, but I refused. Yet, at my husband's insistence, I had acquiesced on the nose. And, despite my misgivings, the results were pleasing. Then, at Christmas, my mom had given me two gorgeous evening gowns, along with other clothes that flattered my slim figure. And, because my husband wouldn't permit me to cut my hair, unruly curls hung almost to my waist.

The first year we were married, though I'd only weighed 115 lbs., Jeff had given me little white pills to help me lose weight. After a week of anxiety-laden hyperactivity, I fell apart and refused to take anymore. Yet, after Josh was born, I lost weight naturally. Now I only weighed 105. Dozing off, I couldn't help but smile. Too bad Svein wouldn't be there. He would have appreciated my transformation. However, little did I know that on this third cruise someone far more intriguing awaited.

Chapter 2

A High-Stakes Gamble

After the Bon Voyage dinner, my mom and I walked up to the nightclub, slid into a booth, and ordered Salty Dogs. We'd arrived in Miami early, then took a tour that included lunch before boarding the ship. Unpacking, donning our lifejackets for the safety drill, and dressing for the evening kept us busy until we headed into dinner. Before Svein left on vacation, he'd arranged for the maître d' to assign us to the new chief officer senior's table. However, we knew not to expect any officers to appear until the second night. Svein had explained, they were too busy the first night at sea.

So, I was surprised to see a couple of young officers walk into the nightclub dressed in their formal white dinner jackets—no doubt prowling for women to keep them company. They didn't interest me. Svein had made me feel safe, but one night on the last cruise, when he wasn't around, an arrogant young officer had become pushy and followed me to my stateroom. Despite my objections, he'd decided we were going to have some fun—at least until I mentioned that my mother was inside. Furious, he'd left, yet his aggressiveness had scared me.

A Hilarious Encounter

Tonight, though we'd already been awake almost 24 hours, the allure of a live band made us ready to dance. Near the door, a portly middle-aged man slid out of a black leather booth where he'd been chatting with two women. As he headed toward our table, I hoped he'd ask my mom to dance.

Instead, he asked to join us. Waiting for my mom to respond, I expected her to say "No." But she hesitated only a moment, then nodded. "Yes, that would be fine."

After introductions, Chris turned toward her: "Where are you from?"

"Southern California. About 30 miles east of LA."

"That puts you about in Fontana." He seemed smug in his knowledge.

"Actually, Ontario," my mother corrected.

"Really. I live in Ontario. Whereabout are you?"

"Northwest Ontario."

Quizzical eyebrows raised. "I live in northwest Ontario." He squirmed and gripped the arms of his chair. "What street do you live on?"

"Armsley Square," my mother responded with a hint of pride. A little before marrying my stepfather, she had convinced him to buy a stately home on the most prestigious street in the city. Overhead, tree branches formed a canopy shading the expertly manicured lawns.

Chris sat back, his face lobster red. Taking out a handkerchief, he mopped his brow. "Now, that's interesting. I live on Armsley Square. What's your address?"

"529."

Blustering, he choked out the words: "I live just down the street!" For a moment, he hesitated, then heaved a sigh. "I guess I better tell you—I, I'm not traveling with my wife." Turning, he waved to the two women in the booth near the door. "That's my secretary and my girlfriend," he mumbled. "I hope you'll keep this our little secret."

Graciously, my mother agreed as Chris rose from his chair. "Guess I better get back and find out what those gals are up to."

As soon as he left, we burst into gales of laughter. Getting serious, my mom frowned. "What am I going to do if he shows up at my door?"

"You go make friends with his wife!" The thought started us laughing again, at least until another male voice interrupted. "Would you like to dance?" I looked up to find a tall Norwegian's question directed at me. My guard immediately went up; however, the band was playing Proud Mary—

one of my favorite songs.

As I agreed, then stood, the officer's clipped Norwegian accent startled me. "My god, you're short!"

"At least I can look up at people, instead of down on them." His discomfort made me smile. "Do you play basketball?"

He scowled. "Why does everyone ask that? No, I don't play your basketball. I play fùtbol!"

"Football?"

"No, you dummy." His rudeness was jarring, but almost immediately his voice softened into a warm timbre. "In the states, you call it soccer. And, I'm good at it!" He grinned revealing a charming Lauren Bacall gap between his two front teeth.

"Oh, I'm sorry. It's just, you are so tall. How tall are you anyway?"

He ignored my question, but there was no mistaking that I barely reached his chest. As the band started playing "Dock of the Bay," Jan's strong arms gently enfolded me into a secure embrace. All too soon the music stopped, and he walked me back to the table.

A little disappointed, I was also a little relieved. This guy was way out of my league. No pretty boy, his rugged good looks complimented his international playboy charisma.

"May I join you?" His question startled me. Those initial gruff remarks made me think he'd prefer to take his chances with someone else.

Hesitating, then despite knowing I shouldn't, I took a deep breath. "Yes, that would be fine." He reminded me of Robert Redford in *The Way We Were*. Like Hubbell Gardner, Jan's cockiness made me laugh. And, the way he swiped the hair out of his eyes made me want to do it for him. Slowly it occurred to me—I was one of only a few young women on board. No wonder Jan wanted to take his chances with me. Another lonesome officer who wanted a "no-strings-attached" relationship. I was not playing that game.

Jan's brashness made it easy to get straight to the point. "Look. You should know, I'm married. And, I won't betray my husband. Please, go find someone who's available to spend your time with."

"I'd rather get to know you," he grinned. Of course. I posed a challenge. Being married might have been part of the attraction. He was trouble. The last thing I needed.

Even though I recognized his game, his magnetic personality enticed me. He was so different from Svein. Though not much taller than me, the chief officer senior was polished, formidable on duty and off. Powerful. Elegant. A gentleman. Even if he hadn't been married, Svein didn't intrigue me the way Jan did. The confident arrogance of a future ship's master showed in the set of Jan's jaw, yet in other ways he seemed easy-going, casual and relaxed, so sure of himself. Third in command of this huge ship at only 25 years old, he'd said. That was impressive. So was his country.

On each of the previous cruises, I'd seen pictures of the Norwegian fjords flash on large screens mounted on either side of the nightclub. "You live in what I think must be the most gorgeous place in the world."

"Yes. It is very beautiful. You should come someday." The warmth in his eyes issued a personal invitation. I ignored it, but apart from him, someday I hoped to see Norway. Not long after, he excused himself, and I couldn't help but wonder if I'd see him again—even though I knew it would be better if I didn't.

An Enchanted Evening

For the Captain's Welcome Aboard Cocktail Party, the second night of the cruise, a stylist pulled my hair up into a loopy knot. Three sets of spaghetti-thin laces held the gossamer silver fabric of my backless gown together. A rhinestone clasp kept the low-cut front from being too revealing. Feeling glamorous, I hoped to see Jan.

As I stood in front of the mirror, my mother glanced at me, walked over, and tapped the silver POW/MIA bracelet on my wrist. "You're not wearing that."

"Oh yes, I am. I promised when I put it on, not to take it off until Daddy comes home or we find out what happened."

"I bought you that dress, and that bracelet looks tacky."

"That's too bad because I'm wearing it." Her guilt-inducing threats made no difference to me. She'd never understand the importance of upholding one's convictions. Usually, her manipulative demands didn't matter to me, but this time I wasn't giving in. Glaring her disapproval, she turned away, and we finished dressing in silence.

Determined to get a seat in the lounge before they were all taken, my mom slyly maneuvered her way to the front of the receiving line forming at the entry to the Merry Widow lounge. A bit embarrassed, I followed close behind. Approaching Captain Andreasson, she cooed up at him, shook his hand, and smiled for the ship's photographer. Then, observing the etiquette we'd been taught in National Charity League, she regally presented me as her daughter.

The captain grasped my hand in both of his, looked me in the eyes, and spoke a kind greeting. As I glanced up at him, across the crowded room, a lanky tanned officer caught my gaze—Jan. I couldn't even pronounce his name right—kind of like "yawn" only the "a" had an "ao" sound that eluded me no matter how much he'd tried to help. Nevertheless, this evening he'd obviously been watching for me.

My heart fluttered as he strode in my direction. Deep navy epaulets on the shoulders of his immaculate white dinner jacket revealed two-and-a-half gold bars, signifying his first officer status. A small gold anchor embossed his navy-blue tie with Royal Caribbean's insignia.

Coming face to face, he said, "Good evening, Pat-ti." Then he stared, his strong tanned jaw unflinching.

"Wha-at have you done with your hair?

"I put it up to show off the back of my dress. See?" Slowly I turned.

As I faced him again, his voice softened and his chocolate brown eyes traveled the length of my body. "It is bet-ter down." He pronounced each word distinctly. The musky bittersweet orange fragrance of Old Spice wafting in my direction along with the captivated expression on his face stole my breath. Electrical sparks flashed between his eyes and mine. My thoughts raced. *This man is trouble. He's so arrogant. Why is he here? The night before, he'd mentioned being on duty from 8:00 until 12:00, morning and night, every day with rare exceptions.* "I didn't expect to see you. Don't you have to be on the bridge?"

"I'm only here long enough to be introduced by the captain, then I must go. But I want to know if you'll be in the nightclub later. After my shift, I can only remain until 1:00 a.m. For such short time, I won't change into my dinner jacket unless you'll be there."

Despite knowing I was playing with fire, I quietly responded: "Yes, I'll be there."

Smoldering Embers

At the Captain's Welcome Aboard dinner, my mom and I met the second in command who replaced Svein. Tor was in his mid-40s like my mom, but despite his efforts to win my favor, there was something about him I didn't like. I much preferred talking with Chase, the elderly gentleman to my right. A dear passenger friend of Svein's, Chase easily became my friend too. We swapped stories of previous cruises as we enjoyed our meals. He'd been on dozens.

Without hesitation, my mom accepted Tor's invitation for us to join him in the nightclub. So, when Jan walked through the doorway a little after midnight, we were sitting with his superior officer.

The handsome Norwegian stared straight at me, and he was not smiling. After a long moment, he walked to the back of the room and ordered a drink at the bar. I didn't know what to do. He'd come because I'd agreed to meet him. He couldn't possibly know I hadn't preferred his boss. My mother might go for the highest possible rank, but that didn't impress me at all.

Excusing myself, I left the table and walked over to Jan. My smile did little to erase his scowl. "Why didn't you come join us? My mother made arrangements with Tor without consulting me. I'm not with him."

His clipped accent made his words sound harsh. "I don't want to intrude."

"Jan, I'm inviting you to sit with us. Doesn't that matter?"

His voice softened and looking into his brown eyes was like bathing in hot chocolate. "It does. But do you understand the awkwardness of my position?"

Tor was his boss, what was I thinking? "Of course. I'm so sorry."

"I wanted to get to know you better," I said softly. "If I make it clear this was my idea, will that help?"

A slight smile revealing the tiny gap between his two front teeth turned him into a mischievous young boy. His smile crinkled his eyes as he said, "OK. I guess I can't refuse."

When we sat down, the two men exchanged a curt nod. Tor flashed a fierce look at his subordinate. Hoping to lighten the mood, I tried to cajole him. "I invited Jan to join us."

My mother gave me a scathing look. She'd much prefer I flirt with the chief officer senior than his subordinate. The two men had a brief exchange in Norwegian that didn't sound pleasant. I hoped I wasn't getting Jan in trouble.

For a while we danced and chatted. At five minutes until 1:00, Jan asked me to go for a walk.

He pushed open the heavy aft door, and we escaped into the balmy dark night. Slowly we wandered amidships, away from the nightclub's lights and noise and over to lean against the wooden rail. I looked out over the indigo sea illuminated by a full moon. Lost in thought, I stared at the oceanic realm, nothing but calm water clear to the horizon.

The way Jan looked at me gave me chills and made my heart beat faster. *I must not get caught up in this. He's sexy for sure but I'm married. If I offend him, maybe he'll go away—that might be best in the long run. With his charm, he's got to be a player, and there's no way I'm going to be duped into getting physically involved with someone for two weeks. Oh, but the way he asks questions and listens to my answers. . . the way he looks at me. . .*

After a few moments, Jan asked what I was thinking. I spoke from my heart. "I shouldn't be here with you. I have a husband and a son."

"And, I have a girlfriend in Spain." His eyes smiled.

"Are you in love with her?"

He avoided the question, but spoke thoughtfully. "She does whatever I ask. If we're out somewhere and I want to talk to my friend—I tell her "go over there and wait for me. One time, I told her to go to a different city. And, she did!" His eyes widened declaring astonishment at his audacity and her compliance.

The surprised look on his face made me laugh. "That's terrible!"

"I know," he chuckled too. A strand of thick honey-colored hair fell across his brow, and I resisted the urge to brush it out of his eyes. Instead, I turned and looked back out over the sea.

"So why do you come without your husband? And, why does he let you?"

"He doesn't care. My mother needs a traveling companion. I worry about my little boy, though, and I miss him."

"Not your husband?"

"No."

"Does he mistreat you?"

There was no reason to lie. "He thinks I'm ugly, stupid, and worthless. Before we left, he threw me up against a wall when he got angry. I'd always said, I'd leave if he ever hit me, but he insisted he didn't. And, technically he's right. He only shoved me."

"Why do you stay?"

"More than anything, I want my son to have a family that includes his father. I missed my dad so much as a little girl. And, a boy needs his father even more. I can't do that to our son."

"Is he a good father?"

"No. He didn't want a baby to take my time away from himself, and he won't even watch Josh while I run to the grocery store. It's a catch-22. I'm damned if I stay and damned if I don't." Not knowing what else to say, I quit talking. Jan shouldn't bother with me. There was no mistaking the sexual tension between us. "So, why do you want to get to know me, when others might offer you more?"

His bronzed forearms rested against the wooden rail; his lean body so close we almost touched. Again, I breathed in that woodsy Old Spice aroma. With a slight turn of his head, Jan looked at me with unmistakable intensity: "What do you mean?" He knew I was referring to a physical relationship but seemed determined to get me to say the words.

Emboldened by drinks before dinner, wine at dinner, then after-dinner drinks, I didn't want any misunderstandings. "Well, it's just—OK, I'm going to say it straight out. Scandinavians have a reputation for being very free about sex. I suppose that it might even include casual friends. But I don't think most Americans are that way." News images from Woodstock flashed in my mind. At Whittier College, one of my friends had slept with an entire fraternity. "Well, maybe Americans have become more free, but I'm not that way. To me, sex should mean something. It should be special. Though I have a difficult marriage, I will remain faithful to my husband. You need to know . . ."

He smiled. "Why must it be about that, Pat-ti? I like you and want to know you. That's enough. Why must we worry about the other?"

Deftly, he changed the subject telling me how he left home to go to sea at 15, and his mother wasn't happy.

"I wouldn't be happy either." Saying good-bye to a son so young must have been excruciating. Having my dad leave had been hard, especially when he went to southeast Asia, but I couldn't imagine not seeing my son for months at a time. "All I've ever wanted is a family—a mom and dad who are home at night. More than anything, that's what's important to me. Besides it would be almost impossible to support my son if I left my husband."

"My mom was single, and yes, it is hard. But Norway would love you. We take care of single moms, even those who do not work. They are given an apartment and enough money to live on."

Now, that was an intriguing idea. But someone had to fund the expense. "You must pay a lot of taxes."

"Yes, you are right. Sometimes as much as 70 percent. Yet the government takes care of many things. Not long ago, oil was discovered in the

Norwegian waters of the North Sea. Exports became an important element of our economy. The government uses that money to help Norwegian citizens."

Later, after leaving Jan and going to bed, sleep eluded me. My thoughts centered on the Norwegian, the most fascinating man I'd ever met. About my age, yet world-wise, he even spoke several languages—English, Spanish, and German, plus dialects from different areas in his own country. Though passionate about his homeland, he worked in the Caribbean and vacationed with his best friend in Spain. Somehow his open admiration and deep bond with that guy friend made Jan all the sexier. Unlike anyone I'd ever met, his warmth and kindness embraced me without a touch. Somehow that gentleness fueled an undeniable spark between us that threatened to ignite and burst into flame. If anyone could determine the truth of whether I was frigid, Jan might. Dangerous as that idea might be, I could hardly wait to see him again.

Freezing Hot

As the clock in the nightclub ticked slowly toward midnight, I nervously smoked a cigarette. Would Jan bother to change into formal attire again, for only an hour? When he appeared in the doorway, I watched as he scanned the room. When he saw me and headed toward our table, my heart leapt into my throat. After asking permission, he sat down and the waitress appeared to take our order. Since dinner, I'd been drinking water but decided to try a Pink Lady.

Moments later, the waitress carefully set the cocktails on our small round table. After Jan signed the check, I continued telling a story, waving my hand for emphasis.

The moment the back of my hand struck the cold hard glass, I stopped breathing. Horrified, I watched as, though in slow motion, the full drink tipped over. Sticky pink liquid poured into Jan's lap. His shocked expression made me want to laugh, yet my clumsiness brought tears to my eyes. Speechless, I wanted to flee.

Jan did. "Excuse me, please." After he left, I hurried out the back doors, moving aft to the rail. Watching the engines churn up the white wake behind the ship, I tried to calm the churning inside of me. But that was impossible. My husband's voice filled with disgust droned in the engine of my mind. "You are so stupid. How could you do such a thing?"

The night washed darkness over me. While trying to convince myself it was better for Jan to stay away, I felt a slight touch on my shoulder. Turning slightly, I glimpsed a look of deep concern on his face before I looked away blinking fast so the tears in my eyes wouldn't spill over.

"Are you OK?"

"No," I replied in a small voice. Unable to face him, I looked back out over the ocean. He must not see me cry. "I'm so sorry. Sometimes I do such stupid things."

"It was an accident, Pat-ti. Do not feel bad. It's OK."

"But you went to all the trouble to come, and I spoiled it."

"No," he replied. "You are very beautiful; I am glad to be here—even with wet pants." The smile in his voice lightened my internal weight of shame.

With a zillion stars glittering on the black velvet fabric overhead and the moon shimmering on the dark rippling sea, we stood side by side for several quiet moments. Finally, I composed myself enough to break the silence.

"What are you thinking?"

Desire etched his face as he looked at me. He spoke so softly I barely heard him. "I want to kiss you, but am afraid I'll get slapped."

Looking down, I whispered, "I wouldn't slap you."

Softly, oh so tenderly, he reached over and touched my shoulder turning me to face him. Then, Jan cradled my face in his hands and slowly tipped it up as he bent his head low. I closed my eyes and completely abandoned myself to his kiss.

For one brief moment, nothing else mattered.

Afterward, breathless, I said goodnight.

Shrouded in Mystery

Morning rushed in, and I crawled out of bed to meet my mom for breakfast. Shopping in old San Juan soon captivated my imagination. Browsing exquisite shops with stunning jewelry and other enticing wares kept me content. Encouraging my mom to buy an opulent opal ring made me even happier.

Yet, unexpected emotion surged while we stood in A. H. Riise looking at a delicate porcelain figurine. Inexplicably tears filled my eyes, threatening to spill over and run down my cheeks. I blinked quickly not wanting my mother to see. Unsure of how to express my thoughts, after hesitating for a moment, I spoke. "I don't know why, but somehow I feel connected to her."

For a moment, there was silence. Then my mom spoke quietly, in an almost reverent tone. "Why, she's you!"

Her comprehension shocked me. I didn't even understand but somehow my life was bound to this Lladro called "Windblown Girl."

Though many similar statuettes stood on the elegant shop's glass shelves, only this one attracted me. A plain young woman, she stood on a rock, her dress billowing behind her as though caught in a fierce gale. Yet, standing tall she seemed resolute, clutching a book behind her back. Tiny fragile flowers rested in a basket at her feet as she gazed into the distance, watching and waiting, peace on her face.

Though I longed to possess her, I couldn't afford the price—$350.00—far too steep for me. A mystical fog concealed our connection. Though I didn't understand it, some sort of powerful bond united me with this Windblown Girl. I sighed, turning away, knowing I'd never forget her. Strength emanated from her posture and her peaceful countenance epitomized something I craved.

After lunch onboard, we went out by the pool. Soon my tan would be as deep as Jan's. Relaxing on the chaise lounge, I closed my eyes. His kiss lingered, unforgettable. Did it matter if he was a playboy? I wasn't so sure. Ever since Woodstock, the term "free love" had become commonplace. This was considered the "Me" generation." Was I the one who was wrong?

Why had I always believed sex should be reserved for marriage? That was supposed to make it special, but it sure wasn't with my husband. Although I knew I didn't want to be like my mom—playing up to men who had money, determined to get her way no matter who it hurt—maybe she was right, and I ought to put myself first.

At least tonight I wouldn't be tempted. My mom insisted on going to dinner at the El San Juan casino—rumored to be a favorite haunt of Hollywood's famous Rat Pack. We wouldn't return until too late for the nightclub.

What would Jan think if he couldn't find me after his shift? Would he suspect that his kiss drove me away? There was no way to get a message to him. Besides that would be presuming he'd expect me to be available.

Stakes Beyond My Reach

Arriving at the casino, a man in a tuxedo opened the heavy glass door and the air conditioning rushed out, cooling us despite the thick-hot humid night air. Crystal chandeliers glistened overhead. Women in elegant evening gowns congregated with their black tuxedo-clad escorts in small groups on the polished red floor. Overwhelming opulence—and silence. Unlike the noisy Las Vegas casinos my husband took me to on our honeymoon, everyone here spoke in hushed serious tones. No shouts of joy accompanied the stacks of money players piled in front of themselves at the roulette table.

Mindful of the steep limits, my mom tried her hand at Black Jack. I stood behind her to watch, but my thoughts wandered. That kiss. What would sex with someone like him be like? The thought tempted me. Good thing we weren't onboard tonight. My family was important. My son deserved a mom and dad together. Still my mother's voice rang in my mind, "You should have an affair."

After a short time, I wandered around hoping to encounter Hollywood stars—maybe Dean Martin, Frank Sinatra, Sammy Davis Jr., or Peter Lawford. Men at the poker tables were riveted on their cards. These games were far too serious. I wasn't a risk taker. Fear of loss loomed large. My family at stake. Could I gamble on a two-week fling? Did I really want to be just another of Jan's girls? Yet, no one would ever need to know.

Chapter 3

If It Feels Good, Do It

The next night, a friend of Jan's came into the nightclub to tell me he'd be waiting on deck after his shift. A little after midnight, I walked outside. Jan stood by the rail wearing his white work uniform, watching me.

"You dummy, where were you last night?" he demanded as though he had a right to know. Before I could respond, his voice softened. Reaching out, he took hold of my arm just above the elbow. "Pati-ti I went onshore and bought champagne yesterday afternoon, hoping you'd come to my room." He didn't try to hide his desire or his disappointment.

"My mom wanted to go to El San Juan. She paid for this cruise so when she wants to do something, I have no choice. She took me to a casino, and we didn't get back until late. I wanted to let you know, but there was no way to do that."

"I understand," Jan said moving his hands to my shoulders. "Pat-ti, listen to me. Time on cruise is very short. Four days already gone. We shouldn't waste time, we can't replace. We had fourteen days; now only ten days more. Things might easily happen. Then, we would regret not having more time. I had hoped . . . . Even tonight, I hope you will say yes. Please consider this carefully."

All day I'd thought about little else, knowing tonight, I had to make a decision. Heaving a tremendous sigh, I leaned against the wooden rail and stared out to sea. Strangely I appreciated Jan's forthrightness. Without being aggressive, he didn't mince words. The way he spoke my name so carefully made me feel special. In my mind, the voices of my husband and my mom harped at me.

"You're a prude." "Frigid." "What's wrong with you?" "You ought to have an affair." Maybe I should. What would it hurt? Who would know? Ever since I'd been shoved up against the wall, it felt like my marriage was over. Though I still didn't want a divorce—I really didn't care anymore. And, I wanted to know the truth about me.

What if I played Jan's game? Others could have casual sex, why not me? From the beginning, I'd know it was only for two weeks with no hope of anything else. I could toughen my heart and disconnect my emotions. It would be purely physical. I'd been on enough cruises to know Jan would forget me as soon as I left the ship. He didn't hide his girlfriend. He was honest. That unforgettable kiss enticed me to want more. What would it feel like to be held in his arms for more than a moment? With such volatile chemistry between us, at least I'd find out the truth about myself and sex. When I stepped off this ship, our relationship would end. Period. Simple as that. I was a big girl and could handle it as long as I remained in the truth about reality. In a split second, borne on years of history, my decision was made.

A Hazardous Expedition

"We must be careful Tor does not see us," Jan warned as we headed forward toward the officers' quarters. "He will want to make trouble for me."

While creeping up the stairs like two defiant high school kids, Jan explained that passengers were not supposed to be found with junior officers. Though I didn't mention knowing Svein, I shuddered to think about the woman he'd put off the ship for disrupting his crew.

Expecting my nerves Jan hesitated, looking back at me. "My friends in the radio room will help. Edgar and Hilda are nice couple. If necessary, they'll distract anyone who is there." My heart pounded in my head as we neared the area off limits to passengers.

Through a window in the radio room, I saw an officer standing with his back to us. He looked like Tor. A husky officer faced him. Seeing us, he became more animated, continuing to talk while we rushed past and up a small stairway.

A few steps down a short hallway, Jan shoved aside a curtain, and we stepped into his quarters before he pulled it closed. The room was compact but neat and well-organized. A bathroom and narrow twin-sized bed lined one wall. Below the large windows in front of me was a window seat. I perched on the edge of it and looked out past the bow of the ship cutting through the black night. Jan sat across from me at a desk.

My heart beat faster as he pulled a bottle of champagne out of an ice bucket. Experience had taught me that the instant I drank it, I'd feel it in my toes. "Only a tiny bit for me."

Jan partially filled a glass, then handed it to me. I lit a cigarette and tried to relax. I couldn't think of anything to say. Jan came over, took my cigarette, and stubbed it out.

An interlude followed as he took me in his arms. Small steps moved us to his bed and a symphony began to play as I became the yellow sunshine kite from my childhood. Our steps became longer and larger as clothes forsaken, he drew me up off the ground, gliding here and there until I was tugging at the taut string, dipping and diving, soaring higher and higher until finally I broke free of all restraints and the breeze took me places, I'd never been before.

Afterward, spontaneous tears slipped down my cheeks. In the semi-darkness, Jan had raised up on an elbow to scrutinize my face. "Wha-at?" his voice cracked like an adolescent's. "Wha-at is this?" he asked, searching for answers. Deep concern etched his countenance. Gently he swiped my tears away with his thumb.

In that moment, all I wanted was to ease his fear that I might be having regrets. Passengers had the power to get officers in trouble. "Ih-it's OK," I said with broken breath—trying to reassure him. "I just never knew it could be like that." Finally, the truth. Tears of grief at all I'd missed mingled with tears of joy at all I'd found.

Incredulous, he asked, "Never? Not with anyone?"

"There's only been my husband."

Stunned, Jan looked away. After a few moments, he took a deep breath, then peered into my soul—the wonder in his expression declaring our union precious. "I must say, I appreciate the thought of it."

His tender candor and our lovemaking continued long into the night signifying an inestimable gift. Early the next morning, in the darkness before dawn, I crept back down the stairs of the sleeping ship. Despite my newfound awareness, I fully expected that when the cruise came to an end so would our relationship. Regardless of what happened, I must not, could not, think in terms of love.

The Release of Laughter

While at sea the next day, I laid out by the pool with plenty of time to think. No regrets plagued me, only a sense of wonder. Yet my reverie was mixed with reality. For Jan, I simply offered a diversion while he was at sea, and I must never lose sight of that.

Perhaps that's why it startled me to see him drop by the pool area after his shift. Jan wasn't supposed to be there mingling with passengers. However, he caught my eye motioning for me to join him at a table off to the side. He seemed happy to see me as he ordered himself a Norwegian beer and a soda for me.

When the Jamaican waiter brought them, he leaned toward Jan talking in a conspiratorial tone too low for me to hear. Clearly, they appreciated each other's company.

Already, Jan's respect for people, regardless of position, endeared him to me. People all over the ship enjoyed his company. And, I had no doubt they'd be eager to follow his command when necessary. His kindness to everyone was so different from Svein's formidable behavior or my mother's rude expectations. The day we came onboard, she insisted the cabin steward bring extra towels "*right now* because Patti needs them for her hair." Her condescending tone made me cringe, and later I apologized to the steward.

Laughter pulled me back into the moment. With a grin, the waiter left spinning his drink tray on his finger. Jan turned to me. The first joke he repeated was off-color funny, and I laughed. But the thought of a Jamaican telling a Norwegian the second one struck me as hilarious. With all serious-ness Jan asked, "Where does the lone ranger take his trash?" At the shake of my head, Jan sang "to the dump, to the dump, to the dump, dump, dump."

Finishing his beer, he left, telling me he'd meet me later. Returning to the chaise lounge where I'd left my book, I wondered if he'd go take a nap. He couldn't have gotten much sleep the night before. Though we'd dozed, I hadn't gotten back to my cabin until about 5:00 a.m. My mother hadn't woken up—at least she didn't let me know if she did. Now, I could hardly wait for evening and more time with Jan, alone.

An Extraordinary Shore Excursion

"Hey, you dummy!"

My mom and I were walking back to the ship after going out on a rum runner in Barbados, when Jan's unmistakable catch phrase drifted overhead. He spoke the same way to his friends, so I wondered who he was talking to. Despite the throng of tourists at the gangway, Jan's height made him impossible to miss.

Getting closer, I asked, "Are you talking to me?" Seeing the relief on his face intoxicated me even more than the punch I'd drunk while doing the limbo on the rum runner. The morning had been fun, and now the afternoon looked promising. I'd wondered what he did during his off-duty daytime hours.

His annoyance that I hadn't been at his beck and call charmed me, making me feel like I had the upper hand. "I've been waiting for you, so we can go sailing. Hurry, get your suit."

A little embarrassed to have to ask permission, I turned to my mom. "Do you mind?"

"You'll miss lunch."

"That's all right."

Reluctantly she agreed and I raced up the clanking metal gangway to go change and grab a beach towel. On the first two cruises, I'd only been to the beach a couple of times, once on a tour. My mother only wanted to shop, so I was surprised she didn't resist my going, especially because she thought Jan a philanderer. But, so did I. Regardless, he made me feel special, and I intended to bask in every bright moment of his flattery.

A taxi dropped us at a semi-secluded beach, and we went to sit on the clean white sand. As I settled on a towel, Jan changed from jeans into cut-offs. His brazenness appalled me: "What are you doing?"

"What do you mean?"

"You just change, right here in front of everyone?" His lack of inhibitions rattled me. Yet, Jan's ease challenged me to question my own inhibitions. His teasing about my one-piece bathing suit made me lighten up and value his European perspective. Inwardly, though, I suspected he appreciated my modesty. I'd never forget the way he'd looked at me when I told him I'd only been with one other man. What if he'd been the *only* one?

Aboard the small sailboat he rented, I admired his sun-kissed lanky body busy at the helm. Trying to impress him, I'd told him, I'd sailed in races out of the Balboa Yacht Club. Now I had to confess, "You need to let me know when we're coming about. I haven't sailed since high school, and even then, whoever I crewed for had to let me know when to duck."

We spoke little while getting underway, other than Jan motioning when to shift sides. Then, as the breeze caressed our faces, we drifted along reveling in the peace. Quietly he shared his dream to one day buy his own sloop. His smile radiated as he talked about his love for being on the water.

After returning the sabot, we relaxed on the beach enjoying the brilliant sunshine.

"See that sailboat anchored way over there," Jan stretched out his long arm, pointing to a mere speck. "Let's swim to it."

The turquoise sea was inviting. The sun hot. "I want to but am afraid I might make it that far and not be able to get back."

"You can. I know you can do it. But, I promise, if you can't, I'll help you."

His confidence made me feel like I could do anything. The night before while I sat on the window seat in his cabin, he told me, "Whatever happens, I promise you this. I will never lie to you." So, when he said I was beautiful or sexy or could do something, I believed him. With zero expectations, neither of us had any reason to lie. Such honesty refreshed me like ice-cold water quenching my thirst. There were no games. If he didn't like me the way I was, it didn't matter. Our relationship couldn't last anyway. Having nothing to fear made me honest too.

Nothing could ever change the fact that I now knew sex could be the most powerful experience ever. Our relationship couldn't compare to bad sex—they were two completely different means of expression—one painful, tense, and a violation of personal space. The other beyond beautiful, intimate, a shared closeness that defied description. Our love-making involved feelings of safety, honesty, and openness.

Jan seemed to value truth more than most. If people didn't like him the way he was, that was their problem. He might tell me many things I didn't want to hear, but I doubted that he'd ever lie to me, even if the truth hurt.

He hadn't lied when we'd been sitting side by side on his bed after I'd gotten dressed the night before. He'd been quiet a few minutes as though thinking hard about something. Then he looked me in the eye and said, "Pat-ti, I must warn you. Do *not* fall in love with me." Perhaps the intensity of our physical relationship scared him. Maybe it was because I couldn't hide how much I craved his touch.

Yet, knowing his lifestyle and seeing his serious face, I laughed. "There's not a chance in hell. That's the last thing I need." And, I meant it.

The idea of permanence had nothing to do with my current happiness. For so many reasons, our relationship could not last. Every memory with Jan, however, would remain for a lifetime. Nothing could ever steal a single moment from my mind.

He'd even made me feel safe enough to mention my secret dream of being a writer. As he shared his goals of becoming a captain, I shared my dreams about wanting to write. But knowing it would be too hard, I'd never told anyone. He couldn't understand why I didn't chase that dream, but it seemed impossible, and I was a nobody with nothing to say. Yet Jan could convince me of almost anything—including swimming to that boat.

Walking down to the tranquil sea, we waded into the tepid water. He dove in, while I sunk down to get wet, then followed at my own pace. Swimming hard I made it all the way to the sloop. For a few minutes we clung to the side of the craft giving me a chance to rest. On the way back, I did a lazy sidestroke, and Jan stayed close. Reaching the sand, he took my hand. "I'm so proud of you, Pat-ti." My heart swelled with delight.

A Safe Harbor

Back at the ship, we headed for his room. Sitting side by side on his bed, he took my wrist, turning it so he could read the writing on my nickel-plated bracelet. "You wear this always. Why? Who is Roy F. Townley?"

I sighed, rubbing the imprinted name. "My dad. He disappeared during the Vietnam War. Family members wear these bracelets to raise awareness that our men still need to be accounted for."

His face was etched with concern. "You don't know what happened?"

"No. Evidently there's been some live-sighting reports, but I can't bear to think he's a POW, who got left behind. My dad wasn't in the military. He worked for Air America, a company contracted to the CIA."

"Such work must be dangerous." Jan put his arm behind my back, urging me to continue.

I spoke softly. "It was. From what I understand, Air America performed many of the perilous feats shown on the news. "My dad's cargo could be dangerous, and they often had to land on short runways. With a hillside rushing toward his plane, they once landed with a load of fuel that would have exploded if they didn't stop in time."

"Do you think he might still be alive?"

"Several years ago, Jeremiah Denton did a television interview from the Hanoi Hilton. He blinked out in Morse code that POWs were being tortured. Knowing that changed things for me. At first, we thought Daddy would walk out of the jungle. But he didn't. To think he might have such horrendous things done to him—well," I heaved a deep sigh. "I just can't think of that. Or that he got left behind during Operation Homecoming. I was so happy to see

Denton first off the plane that brought so many of our men back. But watching all those POWs return to their families and hoping against hope that my dad might be among them . . ." I stopped, taking another deep breath.

"I loved my dad, Jan, so much. You would have loved him, too, and he would have loved you." The two of them shared such a strong sense of fun and adventure. I could envision them drinking beer together, telling jokes, laughing. "He used to take us water skiing—we had a boat named 'One More Time,' because when we fell, we always wanted to get back up and go one more time. All the way to the Salton Sea, we'd sing songs back and forth over an intercom—Daddy and my brother-in-law in the front of his truck and my sisters and me in the camper."

"How many are your sisters?"

"Though I think of them as my regular sisters, Diane and Suzie are from my dad's first marriage, so technically they're half-sisters. Valerie, Janet, and I have the same mom and dad. Diane lived with us until I was about ten. Suzie lived with her mom."

"Not knowing what happened to your dad must be very hard for you."

"It's hard, but you need to understand that our family wasn't like other families. Even when my parents were still married, my dad rarely came home at night. He worked in New Mexico, but we lived in California. My mom didn't want to move because she didn't know anyone there. And, he was gone most of the time on trips flying celebrities to the racetrack at Ruidoso Downs.

"We believed my dad to be invincible. For months after I got the phone call telling me he was missing, I figured he'd turn up the way he always did. My sisters are convinced he'd have his captors laughing, and they'd be his friends. As for me, I'd rather think he died quickly than to imagine him in the Hanoi Hilton being beaten or having bamboo shoots forced under his nails." Despite the warmth sitting so close to Jan, I shivered, then struggled with my words.

Heaving another sigh, I admitted, "The hardest part was that we hadn't been getting along. Valerie and I hadn't spoken to him in two years."

"Why?" Though we weren't touching, Jan's attention was so riveted on me, I felt his support. His intense desire to understand emanated compassion. My family didn't discuss these things other than to wonder if my dad was still alive. Diane, Suzie, and Janet were all convinced he'd come home. Val was convinced he was gone. In a vision one night not long after he disappeared, he'd visited her, and they'd made peace. My husband Jeff didn't care enough to listen, much less ask questions. And, I didn't have any close friends. No one ever asked about my feelings, until now.

"It's complicated. He took my younger sister, Janet, to live in Laos. She was only 15. We had no communication with her while she was gone, and we were scared for her. They could hear bombs exploding not far from where they lived in Vientiane. I understand why he did it, but it almost killed my mother, and it was unbearable to see her in such pain. There's no doubt my mom's thinking caused a lot of problems, but she's been good to me in many ways."

Feeling safe, I took a deep breath letting it out slowly. Never-spoken words came slowly, painfully. "While my parents were married, my dad had an affair with my stepmother. That led to my parents' divorce. My mother didn't know what else to do, but losing him devastated her. She turned to the man she worked for—a man who molested my youngest sister. I was only a kid, but as soon as I found out, I told."

"You did?"

"Yes. It was awful. I went to Suzie. She and her husband involved my dad. At first, my mom tried to deny it. Then she tried to do the right thing. I remember her asking the advice of our doctor, plus a lawyer friend. Both said not to make a big deal of it. So, we never spoke of it again.

"But then she married the guy. He offered a way to support her three daughters financially, and she was terrified of being poor. His uncle owned the dental x-ray labs that became a thriving business. My sisters and I wanted our mom to be happy so when they asked our permission to get married, we gave it."

Jan's eyes narrowed and furrows creased his forehead. "You?"

"No. Though I was barely a teenager, I would have killed him if he'd touched me. As I told you, I always thought sex should be special—between a man and woman who have committed to love each other for a lifetime. He tried to proposition me, but after I refused, he left me alone. In fact, he treated me with respect, talking to me like an adult about world events. While they were married, we got along.

"Before the wedding, he and my mom bought me contacts so I could stop wearing glasses. That built my confidence, changing my life for the better. They gave my sister, Valerie, a car—a 1957 black Ford Fairlane convertible. We had many good times in that car. And, my family moved into a large house in the best part of town. It had a pool and a shuffleboard court. Despite all that, their marriage only lasted a few years. It was awful. And, I learned money cannot buy happiness."

Pain-filled memories brought forth silence as I remembered coming downstairs one night to wait for a date. Before leaving, I was supposed to introduce the boy to them—but this night I heard my mother screaming, her husband towering over her, shouting. Peeking around the corner into the family room, I was horrified to watch him pour a beer on her perfectly styled hair. Seeing my date walking up the drive, I ran out to meet him and begged him to take me away. Though he was kind and took me to the beach, the images from that horrible incident remained. Not long afterward, my stepfather found a girlfriend. Relieved, my mom bought the business and our home, so he could sail around the world. Trying to erase him from her mind, she never discussed him or what he did, so neither did I.

With nothing more to say, Jan's strong arms pulled me close, enfolding me against his chest. "You are so sexy," he said with a smile, and I longed to please him. Our lovemaking whisked away every trace of heartache.

An International Freedom Council

That night Jan came into the nightclub, and we joined his friends—Stig (the ship's doctor), Sten (an engineer), and my mom. Though Sten was about our age, he put his arm around my beautiful mother, and she delighted in flirting with him. No wonder she hadn't complained about my being gone in the afternoons or my late nights. Obviously, they already knew each other quite well.

Stig was excited because his "married" girlfriend would arrive the next day. Upon leaving the nightclub, Jan took me to the radio room and introduced me to his friends, Edgar and Hilda, a couple from Belgium. They mentioned that several of the crew were going ashore in Grenada and encouraged Jan to join them. I wondered if he'd invite me to come or leave me behind.

Later, when we said goodnight, Jan said I should be at the gangway by 12:30—no later or he'd leave without me. We talked about water skiing, and I could hardly wait. It had been years since I'd skied, but I hoped to show off.

As my mother and I returned from town, Jan stood near the gangway; waiting by a taxi with its door open and engine running. Anxious to leave, he urged me to hurry. Shortly thereafter, we arrived at a resort with a huge horseshoe-shaped bar on the beach—looking out on the aquamarine sea. More than a dozen of Jan's friends surrounded it, but as we walked up, several of them quickly slid over making room for us and pulling up chairs.

For me, it felt like a mini-United Nations. Representatives from Cuba, Belgium, Norway, Denmark, and England—young world-travelers telling one story after another.

The only American, I listened—a little ashamed, yet fascinated. Their lives were so different from mine. Making good money, with little time to spend it and no living expenses while at sea, they didn't need to worry about financial security or cleaning house. They worked hard and played even harder. While I wanted to stay safe, they lived life on the edge with enough money to do what they wanted—and freedom in their relationships. They spoke with pride of their homelands and frequently mentioned their heritage.

When asked my nationality, I felt like a mutt in a pedigreed world. I didn't know; it wasn't clear. Yet they were all so proud of their lineage.

Mostly I kept silent, disillusioned by our government. Watergate. Nixon's resignation to avoid being impeached. The Pentagon Papers. Government lies about our involvement in Laos. Again and again, we heard on the news: "There are no Americans in Laos." Yet, my dad and Janet had lived there. Adding to America's shame, Jane Fonda, the traitorous "Hanoi Jane," increased the confusion by questioning our POW accounts about being systematically tortured.

The experiences of Jan and his friends were completely foreign to me. Tall tales rang with bits of truth amidst peals of laughter, borne of courage enough to take risks and explore the unknown. When things didn't go according to plan, a new plan emerged. Two young women gave me chills as they described missing the ship in Port-au-Prince, Haiti. All night long pounding voodoo drums terrified them and convinced them never to take that risk again. Others spoke of their homelands with nationalistic pride. Stories ridiculed rude American tourists on board ship. Even I had been ashamed of some of my fellow passengers, their insulting demands and crass behavior.

Feasting on rum punch, I drank my lunch. When Jan said we'd ski later, I described how my sisters and I used to play London bridges crossing under each other's tow ropes. Increasingly concerned that I might have trouble getting up, I avoided complete intoxication by escaping alone to the glistening blue-green sea. Its warmth enfolded me as I floated under the glaring Caribbean sun, my feet occasionally touching the sandy bottom in the shallow water. Peaceful quiet surrounded my rum-punch reverie. Having the inner strength not to cling to Jan brought a sense of confident satisfaction. The afternoon felt so splendid; I wanted to remain there forever.

Nearby, a sudden rustling in the water startled me. Imagining a large sea creature, my heart pumped faster as a fair-skinned, platinum-haired young woman broke the surface right beside me, with peals of laughter. It was Brigitte, Stig's girlfriend. Though she only knew a smattering of English, we giggled like schoolgirls introducing ourselves and trying to communicate. Inexplicably an instant bond formed with the silvery blonde, who wore a tiny brown bikini on her exquisite body. Hoping she was wearing sunscreen, I feared she'd blister in the sun's intense rays.

Jan interrupted my thoughts, calling to me from the beach and pointing to a waiting ski boat: "Let's go, you dummy!"

Attempting to tandem ski, I fell twice. The third time I went down, Jan shouted at me. "Get in the boat! Now!" His abrupt command stung, but when one of the boat's crew mentioned sharks—I shivered and watched Jan ski, embarrassed that I wasn't gliding across the water with him. Once we returned to shore, I remained in the water swimming close to the beach rather than face his disappointment.

Releasing my cares, I reminded myself that it didn't matter what Jan thought. Within less than a week I'd be going home, never to see him again. Still, I craved his approval. Floating, alone with my thoughts, it startled me when someone shouted in alarm.

The Ship Might Sail Without Us

We only had half an hour to get back on board before the Sun Viking sailed. From the beach, I could hear someone insisting, "There's no way a taxi can make it in time."

We might miss the ship! My mother would be furious. Even worse, Jan might get fired. This just couldn't be the end to such a perfect day.

Then, I saw a speed boat racing toward us. Someone had talked its owner into taking us for a hefty price. Several of us piled in and, with a wide-open throttle, we raced across the shining sea.

Jan's silence and set jaw showed how worried he was. He'd be in trouble if he was late or caught with a passenger. I wondered if we'd make it in time or if he was sorry he'd brought me.

With only minutes to spare, we pulled alongside the Sun Viking. The crew must have been expecting us. A cargo door to the hold yawned open—high above. Sailors lowered a thick rope ladder over the side and panic seized me in its grip. I couldn't even get up on skis, how was I going to climb that?

Everyone wanted me on board immediately. That opening must have been at least two stories up! Not at all sure I could make it, I looked at Jan, and he saw the fear on my face. He firmly grasped me by the arms and looked me in the eyes: "You must hold on very tight, Pat-ti. But you can do it. I know you can. And, you must. I'm going to go first so I can help you inside, then you must follow."

After my disastrous performance skiing, I was determined not to disappoint him. Though terrified, there was no choice. It was a long way up. Thankful, I'd given up the rum punch hours earlier, my head was clearer. My arms stronger, although my heart pounded like a drum. After Jan disappeared inside, another officer helped me grab the rough rope high up then placed my foot on the swinging ladder's lowest rung. Jan reappeared in the doorway watching my every move, quietly urging me on. While the crew above watched and officers below offered encouragement I clung tight to the ladder—climbing step by step, placing my foot on one rung and bringing the other up to meet it. "Don't look down, just look at me, you're almost here. You can do this."

Watching Jan, I believed him and became all the more determined not to fail. The drop itself was enough to make me grip that rope with more strength than I'd thought possible.

As soon as I came close to the top, Jan grabbed my arms, and a couple of blue-shirted sailors helped him hoist me inside.

Looking down at me, Jan grinned. "I'm so proud of you, Pat-ti." Those words spoken in front of everyone made my heart race. So did his whispered suggestion that we head up to his quarters.

Later, we lazed on his bed and talked. "How old are you?" Jan asked.

"I'm 24."

"I'm 25." Even his eyes smiled as he spoke. "One year older. One-year difference is just right between man and woman. You are perfect. Just perfect for me."

For a moment, I couldn't breathe. He didn't lie. We were perfect together. Still, I must not have any illusions. Our relationship couldn't, wouldn't last. In a matter of days, I'd be going home.

Chapter 4

Under the Stars

"Come. Have a drink with us." Surprised, I looked up to see Stig asking me to join him and Brigitte in the small intimate bar behind the main lounge. His invitation made me happy. Despite Jan being on duty, they wanted my company enough to come find me in the main lounge. My mom had gone to bed early, so that gave me the freedom to do as I pleased.

Seeing Brigitte standing at the bar, her lobster-red blistered skin made me cringe. "Are you OK?"

Her gleeful laughter was contagious. "I don't know, to tell my husband. He thinks I am in Spain, and it rained there whole time I am away," The absurdity of her being caught, red-faced, made me grin.

Stig's dark brown eyes shone with adoration, and I could see why. Though outrageous, Brigitte was delightful—smart, beautiful, and like a wild colt racing across a meadow for sheer joy.

Merriment sparkled in her eyes and even the normally reserved doctor looked amused as we watched Penny waddle our way. A small plump blonde New Yorker with flashy jewels, her loud voice notoriously hijacked conversations. With no escape route, Stig and Brigitte put their heads together and started conversing in Danish. Without a clue as to what they were saying, I leaned against the bar, rested my chin in my hand, and nodded intent upon their every word, hoping Penny might pass us by.

She didn't. Stopping behind us, at a momentary lapse in conversation, Penny started telling a story. We smiled, made polite comments, and sipped our drinks. Finally, she took a breath, then looked at me. "And you, my dear—I'm simply amazed at how well you speak English!"

She was barely out of sight when our laughter erupted. The thought of me, a Southern California native, passing for a Scandinavian couldn't have been more hilarious. Yet our frivolity screeched to a halt, when an officer I didn't recognize appeared and headed straight for me.

An Unwelcome Intrusion

"Patti, we have been paging you. Edgar figured you wouldn't hear it and thought it might be important. He sent me to find you. We thought you might be here. There's a shore-to-ship call for you."

Edgar had told me when I met him that a call home would cost $9.00 a minute, so this must be an emergency. Jeff and I didn't have that kind of money. The voice on the other end of that call had the power to change my life, forever. Stig and Brigitte offered to come with me; however, I waved them off, knowing they couldn't help.

Rushing toward the stairs, I was terrified, "My son . . ."

"It's OK," the Norwegian officer said softly. Horrible thoughts flooded my mind. "We'll be right there with you." He placed his hand on my back to steady me as we climbed the stairs.

Images of my little boy lying in a hospital bed—or worse—crowded my mind. By the time we entered the radio room, guilt for coming on this two-week cruise became all-consuming. Hilda looked at me with concern as Edgar handed me the receiver. Taking a jagged breath, I said, "Hello." Hearing my husband's voice, I interrupted: "What's wrong? Is Josh OK?"

Jeff's brusque monotone startled me. "He's fine. I just need to know if you want me here when you get home." My thoughts raced as I fought to stay calm. He couldn't possibly know about Jan, could he? We'd met my mom's neighbor that first night. I hadn't seen Chris lately but wouldn't he still be on the ship? Even if he'd gone home, he didn't know Jeff. No, my husband couldn't know. His question must have stemmed from the growing animosity between us.

Silently I shouted, "No, I don't want you there," but the words stuck in my throat. How could anyone be that cruel? Certainly, I couldn't end my marriage with a phone call, no matter how much I disliked my husband.

And, I still didn't want a divorce. Jan offered no future. More than anything I wanted a family for my son—a mother and father, together.

Relief, fear, and despair climaxed in anger. "Yes. Of course! Why would you ask such a question?" I demanded. "Why did you call and scare me that way?"

Hopelessness drummed its beat into my mind as I ended the call, embarrassed and shaken to the core. Though I assured the concerned radio officers that there was no problem, I lied. My life was a mess.

Wanting to be alone, I went downstairs, pushed open a heavy door, and stepped outside into the oppressive evening air. Finding an isolated spot by the pool, I perched on the edge of a chaise lounge and rubbed my throbbing temples. What am I going to do? How can I possibly make my marriage work? And, what about Jan?

This was the decade of "me." I had abandoned all the rules to learn about my "self." With no responsibilities, I thought I could be whoever I wanted for two full weeks. Despite knowing that the sensations of lovemaking, intimacy, and respectful interactions could only be temporary, I'd taken that risk thinking no one outside this oceanic realm would ever know. But how could I possibly put Jan in the past? Though it was clear I must not fall in love, I was crazy about him. Yet those emotions couldn't be any more than temporary. If he knew how I felt, the relationship would be over. I simply must not, could not, fall in love. And, what about the family I longed for? He was not an option.

Jan's highest priorities involved his career and seeking pleasure. Mine were diametrically opposed—stability with a family and conventional routines. He loved his glacial homeland; I loved Southern California's warmth. He constantly made new friends and went on adventures in exotic locations. He spent vacations in Spain with his best friend. All I wanted was security—a home and a husband, who would come home at night and be there for me and my son.

This cruise had put me onboard my own personal Titanic, an emotional ship destined to sink. My mind and body had connected in ways I'd never before experienced. Yet, that problem seemed mine alone. Others had casual sex. Why couldn't I?

At least, this time my feelings weren't wrecking the relationship. Although I had a hard time not revealing how much I adored Jan, knowing our relationship couldn't continue made me seem as elusive as he was. Craving a life with someone like him was out of the question. But how could I live without him?

The muggy night's silence wrapped me in a thick blanket of despair. Knowing what was at stake, I leaned back to look up at turbulent storm clouds with glimpses of the moon peeking through. A gentle breeze parted them enough to reveal patches of a night sky spangled with the brilliance of diamonds tossed on a black velvet jeweler's cloth.

Hope in the Heavens

It would take someone big enough to hang those stars in the sky to fix this mess. Right, I laughed ruefully. Even if such a Creator existed, why would he help someone like me? I left my little boy to go on a Caribbean cruise. I cheated on my husband. Worst of all, I didn't even feel guilty. And, I was crazy about a man I must not fall in love with. This situation was beyond any power I had to control it.

For a moment I sensed an unseen presence—one that understood and cared about the mess I'd made, a mess far too big for me to clean it up. Maybe that was wishful thinking. This was only the tip of an iceberg that lay straight ahead. And, no matter what, I had to stay in the truth. My relationship with Jan would soon be over.

Chapter 5

Anchors, A Way

On the hot afternoon we met at the gangway in La Guaira, an electrical current flashed between Jan's eyes and mine. Despite the heat, I had dressed deliberately in a long-sleeved mint green cotton jacket and matching pants with a tie-dyed slim-fitting tee.

"You look perfect," Jan's voice took on a husky tone as his eyes devoured me. My heart swelled at the pride in his voice.

While walking along the dock to go into town, Jan kept glancing up at the Venezuelan freighter moored behind our ship. "What are you looking at?" I asked.

"Those sailors. They are staring at you."

"They are not." Jan liked to set me up to see my reaction. Convinced he was teasing, I wasn't going to take the bait.

"Yes, they are." He grinned. "They're undressing you with their eyes."

Squinting, I shielded my eyes from the sun and looked up high above the towering ship. A guy with a scruffy beard waved. Though I never blushed— I could feel heat rise into my face, turning it red. Jan laughed out loud at my naiveté.

"Men do that sometimes. The Spanish don't hide their admiration for a pretty woman." His voice carried unmistakable pride. Maybe he wouldn't forget me so easily.

Leaving the docks behind, we turned inland. Walking next to a high curb, I climbed up on it—making myself almost as tall as Jan. Charmed, he smiled with his eyes. It was a spectacular afternoon—bright blue sky, gentle breeze with a dynamic Norwegian lover beside me. Moments later, we stopped outside a jewelry store. "Wait here," he commanded.

Basking in the freedom, I didn't mind. No responsibilities. No husband or mother telling me what to do. A sexy man who made me feel beautiful. I had no idea what Jan was doing, and it didn't matter. Maybe he had to buy his girlfriend something, but that was none of my concern.

Within minutes, he reappeared. "Hold out your hand." When I did, he placed a tiny gold anchor in my palm. Royal Caribbean's emblem, a perfect memento of this cruise. Yet Jan seemed a bit embarrassed.

"I wanted to get you a bigger one, but they didn't have any. I am sorry." He looked crestfallen.

Sorry? Such unexpected thoughtfulness made my heart nearly burst with joy. Men didn't buy me spur-of-the-moment gifts. It didn't matter how big the anchor was. This precious memento was a way to treasure our time together for the rest of my life. "Oh, no! I love this one. It's perfect. Dainty, just-right for me."

I didn't want a bigger one. He owed me nothing, yet was giving me a lifetime of memories. Now I had an incredible reminder of our time together. As soon as possible I'd get a chain so I could wear the anchor next to my heart. I wanted to kiss him, but his public restraint prevented us from touching.

Walking a few blocks more, we turned into a small bar. Jan couldn't disguise his disappointment at the empty establishment. "I'd hoped my friends from the ship would be here. This is where they often come."

An Unforgettable Afternoon

Speaking Spanish to the lone bartender, Jan pulled out two high stools from the bar. "Watch. He's making us sangria." They resumed speaking Spanish, with Jan repeating the ingredients to me in English. Fresh pineapple, oranges, apples, and limes soon floated in the clear pitcher of deep red liquid—a mixture of wine, rum, and other liquors. Overhead, a fan whirred, cooling us with an easy tropical breeze.

As though we were starring in a movie scene, Jan requested a long-handled spoon and began feeding me the alcohol-soaked fruit as he continued conversing with the barman. Not understanding a word they were saying simply added to the dramatic ambiance. At peace, I felt valued, respected, at one with all that was good. Whenever I had a question or comment, Jan quickly turned his full attention to me, but mostly I watched and listened while drinking deep of La Guaira's exotic flavors.

People gravitated to Jan with such ease and respect that I was proud to be with him, even if for only a moment in time. The opportunity to practice different languages made him happy, and his enthusiasm made me happy. The last thing I wanted was to restrict his freedom.

Finishing the pitcher, he helped me down from the bar stool, and we walked to another place where we found more than a dozen of his friends. Quickly, they scooted wooden chairs to make space for us at the long table where platters of fried shrimp were being distributed. Famished, under a whirring fan, I feasted on the fabulous seafood with the spicy/tangy dipping sauce that made my taste buds dance. And, I sipped more sangria.

It wasn't until we walked out to the hot musty street that I began to feel a bit nauseous and dizzy. Determined to maintain my composure, I remarked on how delicious the shrimp had tasted.

"You dummy. That wasn't shrimp; it was squid." Trying to digest that thought took all the effort I could muster. For a moment I feared losing my lunch but when Jan's friend jostled him, it diverted my attention. In a low voice, his fellow officer issued a warning. "You had better be careful taking her back." The only thing worse than Jan being caught with me would be getting me drunk.

"Pat-ti, you cannot walk back to the ship," Jan said gently. "I'm going to get us a ride." At that moment we stood behind a white construction truck with men perched all around the bed, hands gripping a high metal bar overhead that attached to the cab. Finding the driver, Jan conversed with him in Spanish. They chuckled as Jan pointed toward me.

The next thing I knew he came back by my side, picked me up, and set me far enough inside the lowered tailgate that I wouldn't fall off. Then, he hoisted himself up to stand in front of me, grabbing onto the rail alongside the other men. When they dropped us near the Sun Viking, we all waved goodbye, then Jan turned to me with a serious expression. "You must walk carefully, Pati-ti, up the gangway. You must not attract attention."

Time Keeps Ticking

Despite having no future, my relationship with Jan existed outside of all boundaries. Time, space, marriage—nothing detracted from the intimacy we shared. I'd never been so close to anyone. The cruise was rapidly coming to an end. Other than spending an hour each night in the nightclub— having drinks and joking around with Stig and Brigitte—and our few outings away from the ship, we spent as much time as possible in Jan's cabin.

When we weren't making love, we talked about everything—even my marriage and my determination not to destroy my family. Jan asked questions about my son and listened as I described how beautiful and bright Josh was. Expressing tender love for his mother, Jan told me about his brother, his grandparents, and his dog, a big German shepherd. He described Norway, and insisted his country would love me. Should I leave my husband, I'd have no worries about health care or day care. I wouldn't even have to work because the government took care of single mothers. Disenchanted with America, it sounded enticing, though I couldn't escape reality. Like my dad, Jan wouldn't be there. He'd work elsewhere.

Memories of my dad going to work for the racetrack in Ruidoso Downs, New Mexico, when I was in fifth grade remained far too vivid. He only came home every few months for a visit. During my junior year of high school, my stepfather had to take me to the National Charity League father/daughter brunch because my dad was thousands of miles away. He didn't talk to me about boys or books because he wasn't there. I adored my daddy, but that didn't keep him home.

My fears of living elsewhere were probably even greater than my mom's had been. Jan wouldn't be in Norway; he'd be in the Caribbean or wherever else he might choose. I'd be alone with a small son in a country where I couldn't even speak the language. Moving might sound nice, but it wasn't an option. My dad hadn't remained faithful even though he loved my mom and was married to her. The temptations on a cruise ship would be constant, inescapable.

Brigitte and Stig wanted me to come visit them in Denmark. With Jan, we discussed the idea of traveling to the coast of France, but I knew that trip was only a dream. Dreams like that, even if I didn't have a husband, could not come true. I had a son, a home, responsibilities. I needed to make decisions based on what was best for Josh and for me. The security of a home and family was all I'd ever wanted. Jan couldn't provide that, and it would be disastrous for me to pretend he could.

Seeing how happy Jan was speaking different languages, embracing different cultures, and flirting with different women, he'd quickly become bored with me. Jan had been working hard ever since the age of 15 to advance his career. He loved holidays in Spain with his best friend after spending time in Norway. He was nowhere near ready to settle down. Even if he cared for me, our futures led in different directions. He'd been honest, warning me not to try to tie him down.

Sometimes, though, Jan made comments that confused me. Several times he spoke about growing old and sitting on the front porch in *our* rocking chairs. Powerful imagery at odds with reality. What was he thinking? The present was too immediate, the future too far away.

Thinking about my night under the stars, one afternoon while sitting on his bed, I asked him: "Do you believe in God?"

Hesitating for a moment, a guarded look came over his face. "I think there may be something. But mostly, I think he's for women and children, not for me." His response shut down that conversation. But I wondered, was there something more?

Our Final Excursion

The day arrived when we docked in Port-au-Prince, Haiti, our ship's last port. On the previous two cruises, Haiti had fascinated me. When his father died in 1971, at the age of 19, Jean-Claude Duvalier, Baby Doc, had assumed power as the country's ruler. He'd been even younger than me.

On the first cruise, a native "protector" had taken my mom and me from the ship to see Baby Doc's opulent residence. Decorated for his celebrated return from a trip, the wrought iron gates adorned with flowers provided a stunning contrast from other areas of the city.

While making our way through the crowds into the marketplace, our protector explained how Haitians had hoped the dictator would be kinder than his brutal father. But Baby Doc was ruthless. Citizens feared arrest, torture, and death. Goats wandered alongside us on the dirt road until we reached brightly colored stalls where vendors hawked their wares. My mom and I had bought carved mahogany statuettes and pictures crafted from banana skins, paying full price rather than bargaining as was customary. It was the least we could do to help alleviate the crushing poverty.

Today, throngs of Haitians crowded the gangway offering their wares to tourists as they disembarked. Jan had said to be on time, so we could meet his friends for lunch at a luxurious hotel on the hillside above Port au Prince. My mom and I had remained onboard, so I arrived a few minutes early to wait in the stifling heat. As soon as Jan appeared, he engaged a driver, and we climbed into the taxi's back seat.

As usual, Jan instantly struck up a conversation with the driver, and we soon discovered that this friendly guy spoke several languages. I wondered why he was driving a cab, and he explained it was the only work he could find.

His gratitude for such a menial job astonished me. Far more educated than I was, he chatted with us easily. Our conversation permitted him the freedom to ask if we'd mind stopping by his home so he could give the fare to his wife. Jan didn't hesitate. Her need to go to the market outweighed any delay and the impropriety of advance payment.

A short time later the driver pulled to the side of a dirt road announcing that this was his home. After Jan gave him some cash, the driver got out, saying he'd be right back.

The bright turquoise-painted hovel's interior could be seen in its entirety from the car. Dirt floors piled with a kaleidoscope of stuff made it look crowded and filthy. A skinny dog wandered in and out. Hot and heavy air made the stench even more putrid. The living conditions horrified me. Taking shallow breaths, I asked, "How can he live in such a dilapidated shack? I wouldn't want my dog to stay there. How do people live like this?"

Jan's swift rebuke stung. "Shhhh! Pat-ti, you must be quiet. That man is very proud of his home, and he might hear you. You must not make him feel bad about it." Embarrassed and ashamed of my arrogant ignorance, I felt terrible. Determined not to cry, I sat in silence the rest of the way to the resort while Jan continued chatting with the driver.

Entering Habitation Leclerc's luxurious grounds on an asphalt road, we wound through a gorgeous green maze—plants and trees flourished all around us. After exiting the cab, Jan escorted me along a pathway with lavish ferns towering overhead. Extravagant overstuffed beige leather couches and chairs enhanced natural alcoves. Hesitantly, wondering if Jan was still upset with me, I marveled at the grandeur. Easing the tension, Jan speculated on the resort's benefactor: "It's rumored that Aristotle Onassis was involved with financing this place."

Eventually we wandered out of the foliage into a clearing where people played in a large pool, swimming up to the bar or careening down its overhead slide. Nearby about twenty officers from the Sun Viking were seated at a long table set with crisp linens, shiny silverware, and crystal glasses.

The buffet featured all sorts of splendid seafood and other delicacies, but after my experience with the squid in La Guiara, I filled my plate carefully, avoiding the prawns with bulging eyes. Returning to the table, conversation flowed along with the drinks until the sound of shattering glass halted all conversation. For a moment, the air hung heavy with complete silence. When the hum of people enjoying themselves returned, Jan remarked on the grave situation. "Well, he's gone."

"What do you mean, he's gone? It was only a glass," I whispered.

Whether still annoyed by my naivete or this particular situation, I wasn't sure. Though Jan spoke quietly, his reply sounded harsh: "They have more than 200 people waiting for that job. Why should they keep someone who drops a glass?"

Rubbing the tiny gold anchor that hung from the chain around my neck, the injustice stunned me into silence. Though Jan sounded almost cruel at times, he only spoke of reality. Quite soon I'd face my own cruel realities. After one more day at sea, I'd fly home to my husband.

Facing the Real World

The sun was still high in the sky when we got back aboard. We weren't sailing for a couple of hours so Jan and I headed for his cabin.

Saying he needed to take care of some paperwork, Jan sat at his desk, so I perched on the window seat to stare out the window at dirt roads, bumbling traffic, and the colorful buildings across the street. Noticing blond crewmembers wearing civilian clothes entering a particular building, I began to wonder what they were doing. It didn't look like a shop; no sign hung over the door—but one guy after another kept walking in. Yet, no one came out. As much as I hated to disturb Jan, eventually curiosity got the better of me.

"Jan, see that building? What are those guys doing? What is that place?" Jan looked up. "Those men are at sea a long time, Pat-ti. They miss their wives and girlfriends. That's a place where they can pay to be accommodated."

As his words sunk in, so did my comprehension. The thought was abhorrent, birthing one even worse. "Do you ever go there?"

"No. I don't resort to that."

"I didn't think so."

Jan had said he'd never lie to me, and he had no reason to now. I'd be gone soon enough. One of the things I liked most about him was his being so straightforward. He wasn't defensive but clear and to the point. One night he'd told me how "rich blue-haired ladies" had tried to get him into bed, but he'd have no part of it despite concerns that someday his refusal might cause one of them to trump up a complaint. Though he wasn't supposed to fraternize with someone like me, his superiors expected him to "get along" with important passengers and at times he struggled with that—probably more than any other aspect of his job.

Even though our relationship was temporary, I adored him and didn't hesitate to show it when we were alone. Later, as we sat on his bed, he looked worried. "Pat-ti, you must not think of me as . . ." his voice trailed off while he searched for the right words—"as perfect. You must not try to compare your husband to me. Remember we have been on a romantic time. If you knew me in more regular situation, you would see my flaws. And, there are many."

His serious expression almost made me laugh. Yet, his concern was genuine. And, I respected him for not wanting me to think a fantasy could be reality. As crazy as I was about him, he couldn't hide his imperfections. He drank too much—though, unlike me, he never seemed to get drunk. He just always seemed preoccupied with having a drink in his hand. And, I couldn't imagine him ever settling down or having to put children ahead of himself or mowing the lawn or taking care of household responsibilities. He openly flirted with other women in front of me. At times he seemed almost arrogant, yet he was so endearing that his imperfections didn't change my feelings.

"I won't." I said, quietly. He needn't be afraid that I might leave my husband in hopes of a future with him. That simply wasn't part of the plan. I'd known from the beginning our relationship was temporary. It wasn't like Stig and Brigitte, who planned to move in together after they returned home. Stig was leaving the ship for good. Jan was not.

I missed my son. Besides, as much as I hated the thought of never seeing Jan again, I knew that the longer we were together, the harder it would get to say good-bye. It never occurred to me how hard that might already be for Jan.

Chapter 6

Devastating Goodbyes

That last night, Jan lay facing me in his twin bed—both of us sleepless—knowing that dawn was creeping ever closer. He took my face in his hands and in the moonlight that filtered into his cabin, I could see him staring at me as though trying to memorize every detail. "Pat-ti, I will tell you one thing for certain. I don't know how or when, but I will see you again."

He meant it. Of that I was certain. But things could easily change once I was gone, so I remained silent—just as I had when my dad left home. Earlier in the day while laying by the pool, I'd steeled myself against emotional outbursts. The last thing I wanted was to leave Jan with tears or pleading or any of the things that might make a woman annoying to a man. Later, the tears would come, but not now. And, not on the way home.

My mother must not see me cry, nor my husband. No one must ever think that this cruise had made me sad. It was the most magnificent time of my life, and I'd treasure the memories forever. No human being could ever wrest them from my mind.

I was tired, but probably not as much as Jan. When he'd walked by the pool after his earlier shift, he looked exhausted. Though I was disappointed when he said he was going to take a nap, I understood. It was going to be a sleepless night. And, before that he still had responsibilities on the bridge.

After he left, I lay by the pool thinking about how our lives were about to diverge. I was going home. Once again, yielding to the demands of a husband I didn't love. Caring for my precious son, making decisions based on what was best for him. Career choices needed to be made too. After being with young adults who chased their dreams, I couldn't keep working for my mother as a receptionist. For Jan, there would be new passengers, new adventures, and sooner or later another girl.

Steeled for Separation

All night, conversation and lovemaking mingled until almost time to dock in Miami. Right after we'd gotten to his room, Jan had broken news that he feared would devastate me. "As part of my duties, Pat-ti, I must be at the gangway when you disembark. I will have to treat you like any other passenger." He hesitated, then added, "If I seem cold and distant, you must understand—it is not the way I am feeling. I don't want to be there, but there was no choice. I cannot leave my post; it is my duty." My heart sank, but he looked so miserable at the thought of having to watch me leave that it deepened my determination to stay strong.

How many times had I told my dad good-bye—hugging him, then watching him walk away, not knowing when or even if I'd see him again. That agonizing memory increased my resolve not to make it any harder for Jan. I'd learned as a child how to paste on a smile when my heart was breaking. "It will be OK. I understand, and I will be all right." He'd never know how inside, I'd be dying.

Life was about to change, radically. With Jan, every precious moment was significant. Spontaneous adventures challenged my capabilities and brought a sense of achievement. He told me I was sexy, so I played that role without inhibitions. Seeing the delight in his eyes when he looked at me gave me confidence. Never again would I wonder if I was frigid. With him, I gave myself away with complete abandon. And, he appreciated me just the way I was. No matter how many miles separated us, no one could ever take any of those memories away from me.

Grief, plus lack of sleep, numbed my mind and body as my mom and I gathered our suitcases. She preceded me as we walked to the disembarkation door. A moment before reaching it, I saw Jan.

He looked as wretched as I felt. His usual white uniform, rumpled. Bristly stubble indicated his need to shave. Unkempt hair. He said good-bye to my mom with a quick hug. As she walked toward the gangway, he took my hand in his and pulled me close for one brief instant. Then his face crumpled like a newspaper squished by a giant hand. Turning on his heel, he walked away from his post.

Intense pain anesthetized my mind on the flight home. Though exhausted, I couldn't sleep or think. Sheer misery enveloped me as I leaned my head against the plane's window, so my mother wouldn't try to talk to me. After we landed at LAX and walked through the gate, I embraced my husband, pretending to be glad to see him.

Immediately I asked about Josh and Jeff said he'd asked Valerie to watch him one last night so we could go dancing. That was the last thing I wanted to do. All I wanted was to hold my son.

Arguing with Jeff was useless, so we dropped my mother off, then went home for me to shower and change. Still hoping to save my marriage, I dressed in the long blue backless gown everyone had admired on the cruise. When I came out of the bedroom, my husband took one look and said with disdain, "Do you have to wear that?"

I bit my lower lip and blinked fast to hold back the tears. Muttering something about everything else being dirty, I grabbed my purse. We went to a club he'd discovered while I was gone, and I couldn't help but wonder who he'd met there. Not that I cared. Later, back home, I tried to conjure up my newfound feelings, but now forcing myself to do my duty felt like a knife held against my throat. No emotion. No desire. No pleasure. Before my husband turned over to go to sleep, a tear slipped down my cheek. He didn't notice.

Every day I tried to be a good wife. Though I went through all the right motions, in my heart I failed. Josh gave me hugs, made me laugh, and kept me going. So did the letters Jan sent to my mother's address. He said he was proud of me for trying to make my marriage work. However, after a couple of months, one night while I was sitting under a hair dryer— my husband came over to me and wanted sex. In that instant, I couldn't pretend any more.

"I want a divorce," I said without feeling.

He reeled backward as though I'd punched him. After the initial shock, he asked if we could get counseling.

"No, I want you to move out. As soon as possible."

He asked if I'd had an affair, and I lied. There was no sense hurting him any more than I already had.

His grandfather had recently passed away so his apartment was still available. Jeff moved into it the following weekend. He said he still wanted to make our marriage work, but I was done. Having made up my mind, there was not one instant of regret. Though the idea of divorce made me cry, I never wanted to see him again.

Because we had been renting my childhood home, my neighbors, who lived on the corner opposite mine, had known me since I was a little girl. Betty, the mom, had helped me color a map of the United States when I was in fourth grade with her son. In fifth grade she gave me an angora bunny I named Thumper. After watching my husband drive away in our 1973 Ford Torino, one Saturday afternoon, Betty's husband Dave turned off his lawn mower and came across the street. "What was that jerk thinking?" he asked. I didn't know how to respond, so I just shook my head.

Dave had seen the sexy brunette my husband had brought with him to take Josh for the weekend. We'd been separated less than two weeks. Rather than making me jealous, I was relieved.

"Come on over, Patti, you need a drink." Dave, Betty, and I sat outdoors by their pool as the strong icy screwdriver worked its magic. For those few moments, I stopped wondering what I was going to do next.

Taking Risks

My mom tried hard to encourage me. One day while I was answering phones in her Riverside lab, she came to do the accounting and take me to lunch. This time she brought a paper she'd saved from my school days. It revealed my IQ results. She wanted me to know I was smart enough to manage on my own.

Because she was the boss, she often took me out for long lunches. Over Bloody Marys we'd even named Josh, because Jeff hadn't wanted to discuss what to call our unborn baby. Still, I hated working at the lab. She owned the business, and Valerie ran it. There was no incentive for me to be promoted and the tedious work of mounting x-rays day after day made me long for something more intellectually stimulating. Soon, I began searching the want ads.

Crazy creativity got me a new job! Originally the advertising executive told me he was giving the position I'd applied for to someone else—a friend of an existing employee. So, remembering the confident young woman I'd been on the cruise, I refused to take no for an answer. Calling him back, I imitated Vito Corleone as The Godfather in my gruffest voice: "I'm going to make you an offer that you can't refuse." That and some flirting brought laughter and an invitation to lunch.

By the end of our meal, he saw the value of putting me on staff with the agreement that my position would not include fringe benefits. Finally, I had become independent—no longer working for my mom nor married to a man I didn't love.

But after a few weeks, even though I had worked hard, often taking proofreading home at night, while the other girls partied, I lost my job. Only one of us could stay and Mike chose the other girl.

My mom encouraged me to live on unemployment until after my divorce settlement, but wanting to work I submitted my resume to an employment agency. Finally, the direction for my career became clear— my next job needed to involve working with words. It's what I was good at and what I loved. Still, the timing couldn't have been better for me to be off work.

Ready Or Not, Here He Comes

The phone's shrill ring woke me from a sound sleep. Glancing at the clock, I saw it was only 3:00 a.m. After Jeff left, I'd told Jan to call any time and before dawn worked best for him. As soon as I said "hello," I could hear his excitement. That, on top of my being groggy, made it almost impossible to decipher his accent.

Why did he keep saying he was going to Kansas? After asking him to repeat it about three times, I finally admitted: "I can't understand what you're saying. Please slow down."

"I'm coming to California, you dummy!" He'd already booked his ticket and would be arriving in a matter of weeks. He'd also developed a friendship with a couple who lived in Hermosa Beach and wanted to visit them too. After we disconnected, I sat up in bed and hugged my knees to my chest, wondering what it would be like to have him in my home.

He'd seemed relieved when I'd called to tell him my husband had left. In that moment, all I'd wanted was to hear his voice. Since then, we'd talked and written often.

He'd switched from 8-to-12 to 12-to-4 shifts, reassuring me that he was saving money and didn't have time to get involved with passengers. Jan claimed to have written me the longest letters of his life saying that "not even to my mother did I write so much."

At the same time, the environment on the ship was so different from my middle-class home. It had been easy to pretend to be carefree for two weeks, but I couldn't do that now. Tremendous responsibilities weighed on my shoulders—my son, my home, the need for a decent-paying job. Though I rented from my mom, I'd never missed a payment.

Jan didn't realize I had very few friends. He had so many. My husband had kept me isolated, and now I wasn't even working. My mother had been right—most couples don't continue to include single women. "It's different for men," she'd said. "Wives of friends tend to want them around to fix them up with their friends. But women all too easily become jealous of other women."

Jan would also discover that, as hard as I tried, I wasn't a terrific housekeeper. Though I did my best, some women—like my oldest sister, Diane—kept their homes immaculate. She often teased me about things I didn't even notice—like baseboards. Jan's mom had a job keeping entire airports clean. And, he was used to a cabin steward taking care of his room every day. How could I possibly live up to such expectations?

And, how would Jan feel about Josh? My son was now 18 months old. It had been easy enough to feign interest while we were on the ship, but Jan might easily consider Josh a nuisance—what then? So many questions plagued me in those early morning hours. Only one thing I knew for certain. I couldn't wait to feel his strong arms enfold me against his chest once again.

While waiting for him to arrive, I dated others. Regardless of his visit my relationship with Jan could never last, and I refused to even consider that a possibility. He was my friend—an incredible lover—but that was all it could ever be. He'd warned me not to try and pin him down. To even try to imagine a life together would destroy what we had. He might stay a couple of weeks, but then he'd leave. And, this time it would be harder. I'd be devastated, but the agony would be worth it—just to see him again, just to have a little more time, make a few more memories.

The only way to guard my heart was to never let myself forget—this relationship could not last. I'd treasure our time together for as long as possible, but this fairy tale didn't include a happy ending. I could pretend for short periods of time, but sooner or later if we tried to stay together, Jan would discover the truth. I wasn't the confident woman he envisioned. I only pretended to be sexy, intelligent, and fun. Far more of me was insecure and scared to death.

Fun and Games or Not

Like a contagious disease, my divorce infected my sister's marriage soon after my husband and I split up, so now Val was separated too. At least once a week, we met my mom at the Boarshead—a small bar with live music. One night my mother introduced me to David, an entrepreneur who owned a local restaurant among other businesses. Though everyone seemed to know and like him, and he sometimes sang with the band, my mom said she'd never seen him with a girl. She claimed he was wealthy and when he became interested in me, she encouraged me to make the most of it.

David treated me with tremendous respect. He'd do almost anything for me. One night I convinced him and another guy to take a turn-around trip to Las Vegas. Others often raved about such spontaneous adventures, and I wanted to know why. My sister agreed last minute to watch Josh, so the two guys and I left at midnight for the four-hour drive. Once we arrived, I desperately wanted sleep. David didn't even suggest a hotel, but drove us to a friend's home where all of us slept for a couple of hours in separate rooms. After we awoke, I wanted to come home, and David drove without complaint—even when I had bad dreams about us running off the road and woke up shouting "Look out, look out, look out!" He simply smiled, pulled me close, and spoke kind words to me until I dozed off again.

Not long after that trip, on a Saturday night, he took me to a "big game" lodge somewhere in the foothills. Warm and cozy, the exquisite romantic atmosphere startled me. After David ordered pheasant under glass, it occurred to me—Oh my gosh, maybe he's going to propose! David might be making an offer most girls couldn't refuse. What was I going to do? There was no way I could say yes. But hurting him seemed unthinkable.

It didn't matter how much money David had. Or, what a catch everyone thought him to be. There was no spark, no fireworks—not the way there were with Jan. I never again wanted to be married to someone my body didn't crave.

Jan had stretched me in every dimension—believing in me, making me tall enough to reach higher than I'd ever imagined. He'd broadened my horizons and satisfied my soul making me more than I ever could have been without him. While David would take good care of me, I wanted more.

My heart sank as David reached for his napkin, swiped at his mouth, then started to steer the conversation in a more intimate direction. I stopped him mid-sentence: "David, before you go on, there's something I have to tell you."

He looked me in the eye, and my heart raced as I struggled to find the right words. "I . . . I, I need you to know that I've been involved with someone else." I went on to tell him about Jan and our cruise. That in a matter of weeks, Jan was coming to stay with me.

There was a long pause as David stared at me, disappointment filling his eyes as comprehension set in. If he'd yelled at me, I'd have felt better. But he didn't. He said he understood and reclaimed the role of my friend, turning our conversation in an easier direction. In that moment I knew he cared about me, more than himself.

But, by the night's end, my thoughts began racing forward to Jan's visit.

Chapter 7

A Cosmic Moment

For two weeks before Jan was to arrive, I cooked, stocking the freezer with stuffed bell peppers, casseroles, and easy-to-heat meals. I scrubbed floors, vacuumed the baseboards, dusted, and even washed the top of the refrigerator. I cleaned out the bedroom closet making room for his clothes and put clean sheets on the bed. Valerie agreed to watch Josh overnight so Jan and I could be alone.

Jan arrived at LAX in the afternoon on the Saturday after the 4th of July. Though I was waiting at the gate when he got off the plane, I wasn't used to public displays of affection with him. Coming from Miami, he'd already had a long day and needed a shower. My hug was stiff, quick, and awkward—then I turned, leading the way down the escalator, but not before seeing his disappointment. He caught up to me and grabbed my arm. "Pat-ti, aren't you going to kiss me?" Breaking through my reservations, we kissed, but my fears prevailed keeping me aloof.

We made small talk on the way home in my 1970 white Maverick, a car I loathed. My lawyer had asked me what things would mean something to me in ten years. All that really mattered was my son so I gave my husband everything of value—our land at the Colorado river, the blue 1973 Ford Gran Torino, and his motorcycle. But when his parents insisted he take the silverware they gave us for a wedding present, I refused. No other woman was going to use my silver. I didn't care who gave it to us.

Jan was simply impressed that I had a car. With the high taxes in Norway and gas more than triple our cost, he couldn't afford one despite his impressive career.

The traffic crawled. Freeway congestion escalated my anxiety. I barely knew the man sitting beside me, and he'd be staying in my home for the next two weeks.

My heart raced at the sight of his lanky blue-jean clad frame, and I longed for his embrace. But what if he wanted to use my home (and bed) for a Southern California adventure. My fears kept escalating until they got the better of me. Though normally easy-going, I needed to make clear there was something I wouldn't tolerate.

Self-Protection

Jan had often put his arms around both Brigit and me at the same time. Stig didn't seem to mind, but despite knowing we had no commitment, his flirting bothered me. Not that I could say anything. There was also no denying that Jan had taken me into his bed, even though he had a girlfriend in Spain. No doubt he'd eventually be with other women, but not while he was living in my home.

Gripping the steering wheel, I watched the cars ahead. Nervous, the hard tone in my voice sounded foreign to me. "There are some things I need you to know, Jan. Of course, you can do whatever you want, we've no strings attached—I understand that. But I need you to be aware that if you want to spend the night with another woman while you're here, you can't come back to my house. Do whatever you want, but please keep that in mind. I'm serious. I couldn't handle that."

"Also, as embarrassing as this is to say, because I'm unemployed, if you want me to do anything with you, I can't afford to pay my own way. I can only go places with you if you are willing to pay for me, too. I have no choice. Right now, I can barely cover my bills."

My boldness shocked me. Never had I spoken to a man that way, especially one who meant so much to me. However with overwhelming turmoil in my life already, plus having just suffered the tremendous pain of a loveless marriage, I never intended to let anyone treat me badly again. Not even Jan.

He was silent for a few moments. "That is fine," he said evenly. Letting out a sigh, I tried to smooth things over the rest of the way home and Jan seemed OK, so I tried to relax.

Finding a Rhythm

As he put his suitcase in the bedroom, I opened a bottle of wine. Then we sat in the living room—he on the couch, me in a chair. He was confused.

"Pat-ti, what is wrong? You are so distant. Even in the airport, I don't understand. I know I should go take a shower, but I just want to be with you."

Taking a deep breath, I heaved another sigh. "I'm sorry, Jan, but I've never done this before. I'm nervous. Why don't you go take a shower and give me a few minutes?" Though he seemed to want to say more, I gave him clean towels and pointed him in the right direction.

Taking our wine glasses into the bedroom, I placed them on the nightstands. Knowing Jan wouldn't be long, I quickly slipped into a skimpy black nightie. Somehow that transformed me back into the woman I'd been onboard ship. By the time Jan came into the bedroom wrapped in a towel, I greeted him with open arms. His touch chased my fears away. At least, until the next morning.

The sun was high in the sky by the time we were ready for breakfast. Jan's tenderness overcame most of my insecurities, but when I went to make breakfast, I had to confess that I didn't know how to fry an egg.

Every woman in the world probably knew how to do that, but I'd never learned. My ex-husband had always cooked them. Though I offered scrambled, Jan said he'd cook. But first, he wanted to get something.

While he rummaged through his suitcase, I took out the cast iron skillet and started the sausage sizzling. Then I placed the hash browns on the griddle and sprinkled them with seasoning salt and pepper, grabbing the sour cream out of the refrigerator so I could layer it between the patties.

Jan came up from behind. "Close your eyes and turn around."

He took my hand and placed something in it. When he said to open my eyes, I saw a bigger version of the anchor he'd bought me in Venezuela.

My heart sank because I treasured the little one and couldn't bear to replace it. "That's the one I wanted to give you, but they didn't have any," Jan explained looking pleased with himself.

I didn't know how to respond. My tiny anchor was so delicate and laden with memories. I wore it all the time. The long chain easily tucked inside my blouse and kept that priceless treasure close to my heart. Not wanting to seem ungrateful, I put my arms around him and thanked him. "I'll wear them together—the bigger one for you; the smaller one for me."

That was as close as I could come to thinking of us as a couple. Jan had made it clear both during the cruise and again in a letter that I'd "been smart not to try and tie him down" because that would chase him away. My only hope of keeping him near was to pretend I'd be OK whenever he left.

With Jan's carefree spirit, I also wondered, how he'd relate to my son. But soon after cleaning up from breakfast, Jan said, "Let's go get, Joash!" Valerie was surprised we showed up so early.

No one could resist my little curly-haired moppet, and the way Jan stooped down to look Josh in the eyes and talk to him delighted me. My son was completely enamored, and within moments he and Jan became fast friends. Still, I worried about Josh getting in Jan's way.

One morning as I put the bacon in the frying pan, I saw Josh toddle into the bathroom to watch Jan shave. Leaning the spatula against the cast-iron skillet, I decided to go get him before Jan might get annoyed. However, the two of them met me in the den. Grinning from ear to ear—white foamy lather covered the lower half of their faces. That precious moment made me realize I wasn't the only one who'd be devastated when Jan left.

He'd thought he'd stay two weeks, but things didn't quite go according to plan.

Because I wasn't working, Jan and I were together 24/7 for two full weeks. It didn't matter whether we stayed home or went out, every minute of togetherness was special. Even when we disagreed. About 10:00 o'clock one morning, he opened a beer.

"Isn't it kind of early?"

"Pat-ti, I am on vacation."

As I expressed concern that he might become an alcoholic, a storm cloud passed over his face conveying that he'd heard me, and I shouldn't say more. It wasn't my place, so I didn't.

The nights I cooked, we ate by candlelight, sipping wine, and talking for hours. It was rare we watched television—most of the time, we reveled in being together.

Some nights, my next-door neighbor Lori, a tall blond teenager, came over to watch Josh so we could go out. Though she was only in high school, Jan flirted with her until his teasing made her blush. It made me a little jealous, yet once we came home, there was no doubt, I was his girl.

Everywhere we went, Jan made friends. If we met someone who spoke a different language, he did too, practicing Spanish and asking questions to learn more. I loved listening even when I didn't understand what was being said. Most people delighted in his stories and ability to make them laugh.

We spent time with Diane and my brother-in-law Bruce. After splurging on a steak dinner at the Cask and Cleaver one night, we went back to their home and Jan talked Diane and me into playing "frigate."

"Kneel on the carpet," he instructed placing a 9"x 13" dish full of water between us. "Get closer. The first to blow this matchbook to your opponent's side will be proclaimed the winner."

He stood above us, ready to drop the matchbook as he dramatically counted down. "Ready, set . . ." Our faces within inches of the dish, Diane and I leaned in even closer and took deep breaths ready to blow.

"Go!"

Yet, instead of releasing the matchbook, Jan slapped the water hard with his open hand.

Stunned and dripping wet, Diane and I stared at each other. Seeing the shock on our faces made us erupt into gales of laughter. At the sight of the two of us, Bruce and Jan roared.

My Norwegian delighted in catching me off-guard. The night we popped popcorn, he watched mesmerized as the kernels burst into snowy white morsels. "How do they do that?" he asked, his eyes wide and his voice crackling with surprise. He almost convinced me that they didn't have popcorn in Norway, but his sly little grin and the twinkle in his eyes gave him away. Sometimes I caught him off-guard, too, surprising us both with my creativity.

Still, I don't think either of us was prepared for what happened after having been together constantly for fourteen days.

Time for a Break

Jan announced one morning that he had decided to go visit his friends. Though I didn't want him to leave, I couldn't let him know so I encouraged him to go. "That will be good, Jan. Many things need my attention; this way I can get them done. The house needs cleaning, and there's yard work to do."

Still, when I dropped him off at a car rental place, I calmly asked if he'd be back before leaving for Norway. His voice tender, he reassured me. "Sure, I will. I wouldn't leave you like this." Driving home, I dreaded the day he'd be leaving for good.

A few hours later, while dusting in the bedroom, the phone rang. Jan's "Hi, you dummy," caught me completely by surprise. "I already miss you and want you to come meet my friends. Will you please come be with me?"

Though thrilled, I wasn't sure I should go. "Well, I guess I could leave the rest of the cleaning until we get back, but I really need to get some things done."

"Please? I will help you on Monday." Jan's promise made me smile. I couldn't imagine him cleaning but Josh had just left for his dad's, so there was no reason not to go. And, my heart soared at the thought that he desired my company after only a few hours apart. Plus, he'd be coming back when I did.

Wanting Jan to be glad he invited me, I dressed carefully, pulling on a blue and beige pin-striped halter top with three tiny buttons that hooked it together in the front. A dusty blue short-sleeved safari jacket went over that. Cream-colored linen pants and high-wedged sandals made me taller. Thoughts of him wanting Paul and Renee to meet me filled the trip to Hermosa Beach with delectable expectations.

As soon as I pulled into the driveway, Jan walked out of the house. While I opened the car door to get out, then walked toward him, he slowly looked down to my shoes, then worked his way back up, lingering at those tiny buttons on the halter top before looking me in the eyes. "I am so proud of you," he said in a husky voice before pulling me into his warm embrace.

His words poured confidence and happiness into my heart. Though he'd said it to me before, more than once, no one else ever had. The intense look on his face made me wonder if he still planned to leave soon. Reflected in his eyes, I felt beautiful, desired, cared for. Paul and Renee welcomed me with open arms and soon became my friends too.

After that weekend, Jan didn't say any more about leaving. Though we both knew it was only a matter of time, we didn't talk about it. Instead, we lived each precious moment to the fullest. To my surprise, he divided the household chores. We each cleaned a bathroom. He vacuumed, I dusted.

When it came to mowing the lawn, I didn't understand why he insisted he'd only work in back. The front yard was twice as big, and I knew he wasn't lazy. Eventually the truth dawned on me; Jan had done his best to protect my reputation with the neighbors. He did the same with my mom insisting I not open the door for her unless he had a shirt on.

Playground Intimacy

In the bedroom, with childlike innocence we explored our thrilling teeter-totter relationship with way more ups than downs. Frequently we swung on swings that took us higher and higher—synchronized in movements designed to reach the stars.

One night, Jan walked into the bedroom straight out of a shower. My heart swelled as I looked at him wrapped in a towel and the words slid out of my mouth despite my determination *not* to say them: "I love . . ." *Oh no! That was off limits.* My heart pounded in my throat as I tried to figure out how to complete that sentence. I couldn't love Jan, much less tell him. We were friends. That's it. No commitments. He'd made it clear that if I tried to pin him down, he'd leave. And, for my own sake I had to separate the physical from the mental, however that was becoming impossible. I took a deep breath, letting the air out slowly. ". . . your body."

Unexpected interactions—almost, but not quite, out of control. Laughter, seriousness, and romance mingled as night after night we fell asleep in one another's arms.

Then came the night we went beyond ourselves. Climbing the steps to the slide together, we slipped down, down, down meshing into one another until a cosmic melding took place like warm butter melting into heated chocolate.

Afterward, I took his face in my hands and looked him in the eyes. "I want to make you a promise. No man will ever keep me away from you."

Jan's eyes widened at the thought; his voice cracked when he spoke. "Pat-ti, you cannot know that. You can't promise me such a thing."

Unyielding in my resolve, I repeated the words I knew were true. "Yes, I can. No man will ever keep me from you."

Making love was not the only reason. Jan satisfied me on every level. Mentally, physically, emotionally—in a connecting of our souls, he simply filled me up. Together, we stood on a mountaintop looking toward another mountain, the one where God resides. There we could almost reach out to touch Him—yet the deepest of valleys lay between us and our Creator.

Chapter 8

Reality Leaves No Escape

Walking into the Mission Bay hotel, Jan walked up to the front desk, while I stood a little apart from him.

Hearing him say "Mr. and Mrs.," I was stunned.

Leading the way to our room, he confessed: "I've never done that before, you dummy." His deferential respect claiming me as his wife filled empty places in my heart. Many unmarried couples were starting to go to hotels. Perhaps our relationship meant more to him than a fling. He didn't even hesitate to share his razor when I discovered I'd forgotten mine.

Moving to a less expensive hotel after the first night, we stayed in San Diego a couple of days exploring Sea World, watching the windsurfers, and taking the ferry to Coronado. Sitting in the hotel bar the last night, he leaned close to instruct me in the ways of the world. "See that woman at the bar? She's a prostitute."

"No, she's not," I laughed certain he was teasing.

"Yes, she is. Watch."

Within a few minutes a man came in, and they obviously engaged in a transaction. When they left together, I was shocked. Sex work. How could I be so naïve that I didn't know anything about it? And, I couldn't understand why any woman would sell her body. Were women just a body or was there more to us than that?

Appearances meant everything to my mom. But I'd learned at a young age that appearances could be deceiving. Was that the case with prostitutes? Did they really engage in that profession because they wanted to or was there more to it?

A Beach Road Retreat

The next day on the way home, I suggested stopping by my family's cabin in Capo Beach. Somehow Diane and Bruce had finagled it for the weekend. The private road's speed limit was only 15 mph, so as we crept along, I described how my extended family came to own such a prime piece of real estate.

"My grandmother bought the land in 1948 for $2,500. Then, my dad, mom, aunts and uncles built this little two-bedroom, one-bathroom cabin that we all used for vacations and Easter. But after my parents divorced, my dad's family wouldn't let us use it anymore unless he came with us. And, he didn't come home often. Then, he disappeared. I haven't been here in several years. It's a miracle Diane got permission to use it!"

Walking across the pale green concrete patio to the kitchen door, the pungent fragrance of red geraniums signaled that I was sharing my favorite place with Jan before he left.

Each day brought him one day closer to leaving. He needed to spend time with his mom in Oslo before going on to Spain to spend the rest of his vacation with his best friend. His original two weeks with me had already turned into six. Hearing his side of long-distance phone calls left no doubt that the pressure on him to leave was mounting. Once we got home, it might be a matter of days. This constant reality threatened to catch me in an undertow of grief that would pull me out into its darkest depths.

Though Diane and Bruce weren't expecting us, they were thrilled we came and so were their best friends and teen-aged daughters. After playing some games, while Jan flirted with the girls, I slipped out the kitchen door. A full moon lit my way as I walked over and jumped off the retaining wall into the cold mushy sand below. Facing an angry ferocious sea, I hugged the wooden seawall as closely as possible. The huge shore break crashed and pounded the sand; perhaps being swept out in it would sweep away my agony. Blinking back stinging tears, waves of despair crashed and pounded in my mind.

He hadn't said when, but it couldn't be much longer. If he was to have any time with those he loved before reporting back to the ship, he had to leave soon. Besides, the longer he stayed, the harder it would be to say good-bye.

Waves crashed and the foam receded again and again while I wrestled with my fate. How was I going to live without him?

When I went back inside, Diane took me into one of the bedrooms. "Are you all right?"

"It's so hard to know he's going to leave."

"Jan wondered where you went. He asked if I knew, and I told him I thought you were outside. He was worried and wanted to come find you, but I told him you were probably trying to deal with the idea of his leaving—that maybe he should give you some space. Patti, he said if it was going to make you unhappy, then he just wouldn't leave."

Going Home

A few nights later, Jan pan-fried steaks smothering them with the savory brown gravy I'd come to love. I lit the candles on the dining room table. As he put the T-bones on plates, I took the baked potatoes out of the oven; the green salad, dressing, sour cream, and butter from the fridge. He uncorked a bottle of wine.

We sipped the robust cabernet and talked long after our plates were empty. As candles burned low, Jan said: "Maybe I could move here. Get a job in Newport on a yacht as a captain. It might work." We'd stopped in Newport, the day after leaving our cabin, staying late into the night singing bawdy songs at the Beach Ball, a tiny dive bar where patrons sat on bleachers and sang along with the entertainer. The flamboyant flirt I turned into that night after a few drinks belied the reserved quiet life I was accustomed to—the type of family life I really wanted.

"Jan, you can't do that. We'd end up hating each other. I'd rather have our memories the way they are now than have you resent me because you didn't pursue the career you've worked so hard for." And, though I didn't say it, I couldn't continue living this way for much longer—the drinking, the late nights, my sisters watching Josh. The truth pressed in hard. No matter how much I wanted to deny it, our relationship couldn't last. Otherwise, all of what we'd shared would be ruined.

While driving from Paul and Renee's house to the Forum one night to see the Rolling Stones, someone had passed a joint around the car. When handed to Jan, he'd taken the toke inhaling deeply. He tried to pass it to me, but I shook my head. So, he puffed on it again before passing it back. I'd watched marijuana destroy my beloved brother-in-law. It robbed him of his marriage, his family, and his career as he lost all motivation to work.

Jan drank too much. So did I when I was with him. Sometimes I got sick, and Jan sweetly cared for me. But when he overindulged, he ignored me, flirting mercilessly with other girls. His behavior was so disrespectful toward me one night that Paul and Renee got upset.

The following morning, I stayed in bed, not ready to face them. Jan went to the kitchen for coffee, and Paul confronted his bad behavior. They were my friends, too, and didn't like him treating me that way. Immediately Jan came back to bed, took me in his arms, and expressed deep sorrow for any grief or embarrassment he had caused me.

"You don't have to apologize," I said coldly. "We have no commitments. Either you want to be with me or you don't. If you don't, you can leave." He'd already stayed longer than I expected. And, after Jeff, I simply couldn't/ wouldn't let any man—not even Jan—treat me badly. But I didn't want him to go and within minutes he was showing me that he didn't want to leave.

Yet, we hit another trouble spot when we went to Disneyland. Shortly after paying to get in, Jan wanted a drink. So, we left, walking across the street to a nearby nightclub. The later it got, the more I worried my car might get locked inside the parking gates, like it had while I was in college. "So, if you are worried, go get it," Jan said.

Annoyed that he didn't offer, I left and walked several blocks alone in the dark. Upon returning, I was even more irritated to see a pretty girl sitting next to Jan at our table. They were laughing. I'd made it clear from the beginning that if he went home with another woman, he wouldn't be coming home with me.

Finding an empty table, I sat down—fuming. "Pardon me, would you like to dance?" Looking up, an attractive man smiled at me so I joined him on the dance floor. After he walked me back to the table, I declined his offer to join me. Jan immediately came over, saying he never meant for me not to return to our table. "You looked like you were busy so I decided to enjoy myself." No matter how much I wanted to deny reality, denying it would be disastrous.

Preparing for the Inevitable

A few days later, when I heard Jan speaking Spanish on the phone, I knew. Desperate to prolong our time together, I went into the bedroom, rummaged in my lingerie drawer and found a white lacy chemise he'd never seen. Slipping it on, I went and sat by him on the couch. His eyes lit up with the electric delight that still charged between us. A slow smile spread across his face. Laughing, he said something to his friend that I couldn't understand, then turned to me. "Go wait for me. I'll be there in a minute."

When Jan walked into the bedroom, I spoke only one word. "When?"

"In a week," he said. "I didn't want to leave before you found work. Now that you have a job, it's time."

The job had almost magically materialized, right after we returned from San Diego. The employment agency called wanting to set up an interview for an "advertising production assistant" position at FMC Corporation. Though I had agreed to go, after several phone calls I couldn't find a sitter. "Jan, I don't know what to do with Josh. The sitter who watched him when I was working isn't available. It's such a good opportunity, I hate to miss it."

"I'll watch him."

Astonished at the thought, I grinned. "What will you do with him? Have you ever changed a diaper?"

"Don't worry. We will get along fine."

Something about Jan's authoritative confidence taught me how to trust. Everything didn't have to be my way, and sometimes his ways worked out even better. There was no doubt Jan did things different with Josh than I did, but my son positively thrived on their interactions. Even though he was barely a toddler, Jan treated Josh with respect. Plus, Jan had demonstrated his sweet compassion when I'd been sick with bronchitis. He'd kept me supplied with aspirin and held me close, more concerned about me than with getting sick. I had no qualms about trusting him with my son.

The interview went better than anticipated. A perfect fit for the street sweeper company and for me—with pay higher than I'd imagined. Enough to live on: $500 a month! Letting me know that my former boss used to work for him, my potential supervisor called Mike the advertising executive. His glowing recommendation sealed the deal. My new supervisor, an assistant advertising director, kept me meeting with a variety of people and filling out paperwork for several hours. As soon as we finished, I rushed home.

Walking into the house, I saw Josh still sitting in his high chair chortling over Jan's funny faces. A sopping wet diaper didn't bother my son at all. Jan had been feeding him bananas and teaching him to speak Norwegian.

Within days, a reputable nursery school accepted Josh, and my job started. The work typing tech manuals, processing orders for literature, and proofreading made my days go by fast. Jan slept in and started taking flying lessons at Cable airport, but our late nights were hard on me and the empty hours difficult for him to fill.

He'd lived with me for almost two months, and now we had to face the inevitable. He booked his flight for a week before my birthday.

"Would you like to know something I'd like for my birthday?" I teased one night.

"Yes."

"I want to cut my hair." Down to my waist it took too much time and trying to get ready to take Josh and be at work by 7:00 a.m. was hard. "That means I'd also need a curling iron, but I can't afford it either."

Jan responded quickly. "I guess that might look good. Make an appointment."

"It won't be cheap."

"That's OK. If that's what you want, I'll pay for it."

The following Saturday, he waited in a bar next to the beauty salon. When he saw my new look, Jan said he liked it, but I wondered if he still felt the same.

That last few days, I was determined not to cry. My childhood training had taught me that no one really cared about my tears. Oh, my mom comforted me when my friend got hit by a train and died while I was in high school. That event was memorable because usually I hid my tears from her, from everyone. From my earliest memories, my parents had warned, "Don't cry or I'll give you something to cry about."

And, I also decided not to let Jan make me angry. Trying to make it as hard as possible for him to leave me, I pretended a strength I didn't feel.

My determination faltered over the weekend when we got into our biggest fight. Paul had told Jan about a party they were having, and he decided to go. Yet he didn't mention taking me, so as that Saturday drew near, I kept my mouth shut. That night, we went out for dinner and dancing at a nearby Italian place. Just as Jan started to take a bite of his raviolis, he remembered.

"Tonight was that party," he lamented.

Though I tried to hide it, my expression gave me away. "Why didn't you remind me?" he said angrily, his fork clattering against his plate. "You knew I wanted to go!"

"You didn't invite me. Why would I want you to be gone your last weekend here?" The rest of the night Jan busied himself talking to others in the nightclub. He barely spoke to me. And, I was furious.

The next day as we drove to the store to pick up some potato salad for a final dinner at Diane's, he apologized. "I am sorry. You were right. It was not your place to keep track of something I wanted to do. It was my own fault." He reached over and took my hand, and I melted.

Men didn't apologize to me. Or care about my thoughts. Or appreciate me. Or gently take me into their strong arms and hold me the way Jan did. They didn't tell my sister how sexy my haircut was.

How could I live without him? Dwelling on it tore me apart, so I did my best not to think about him leaving.

The Last Night

Because Josh was spending the night at Diane's, she'd take him to nursery school the next morning. Then she'd come pick up Jan and take him to the airport. We all agreed I should not try to see him off.

As if it were an ordinary day, I'd go to work. Jan would take a commuter plane to LAX, where Paul and Renee would pick him up. They'd spend the day with him before he left for Norway that evening.

For our last dinner, Jan offered to cook the pan-fried steaks and gravy I loved. When the baked potatoes were almost done, I told Jan, it was time to put the meat on. But he was busy watching television, something he rarely did.

"I'll cook them later," he said dismissively. "I want to see this."

"But Jan, it's your last night. Is it really that important?"

"Yes."

He was trying to pick a fight. That made me all the more determined not to argue. Dinner was not worth spoiling our final night together. If Jan didn't care when we ate, I wouldn't either.

"That's fine," I said keeping my tone even. "The potatoes can keep. I'm going to take a bath."

Filling the tub with bubbles, I lounged in comforting warmth for a long time—wanting to delay everything, to push back time.

When I finally finished, Jan went into the kitchen and started cooking, while I made the salad.

We ate slowly by candlelight—the way we always did. Jan reassured me he'd keep in touch. He wanted me to write his mom and had already asked her to write me. As we finished the wine, we talked about his beloved grandparents and how he was anxious to see them. And, his dog.

Despite knowing it wasn't true, I said I'd be fine. Later, we made love—holding each other, dozing, waking to love one another again.

When morning came, I was exhausted. Numb, I got up and dressed. There were no words left to say.

Instead of kissing Jan good-bye while he stayed in bed as I usually did, he walked me to the door. Opening it, I turned and breathed in the way he looked—his long legs in blue jeans. His rumpled honey-colored hair. His strong tanned chest and big brown eyes. He took me in his arms and pulled me close. I looked up at him, and he let his gaze linger on my face, then kissed me, long and hard. He pressed me to his chest again. Finally, I leaned back, putting on a shaky smile. "Stay safe," I said, then turned and walked away.

But not fast enough. As he closed the door, I saw his face crumple, and my heart broke.

Tears welled up in my eyes, threatening to fall as I tried to focus on the road ahead. "He's still here," my internal voice admonished. "There's nothing to cry about. As long as Jan is still in Southern California, I'm OK. Maybe something will happen, and he won't leave. I just have to get through this day."

Taking several deep breaths, I forced myself to be strong. Though I liked the people at work, my job was new. They must not discover how much I hurt. If the pain showed and anyone tried to comfort me, I'd fall apart and wouldn't be able to put myself back together again.

I'd get off work at 4:00. Then, I'd pick up Josh. He'd miss Jan, too, so I'd have to stay strong until I put my little guy to bed. Maybe then, I'd allow myself to feel.

The Dark of Night

After getting Josh settled in his crib, I sat on the couch in the den staring at the clock. Tick 7:55. Tock. 7:56. Tick 7:57. Tock 7:58. Tick 7.59. Tock. 8:00 o'clock. The cuckoo sprung from its nest, flying wildly inside of me. Dense dark storm-clouds rolled into my mind, threatening destruction. Before they could burst, I called Dorothy. Her phone rang, once, twice, four times. Just as I was about to hang up, she answered.

"Did he leave?"

"Yes. We watched until his plane took off."

"Thank you. I have to go now." Not waiting for a reply, I hung the phone's receiver back in the cradle, and the deluge came, flooding my face while I gasped for air. Grief washed over me in drowning sobs as the bleak emptiness climaxed.

Within weeks, I began to seek comfort the only way I knew how.

Chapter 9

Hooking Up

Resting on my knees, I looked at the order sheet and pulled spec sheets from the bottom shelves to fill customer orders. As I stood to reach the brochures that were above my head, Ron startled me by coming into the secluded literature room. He smiled revealing straight white teeth and dimples. His baby face, blue eyes and thick brown hair made my heart beat a little faster. "What do you need?" I asked.

"You."

Not knowing what to say, I just stared at him.

"Nothing really. I just wanted to see if you're going out with everyone after work. We're celebrating Jim's birthday."

It was nice to be asked. Friday nights were hard, especially when Josh was with his dad. Though Jan called—and wrote once in a while—it wasn't enough. He'd been gone less than a month, and it felt like a lifetime. Besides, he'd just left Norway to go spend time with his friends in Spain, and there was no doubt in my mind he'd be with other girls. We had no commitment.

Lonely

As soon as I walked into the restaurant's bar, Ron caught my eye and nodded toward an empty seat across from him. "Let me buy you a drink. What would you like?"

"A Salty Dog."

My new friends from work soon helped me forget the pain. Each time my glass was half empty, one of the guys ordered another round. Quick-witted banter infused the spirits with our laughter.

Later, as people wandered out, Ron caught up to me in the parking lot asking if he might follow me home. He was married, but his attentiveness sparked desire. We sat in his car and talked. He'd recently lost his little boy to leukemia. His wife couldn't see past her own grief enough to comfort him in his own. I told Ron about Jan and how much I missed him.

The fall winds began to blow and autumn leaves fell into the gutter. So, did I.

Pain broke down conventional barriers. I didn't want a real relationship—I might not be able to love Jan, but he'd taken my heart with him. I only wanted someone to hold me for awhile—long enough to ease the constant pain. Ron wanted the same. He loved his wife, the best he knew how.

Soon Ron started dropping by a couple of nights a week. While he was near, his flattery warmed my heart, but the moment he left, hell froze over and I was stuck in the ice.

The "if it feels good, do it" Zeitgeist directed my choices, but didn't solve any problems. Caught between reality and a fairy tale, my confusion continued, and I wanted to die. Every part of my being hurt. I'd fallen into a chasm and couldn't crawl out. Missing Jan, I craved him like an addiction although constantly aware that to be with him again would bring disaster.

During lonely nights, I embroidered a denim shirt for his birthday. Carefully I placed small emblems like an anchor and a sun. On the back yoke, I outlined a pattern for the initial ring he wore, filling it in with gold thread. I mailed it in plenty of time for him to receive it while he was still in Spain, or so I thought.

A World Away

Franco, Spain's dictator, lay near death for weeks. In early October, Jan wrote a letter mentioning his concern about civil unrest. If the chaos got worse, he'd have to return to the ship early. The situation might soon become dangerous for foreigners.

Before hearing from him again, on October 18, 1975, I received a letter from his mom. Even though Jan had mentioned wanting us to write, hearing from her was a tremendous surprise. So was her kindness. She spoke of how happy Jan had been with me and Josh. How she worried about him being so far from home and his family. She told me about his brother, his grandparents, and his dog. She described her work. The letter was warm and friendly especially as she explained plans for a trip on board Jan's ship around the holidays. Afterward, she'd travel around the U.S., coming to California to meet me.

Why would he have her write me? Why would she visit me? His phone calls had stopped. At first, I wondered if he might surprise me by stopping in California on his way back to the Caribbean. Then I started wondering if he'd found someone else.

One night, the phone's shrill ring startled me out of a deep sleep. My heart started racing. Jan! He'd returned to the Caribbean, and I hadn't even known. He never considered how worried I was—this was his normal. I didn't dare express my fears because it would sound like I was trying to tie him down.

Franco had died on November 20th, Jan's birthday. Finding out that he'd left Spain before receiving the shirt devastated me. He'd probably never see how much effort I'd made.

At Christmas, Ron surprised me with a gift—*The Prophet* by Khalil Gibran. He grinned as I unwrapped the book, then the album. Ron knew I was hurting, lonely, and often afraid during the long dark nights. He did his best to make me feel better, but reading Kahlil Gibran only made me miss Jan more. Knowingly, the poet had said,

> A friend who is far away is sometimes much nearer than one who is at hand. Is not the mountain far more awe-inspiring and more clearly visible to one passing through the valley than to those who inhabit the mountain?

With Jan, I'd reached the mountain's pinnacle. One evening we'd shared Rod McKuen's album, *The Sea*, while laying on the living room floor. That night the yellow sun kite had flown until dawn.

For Christmas, Jan asked for pictures so I splurged on professional shots. But when Josh and I called him Christmas Eve—he seemed agitated, and I had no idea why. He hadn't even sent a Christmas card. Hearing from him often had been hard enough, but now the time between letters and phone calls became longer, and the distance between us grew greater.

Only my son gave me a reason to live. Whenever Josh put his sweet little arms around my neck and said "I love you, Mommy," it warmed my heart. I couldn't bear the thought of letting him down. But I didn't know what to do with the empty hours that ravaged my soul.

At the same time, even though we'd never said "I love you," I suspected that if Jan came to visit again, we might get married. The chemistry between us had been electric. Yet for me, four months of heaven would lead to eight months of agony. We never spoke of marriage, but we had discussed trying to live a long-distance relationship—how time together might be worth the time apart. Sometimes I wondered if I could do it—even knowing he'd cheat on me. Maybe that didn't matter. Four months with him might be better than none. At the same time, in my heart I knew that was a lie. The truth refused to be denied.

On April 3, 1976, I received another letter from his mom. It left no doubt that I needed to end my relationship with Jan. If it continued, too many people would be hurt. The trip she'd hoped for over the holidays hadn't worked out, but she requested pictures, especially of Josh. Expecting Jan to come see me in the summer, she worried that he might not come home this time.

Lori often came over from next door to keep me company in the evenings, so I shared the letter and my deep concerns with her. After babysitting for us, she understood Jan's magnetic personality. Trying to comfort me, she told me about someone who could offer me peace.

Desperate for Help

"You need Jesus," she said. "He'll never leave you, but will be with you always."

But I wasn't like her or her family. I wasn't good and had no desire to live a boring "Christian" life. I cussed and smoked and drank and didn't intend to change. All I wanted was to lie in a man's arms, one who loved me. And, to raise my son with a family.

Still, I wondered if a Savior might provide a way to escape the excruciating pain of missing Jan.

Some nights, when my agony was more intense than I could bear, I'd turn the TV channels to watch Oral Roberts, an evangelist. Too often he asked for money, but when he repeated Lori's message, I wondered if Jesus might offer hope.

For some reason, one night instead of turning on the TV, I pulled *The Living Bible* from the bookshelf. Opening it at random, I started reading a letter by a guy named Paul. Though he'd written to some people in a city named Ephesus, it felt as though he'd written to me.

> You went along with the crowd and were just like all the others, full of sin, obeying Satan, the mighty prince of the power of the air, who is at work right now in the hearts of those who are against the Lord. All of us used to be just as they are, our lives expressing the evil within us, doing every wicked thing that our passions or our evil thoughts might lead us into. We started out bad, being born with evil natures, and were under God's anger just like everyone else.
>
> But God is so rich in mercy; he loved us so much that even though we were spiritually dead and doomed by our sins, he gave us back our lives again when he raised Christ from the dead—only by his undeserved favor have we ever been saved.

Curled up in a fetal position on the couch, it was clear I didn't deserve to be saved from my torment. I didn't even have enough decency to feel guilty for cheating on my husband. Despite being completely unworthy, my soul silently begged Jesus for help. Tears streamed down my face as I pleaded, "Oh Jesus, please Jesus take control of my life. Jan's absence is killing me, and I can't do anything about it. I am a sinner. I don't even feel guilty for having an affair with him. It was the best time of my life, but I know it was wrong. And now my life is a mess. Please come into my life and save me from my sins."

A strange peace settled in me and though the pain was still intense, I no longer felt alone. This living God, an unseen presence, seemed to be with me. That night on the ship when I'd sat under the stars wondering about a Creator, He'd been there. He claimed to be the Way, the Truth, and the Life that is the light of men, and for some reason He'd kept me in the truth. Why He didn't permit me to believe I could have a life with Jan that would be anything but filled with pain, I'd never understand. Still, I was not cut out to be a good Christian.

I tried going to church, but didn't like any of them. Lori's church was boring. Another, too weird. The place I'd gone as a child was full of hypocrites. There didn't seem any hope until one night my doorbell rang.

Lori's older brother, Paul, stood there. "Our plumbing broke. Can I use your bathroom?" He was about twenty, tall, good looking, and spoke with a gentle voice. Though I was only five years older, I'd watched Paul grow from a gangly teenager into a man.

"You've been crying," Paul noticed when he came into my kitchen.

There was no denying it. I heaved a broken sigh. "I'm so depressed." Despite not wanting to cry, tears started slipping down my cheeks.

Though his girlfriend waited next door, Paul stayed for over an hour just talking. "Maybe you should try going to church."

"I already tried several, but didn't like any of them."

"There's a new one in Upland. Most of the people at Cornerstone are about your age. I think you might like it," Paul said, giving me directions and hugging me before he left.

The following Sunday, Josh was with his dad, so I went. It didn't even meet in a regular church building but at the local Women's Club. Sitting on a folding chair in the back, I watched people greeting each other. A tall bald man with glasses came over and introduced himself. When Bob asked my name, his warmth and unexpected friendliness made me feel at home.

Even more, the singing soothed my soul. The pastor strummed an acoustic guitar, the tune reminding me of the folk songs my friends and I used to sing in a cave on the beach at Corona Del Mar. About my age, he looked like one of the surfers with shaggy blond hair. And, his message made sense. After a prayer, a lone baritone voice started singing a cappella. Looking around, I realized the voice belonged to Bob. One-by-one others began to join in. I closed my eyes and began to sing the simple melody from my heart.

> Spirit of the Living God, fall afresh on me. Spirit of the Living God, fall afresh on me. Melt me, mold me, fill me, use me—Spirit of the Living God, fall afresh on me.

My flesh tingled as the gentle breath of God wafted life into my soul. Something happened making my spirit soar heavenward as a vertical relationship with One far greater than a mere human came into existence.

The next time Lori's mom saw me, she noticed a difference and asked if I'd been born again. I supposed so. However, even though Jesus had saved me from my sins, my behavior didn't change. I still smoked. Still drank. Still cussed. And, still craved a man's arms to hold me, protect me, keep me safe. Worst of all, missing Jan, I still hurt. In fact, it wasn't long before my behavior got even worse.

Trying to Ease the Pain

Men. Dancing. Drinking. Different men. Cheap sex without much of a relationship left me disgusted with myself. Yet, no matter how hung over I might be, I kept going to church because for that brief period of time, I felt accepted just the way I was.

Despite my lack of feeling guilty, an internal instinct convinced me that my relationship with Jan was wrong. Although I still thought of him every day, his lifestyle wasn't what I wanted for my son or me.

Truth that I couldn't escape permeated my thinking. Sometimes after putting Josh to bed, I sat on the couch in our little dark den and tried to convince myself that even if Jan had other women, no one else could compare to what we had. That was true for me, and I suspected it was true for him. Maybe being with him a few months a year would be worth the challenges. But there was no denying that trying to prolong our romance would only result in more excruciating pain.

His mom's second letter had brought a sense of urgency. He'd be planning his "holiday" soon, and his mother thought he'd be coming here. If I didn't do something right away, we'd be together again.

Forced to Accept Reality

Thoughts of Jan looking at another woman the way he looked at me, kissing her, loving her, teasing her, laughing with her tormented me. My fears empowered me to do the impossible. Fear of lengthy separations. Fear of abandonment. Fear of rejection. Fear of his drinking. Better to end the relationship before we destroyed our precious memories. In reality, that was not fear but truth. Jesus showed me the way through. But it would hurt like hell.

A glimmer of hope rested in my thoughts of God. Somehow, someway, someday, an all mighty, all-powerful God who loved me, could do something. Yet nothing in my capability could turn me into enough of a woman to satisfy Jan on a permanent basis. To be the only woman in his life.

Praying for strength, with tears streaming down my cheeks, I wrote Jan a letter. Not only did it break my heart, but I also believed it would break his. Mailing it tore me to shreds. The worst part was not letting him know how deeply I cared. If I did, he might convince me we should stay together. In late April, I wrote:

Dear Jan,
"I can't live like this. Please don't come back. . . "

But deep inside, somehow I knew that someday I'd hear from him again.

PART II

Embracing the Pain

Unanswered yet? Faith cannot be unanswered;
Her feet were firmly planted on the Rock;
Amid the wildest storm prayer stands undaunted,
Nor quails before the loudest thunder shock.
She knows Omnipotence has heard her prayer,
And cries, "It shall be done," sometime, somewhere.

"Unanswered yet? The prayer your lips have pleaded"
F. G. Burroughs, 1879

Chapter 10

Death in the Family

Sucking in air, I finished my step-aerobics workout, then sat down at my desk for a few minutes to gulp water from a plastic bottle. After having COVID, it was good to be exercising again to YouTube videos. But I still didn't have much energy.

Using weights for my arms one day, then doing a "butts and guts" class another, had made every muscle in my body hurt. Three weeks of laying around, working on a puzzle, and reading had taken a toll. It still didn't feel like I was getting enough oxygen. Though my symptoms had been mild, I was beginning to comprehend how serious the coronavirus could be.

Ushering in 2021

Many of my Facebook friends seemed to think a flip of the calendar would dispense with the problems of 2020, but that hadn't happened. Despite our gorgeous California weather, the New Year's Day Rose Parade was cancelled.

Kids still weren't back in school, and for many teachers and students distance learning on a computer screen wasn't working well. Teachers were frustrated and children needed the stimulation of friends. Young adults attended virtual raves. Most adults struggled with lockdowns that made zero sense. Target, Home Depot, and Walmart were open but small stores with limited patronage were shuttered.

After restaurants invested heavily to accommodate outdoor dining, Governor Newsom shut them down completely. Yet he permitted a movie studio to set up an outdoor banquet for their crew. He insisted on masks, yet went to an elite dinner without one. Hair salons were closed, yet his hair always appeared freshly trimmed. Now, many people refused to get the vaccine while thousands waited in long lines for immunizations in short supply. Once they received it, they were told they'd still have to wear masks and stay socially distanced.

Supposedly I had immunity for three months, so I intended to wait for those more vulnerable to go first. But my motive wasn't completely altruistic. Maybe by then, the vaccine's results would be better known.

Regardless, this virus was vicious and baffling with no rhyme or reason. Before getting a COVID test, I'd been convinced I had allergies. So, I continued going to the grocery store, having my niece cut my hair, and meeting with friends. It took me over a week with a low-grade fever to become concerned about exposing people.

Checking the test results on my computer, I was stunned to see the word "positive." With a history of pneumonia and bronchitis, plus high blood pressure and age against me, I'd fully expected to end up in the hospital if I got it. Not long before Christmas, a Facebook friend posted that her husband had waited five hours to get into the ER at our local hospital. He died a few days later.

Now, before jumping into the shower, I scrolled posts reporting on an overload of cases so severe that ambulances were being turned away. Additional concerns weighed heavily on my mind. Justice issues like abortion and racial tensions continued to divide America. Biden claimed to want unity, but apparently expected anyone who disagreed with him to give up their stance on the value of human life, protecting our borders, and resolving racial tension without demeaning White people. The news reported that Katie Couric wanted to deprogram anyone who supported Trump. Although I definitely wasn't a fan, many of my friends supported our former president.

Being a problem solver, I was well aware that the societal issues were real and needed solutions. But until we could find common ground, the division in our country was bound to intensify.

On the night of the inauguration, the news showed the extreme left in Portland rioting, damaging small businesses and a Democratic Party office.

Yet on January 6th, just two weeks before Biden was sworn in, the extreme right created mayhem by storming the Capitol convinced by Trump that the election results had been tampered with. People died.

Ineffective and Destructive Leadership

A few years after ending my relationship with Jan, I'd started editing doctoral dissertations on leadership. Fascinated, I began reading some of their source materials. The more I learned, the more convinced I became that regardless of results, divisive leadership had led America to this place. True leaders work to unify—to listen and hear differing positions, then look for effective solutions. Integrity pulls people together instead of exacerbating differences. Name-calling throws fuel on raging fires.

During the 2016 election, Hilary Clinton said that half of Trump supporters belonged in a "basket of deplorables." She called them "racist, sexist, homophobic, xenophobic, and Islamophobic."

Trump escalated the name-calling to new heights, and many Christian leaders refused to hold him accountable. After being elected to America's highest office, he bullied people with opposing views using childish schoolyard language.

While he was president, Barack Obama had smiled adopting a calm tone and pleasant-sounding words to convey disrespectful messages about conservatives. His beliefs permeated the reporting of mainstream journalists, who reinforced them at every turn.

Media loved Bill Clinton, too, even though he had sex in the Oval Office with an intern from 1995 through 1997. When that affair was finally exposed in 1998, he lied.

For years, America's leadership had demonstrated a lack of character. Our country was in a mess.

Still scrolling on Facebook, a Chaffey high school friend's post about the new swimming pool reminded me that this lack of integrity had even existed in my teen-aged years. In the late sixties, liberal-leaning thought began to permeate higher institutions of learning, media, and politics. Conservatives had supported Nixon, the only president forced to resign. I'd been a student at Whittier College, his alma mater, when insurgents burned down the building where his memorabilia were stored.

While walking toward the gym one day in junior high, a friend announced the news that John F. Kennedy had been assassinated. His rumored affairs were legendary. Not long before I graduated high school, his brother Bobby was also murdered. So was Martin Luther King. During those years, we watched the Watts riots on the news. Kent State, too. And the Vietnam War came into our homes every night. Conscientious objectors vilified those who fought for freedom—including my dad.

America's divide had begun long ago and now was escalating to the point where no one knew what might happen next, especially with the Biden presidency and a liberal majority in Congress. Many progressives were advocating for socialism with no idea of what government control would do to our freedom. Some wanted to defund the police. Millions opposed the executive orders being signed by our new president. Many were Christians fearful of what claims of domestic terrorism might mean to the Church.

Wondering what the future held reminded me of a news story I'd written in 2013 about how China's Red Guard had ousted people from their homes and stolen their property. After Dr. Yeh had described losing everything and being imprisoned for his faith, I asked if he thought that could happen in America. Grieved, he said he'd already started seeing the signs.

Sighing, I wondered if I might share his fate. Would I someday lose everything? Be confined in a dark dank cell?

Regardless, I had no regrets. Not even about Jan. As much as I had wanted him, I'd wanted something more. Something better. Something he couldn't give me.

I'd thought it might be a man, and it was. Although Jesus is 100 percent human, He is also 100 percent God. Finding my identity in Him had led to vibrant awe-inspiring adventures where I conquered my fears and developed a deep and genuine love for people of all ages, ethnicities, occupations, sexual orientations, and political persuasions. That alone was worth all the pain involved of daily setting aside my longing for Jan and living for Christ. It had given me stability despite the tremendous national and personal challenges.

The one thing I couldn't comprehend was why God allowed me to find out how Jan really felt about me. Knowing that kept him in my thoughts every day. Maybe someday I'd learn what happened to him, the way I did about my dad. But in the meantime—despite COVID, civil unrest, and an unknown future—I was at peace. My life was good, and I was satisfied. Over the years, developing a biblical worldview had brought an increasing sense of contentment, especially after my mother died on November 1, 2017.

Stricken

Carefully balancing the white phalaenopsis, I pulled open the heavy wooden door and walked into the Cask and Cleaver. The restaurant's manager recognized me and pointed toward the room where we'd soon gather to remember my mother's life. Valerie had thought we might wait until after Christmas for the memorial lunch, but I insisted we get it over with before the holidays. I needed to move on, at least in terms of grieving the loss of my mom.

Why I couldn't do that with Jan, I didn't know. Although it seemed eons had passed since we'd last spoken, I wished he was here. Despite knowing my mom's faults, he respected her and understood my love for her. He even asked about her health during the phone calls that made it impossible to leave our past behind. There were so many things I still wondered about.

Where was he? Was he alive? Did he still think about me the way I thought about him? Was he just a part of my past or was there something more?

The Cask had been part of my past, too. I'd been coming here since high school. While married to Jeff, my brother-in-law had bartended here, serving us special appetizers every time we came.

Throughout the years, my family had celebrated many special occasions here. Most recently, the Cask had been my mom's favorite place for lunch. The staff delighted her by catering to her every desire. Each time we came, the manager sat us by the window at her favorite table in the bar. Our usual server, sweet Lauren, no longer bothered asking for our drink order. As soon as we were seated, she'd bring margaritas on the rocks for Mom and me, iced teas for Val and Janet. Because our mother worshipped at the altar of self, we'd decided to honor her life here rather than a church or a funeral home. Glancing around the room, I appreciated the horseshoe set up of the rustic wooden tables. With people seated on both sides, it would keep our family members close together, and we needed that.

A few years after moving to Dana Point, Mom quit staying in touch with the few friends she'd had. Self-absorbed lies whispered in her mind that "it was too much trouble." "They don't want to see me anyway." "I don't like parties or entertaining." Yet I remembered a time when she did. The older she got, the more she shamed herself until she decided it was better to forget than to remember. Life closing in on her likely triggered the dementia that robbed her and all of us of so much more.

Yet I had so many good memories of my mother taking care of me at the beach when I had chicken pox, then again when I had pneumonia in sixth grade. She tried to encourage me when my second marriage failed, and we shared lots of laughter while shopping. Just for fun I'd try on out-rageous outfits, and sometimes they turned into a special find. All these recollections made today hard for me. Perhaps hardest of all was feeling like no one shared my grief.

I hoped Val would bring the photo of Mom and Martha happily standing in front of a beach rental before our family cabin was built. If my dad's youngest sister hadn't died unexpectedly two weeks before the wedding, Martha would have been my mom's maid of honor. That traumatic loss had scarred my mom from ever again having a best friend. My dad's older sister Eileen probably came closest. Years after my parents divorced, mutual heartache over Martha and my dad reconciled my mom and beloved aunt. Despite being 100 years old, Aunt Eileen would be here today.

Placing the orchid on the wooden table, additional thoughts of my mother's life crept into focus. A few photos would remind us of her cruises, her gardening, and her wedding to my dad. But they told only a fraction of her story.

I touched the gold anchors on the chain around my neck. Whenever I rubbed them, Jan immediately came to mind. However, when I remarried, I'd redefined their symbolism so I wouldn't betray my husband by wearing them. Now, the large one reminded me that Jesus anchored my soul, mooring me in God's presence. No matter how tough life got or how alone I felt, the triune God (Father, Son, and Holy Spirit) stayed with me in ways that Jan, a mere mortal, could not. The smaller one still represented me. Today, only divine comfort provided enough strength to rise above my tumultuous feelings.

Mixed Emotions

Part of me was glad my mom was gone. Dementia had robbed my once "perfect" mother of her dignity. Every time I went to see her in that locked facility, I wondered if she'd remember me. Or whether I might find excrement hidden in her room or if she'd forget to use the bathroom and urinate in her pants while we walked outside on the pathway through the garden. Though she recognized Valerie, Janet, and me as her daughters until the end, her mind's mental decay had taken a fierce toll.

Maybe it was selfish, but while starting my car after leaving the assisted-living residence a few days before her stroke, I breathed a prayer that if my mom must continue living, she'd become bedridden. At least that way the staff could preserve a little of her dignity by keeping a diaper on her.

That was a Thursday. Only three days later, while sitting outside sipping hot coffee with friends after church, I received a text from Val. "Call as soon as you can."

Mom had suffered a major stroke. It happened on October 22, the morning after her 91st birthday. By the time I arrived at the hospital, she was sitting up in bed—bright-eyed, lucid, and talking. But by afternoon, she'd fallen into a deep sleep.

When the doctor came into her room, he leaned over to check her vitals, then straightened up, took the stethoscope out of his ears, and replaced it around his neck. "You should let God and nature take their course."

Months earlier, Val and I had discussed not permitting any extraordinary measures to prolong our mother's life, other than whatever was necessary to keep her comfortable. Janet agreed. So, his words confirmed the decision already made. Especially after his assurance that she wasn't in any pain.

For 10 days our mom slept, the most at peace I'd ever seen her. Then she was gone. And it seemed no one really cared but me.

Poignant Memories

Despite all she'd done wrong, in many ways, she had been good to me. When I was out of work, and my car needed an expensive repair, she bought me a new one instead, dubbing it the "Blue Whiz." I didn't like driving her Mercedes so a reliable car made her feel more secure when I took her shopping, to the bank, or to dinner. But she genuinely wanted me to get a car I liked. And, we'd had fun shopping for it. Within a few weeks, she bought Janet one too, because she needed a safe vehicle. Valerie didn't need financial help, so she received nothing.

For nearly 20 years, I'd spent the night every other week at my mom's condo on the bluff above Dana Point harbor. Over dinner we reminisced about our cruises to the Caribbean, the Mediterranean, and the East Coast to see the fall color.

While taking her home one night after dinner at BJ's Pizza, I mentioned how whenever I accomplished something significant, I'd think *If Jan knew, he'd be proud of me.* His kindness to people from all walks of life had been a living example. His sense of adventure and fun had made me more open to doing things I'd otherwise be too afraid to try. His desire for more out of life made me want more. His passion for learning was so contagious, it made me eager to learn. After hearing these explanations, she finally began to understand how much he'd meant to me.

If she knew, Mom would probably be glad that today there weren't any photos of our annual Mexican cruises while she was in her 80s. We didn't bother with sightseeing, and pictures couldn't have captured our frivolity. As thanks for taking me, I always treated her to an extravagant lunch and margaritas at the Blue Shrimp in Puerto Vallarta. No one else shared those memories—hearing our hilarity through open windows, tourists on the street came into that brightly-colored establishment to join in with our fun. Delighted, the owners didn't want us to leave, so they surprised us with after-lunch Kahlua and crème on the rocks. Another year, they brought flan.

In Mazatlán, the next port, beach vendors hawked their wares as we drank margaritas while sharing huge platters of nachos, flautas, and quesadillas. Without leaving the table, my mom encouraged me as I shopped for dazzling fish mobiles that shimmered in the hot sun, and together we chose inexpensive silver rings from trays of jewelry.

During those years, whenever I visited my mom at her condo, she was always happy to see me. Coming in the back door carrying a big bouquet of pink, purple, and salmon-colored sweet peas or whatever else was blooming in my garden, I'd done my best to make her life better—suggesting trips to local garden centers, favorite shops, and restaurants. Sometimes we'd go to Santa Barbara or San Diego for a brief getaway. After Val, Janet, and I moved Mom into assisted living, we quit going anywhere, but every Thursday I took grinders and chocolate chip cookies for a picnic lunch in the residential courtyard. I took her flowers, too, until the day she picked up the vase and drank the water from it.

Once I took cards and helped her play solitaire—she'd always loved games. As far back as I could remember, she'd been a bridge aficionado. Probably because she was so good at it. Visions from childhood revealed her setting up card tables, getting out her best china, crystal glasses, and silver candy dishes for her homemade divinity. Knowing that was my favorite sweet treat, she always wrapped a few pieces in waxed paper, then hid them up in the cupboard for me to have later. But she refused to make any without walnuts for Val.

Bridge had been Mom's passion, her obsession, her idol. At the altar of self, something usually drives us toward compulsive behaviors. For me, it used to be men. My current struggles involve keeping the right balance with exercise and food. I'm not always very good at it. Being at the gym or going out to eat feels good. Just like winning did for my mom. However, as a yo-yo dieter, she had unhealthy food issues, too—limiting herself to calorie conscious frozen dinners every night unless she went out. There's a downside to letting such things control our lives.

Worshiping the one true God, reading His word, prayer, and accountability keep me from getting caught up in addictions. For my mom, nothing but a trip could interfere with her numerous bridge clubs until one day she decided to never play again. No amount of encouragement could change her mind. Perhaps her partners complained about her memory. Or maybe she just couldn't win anymore. When she was no longer the best, she wouldn't allow herself to play for fun. A large chunk of her identity had betrayed her.

Facing Reality

Nervously checking the time on my phone, I realized how early I'd been. Valerie should be arriving any minute. Hoping I was dressed OK in a maroon jacket, gold tank, and black slim-fitting pants, I looked down at my gold sandals, the last birthday present Mom had bought me. She'd have liked that I was wearing her jacket. She often gave me clothes she no longer wanted. I'd miss that. Sometimes her taste suited me well. Although, I missed our frequent shopping trips and the way she understood my funky style, not having to listen to her berate sales clerks anymore was a relief. Nor did I miss our arguments about my sisters.

All my happy recollections couldn't offset flashbacks of how she treated Val and Janet. Though I'd done my best to refute our mother's preposterous lies, challenging her distortions meant enduring her wrath. Within moments, angry words could escalate into shouting matches even in a restaurant. Rarely did I get angry, but I hated the way she tried to portray my sisters so much that sometimes I couldn't stay silent.

Afterward, like many narcissists, she'd insist, "You're over-reacting." "You're imagining things." "You remember wrong." "Why are you so sensitive?" It was always *my* fault.

Even worse was when after saying something hateful and mean, she'd claim, "I was only joking." After an argument, we'd both end up furious with nothing resolved. Though we had happy times, long before I became an adult, I realized she was too self-absorbed to be trustworthy. She didn't care about truth, only about being right in her own eyes.

Sometimes I wondered if my mom's love for me simply fed her own perspective that she was a wonderful mother. When she asked why I never told her that, I hedged by saying she was a wonderful mother in some ways. If pressed, I might have reminded her how as kids we couldn't have our friends over or even eat dinner with her while Daddy was working in New Mexico. How, as an adult, when one of her friends complimented my Christmas tree, she exalted herself and embarrassed me by reminding that woman how her own tree had always been bigger and better with many more gorgeous packages underneath. Or how she never babysat her grandchildren, not even when I begged one New Year's Eve.

As Mom's dementia got worse, Valerie insisted on taking increasing responsibility for her care. Though my sister rarely spent the night, we alternated our visits so one of us went every week. While I helped in the garden and with outings, Val scheduled appointments, did the laundry, changed the sheets on the bed, and bought groceries—all while being badgered with instructions on how to do things Mom's way. Eventually Val had taken over the banking and a multitude of other details. Yet, Mom was never satisfied and rarely grateful. We both did everything possible to spare Janet from unpleasant interactions so she could limit her visits to a couple of times a year.

Though I did my best to forget ugly memories, they kept intruding. How much more difficult today would be for my sisters. While she was alive, forgiveness kept their relationships with her tolerable, but today, they'd be doing all they could to keep silent about those bad feelings. Still, perhaps there were reasons to remember. I never wanted to forget how easily I could become like her. It had taken hard choices to learn the lessons that set me free not to become consumed with my "self."

Enslaved to Self, A Cruel Master

Whenever Mom wasn't in control, her venomous words would strike like a snake's fangs sinking deep enough to poison a soul. Avoiding triggering situations helped. Every September 18th, Mom insisted Val and I celebrate our shared birthday with her by going out to dinner. Then, she'd berate Valerie the entire time until it became intolerable.

The animosity between them increased to where I refused to go anymore. Every year I came up with an excuse as to why the particular night Val was available, I wasn't. Not even when it meant sitting home alone on my birthday.

While packing to move Mom from Dana Point to a senior apartment closer to us, I started putting her laundry supplies into a box. Understanding her pain at having to leave her two-story home, we'd done everything possible to make it easier. Even so, the day of the move, Mom's frustration intensified until she slapped me across the face. But that feeble hit felt like a mere tap compared to the emotional pain she inflicted on my sisters. By then, I simply expected what I was going to get if my mom didn't have her way—whether it was putting something in a box the wrong way or throwing away an old advertisement without her permission.

The worst of our arguments centered around vindictive allegations that she gave her dental labs to Valerie. My hard-working sister not only paid a fair price but also made every effort to grow the business. Instead of being proud of her, Mom constantly cast aspersions against her. Over time, Mom's denial increased until she lived in a narcissistic fantasy world where she was always right, and everyone else was wrong. She was perfect. Nobody else could measure up.

Years ago, we met with Janet and her psychiatrist so they could confront Mom about her role in the sexual abuse perpetrated by our stepfather. Sitting next to me on that brown leather couch, she denied any wrongdoing.

Refusing to acknowledge Janet's life-threatening bulimia or the ways she'd contributed to it, Mom's denial escalated to the point where she couldn't understand why she was there. That continual denial created a fantasy world where the abuse never happened or wasn't that bad.

Yet reality always lurked in the background. One dark night while driving back from dinner, as her dementia progressed, she mentioned that something bad had happened with Janet, and she hoped she hadn't known. Choking on the words, all I could say was, "You knew."

With good counseling and Christ's help, Janet eventually forgave her but also accepted the reality that they'd never have an honest relationship.

The accusations against Val became increasingly ludicrous until Mom convinced herself that my generous loving sister wanted to kill her. Together we confronted that lie but it made no difference. Sitting at Mom's dining-room table, just as she had on the psychiatrist's couch, our mother's ice-blue eyes stared straight ahead without blinking.

"Why can't you just tell Valerie you're sorry?" I pleaded. Silent, unyielding, Mom became a frozen statue, sitting immovable with her wrinkled hands folded in front of her.

Stunned, Val and I left, stopping in the apartment building's stairwell. "That's it. I'm done," Val said. "Oh, I'll still do whatever's necessary but that's it. Nothing more."

I agreed. In the weeks to come, my sweet sister continued grocery shopping, taking Mom meals, doing her laundry just the way she liked, and more whenever necessary.

But when Mom refused to take her meds after calling the doctor "stupid" to his face, we quit taking her to see him. There was no point. Eventually she had the stroke he'd warned about. But not before she turned her life into a living hell. Refusing a reality that respects and cares about the feelings of others does that. Over time she became increasingly self-absorbed thwarting every relationship. She'd been so rude to Aunt Eileen during their last phone call, that my aunt quit talking to her. Still, she'd be arriving soon with my cousin Nancy.

Remembered for all the Wrong Reasons

Seeing Val walk in with a box of photos brought my tumultuous thoughts back to the present. "The table they set up for us is over here," I said, pointing the way. We arranged the memorabilia, finishing moments before family members began to arrive.

Janet, Diane, and Suzie drove in together from the desert where they lived with their husbands. As my sisters walked in the door, their grief-stricken expressions surprised me. Convinced that sorrow wasn't for Mom, I asked, "What's going on?"

"We just found out that DPAA has started excavating Daddy's crash site," Janet said with a tear-choked voice, while brushing her stunning white hair out of her big brown eyes. "To be honest that's stirred up far more emotion for me than Mom's death." Diane and Suzie, looking ready to burst into tears, nodded agreement.

"What's the DPAA?"

"The Department of POW/MIA Accounting Agency."

"So, they know that's where his plane went down?"

"They're pretty certain. This excavation will tell them for sure."

With tear-filled eyes, Janet expressed her longing to go on this government dig. No one could blame her. As a teen, Daddy had rescued her. For years she and Diane had pushed Washington, D.C. dignitaries for information, and now because of their efforts, we might actually find out what happened. However, Janet's husband had recently suffered a stroke, and she couldn't leave him. Sacrificing her own desires simply because it was the right thing to do stood in stark contrast to our mother's behavior.

In the midst of all that emotional turmoil, I understood why Mom's death didn't really matter. Janet had already expressed her feelings: "She was just a woman I saw once a year."

Usually that happened every Christmas Eve at my house. I'd loved our tradition of Janet's family gathering around my dining room table with Mom for stuffed manicotti, my specialty. Christmas festivities kept conversation on the surface so Mom had no opportunity to gaslight Janet the way she did if my youngest sister visited her at the beach. About once a year, Janet tried to take her son John to see his grandmother, but most of the time when they scheduled a get together, one or the other cancelled.

Sacrificial Love

When Janet's world came crashing down, several years after Daddy disappeared, she had turned to Christ. Before that she'd become so thin, my sisters and I were afraid she'd die. Desperate for help, Jesus gave Janet the courage to face the truth through inpatient care. At Charter Hospital, an astute therapist gave her the tools necessary to separate her well-being from our mother's denial.

With her identity no longer tied to Mom's approval, at 40 years old, Janet met and married her sweet husband. A year later, they had their precious son. When I took our mother to see John get baptized, she declared him a miracle child. Yet, she refused to acknowledge the only One capable of miracles. Now, Christ daily supplied Janet with unselfish love for her husband despite the fact that he could no longer take care of himself or even say her name. Her decisions and strength of character day by day gained the admiration of everyone who knew her. But her life was not easy.

My heart ached that our mother never came to grips with life's pain, learning how to deal with harsh realities the way Janet had. As far as we knew, Mom remained in denial until her dying day.

Self-Protection Became Self-Destructive

Insisting she was a self-made woman, our mother claimed she deserved everything she had. One night after dinner and a couple of glasses of wine, I tried to get her to admit that favorable circumstances had made her comfortable lifestyle possible. Her divorce settlement from my stepfather enabled her to buy him out of the dental x-ray labs. Not long after, bank CDs started earning 18 percent interest.

My mom deserved credit for saving everything she could. However, if that unique opportunity hadn't been there, she couldn't have made the money she did. In addition, she'd capitalized on financing Val's and my home loans by charging us 12 percent interest—a little less than the going rate. Considering today's rates at less than 3 percent, that interest income was substantial. At least, it was, until my second husband and I refinanced and paid her off. Furious, she threatened never to speak to us again.

I figured that was her problem. However, Val, still longing for our mother's approval, succumbed to the constant badgering and continued paying that exorbitant interest until her home was paid off.

Perhaps we all have narcissistic tendencies to some degree—that desire to meet *our* needs, to protect *ourselves*. But watching my mom made me determined not to allow my "self" to dictate my well-being. Especially when internal or external voices whispered lies: "You're not good enough." "You need to take care of yourself. Don't worry about anyone else." "You're better, smarter, prettier, than [fill in the blank]." The one I came to hate the most: "You deserve to be happy." Why do I deserve that more than someone else? Lots of good people live in difficult circumstances.

Due to my mother's example, denial became my greatest enemy. The truth was I needed a Savior and He claimed me as His precious child no matter what I did or *who* didn't like me. Intentional about who I wanted to be, my desire to live in the truth forced me every single day to deal with reality's pain. But only supernatural help taught me how to cope with suffering.

Dying to My "Self" Took Time

For a couple of years after Jan left, I tried to anesthetize the pain by drinking, partying, and searching for a man.

Todd gave me hope. He drove a red Porsche and had a good job. But as his phone calls became few and far between, I realized he didn't really care. For a while, I catered to him, hoping he'd pay more attention to me. Eventually my lack of self-respect destroyed our relationship.

Brandon, another Porsche guy, treated me well. Keeping him at arm's length improved my self-respect, but I just wasn't that into him. When he took me for brunch at a gorgeous beachside restaurant, a harp player serenaded us. All indicators made me think he was getting too serious. I wasn't, so I ended the relationship.

Matt drove a Corvette and was movie-star handsome. He might have stayed if I'd let him, but we had nothing to talk about.

When a former crush came back into my life, I started hoping for a future. But within weeks, he ended our relationship and started dating someone new. Rejected by a man I trusted made my heartache worse. My self-esteem sunk into the mud. Seeing myself through the eyes of rejection made me feel worthless. Always, my thoughts returned to Jan. Reflected in his eyes, I saw a woman adored, precious, sexy, and desirable. Even more, he'd made me feel intelligent.

But back then, I was convinced it was only a matter of time before Jan would leave me. Better that I ended our relationship before he could. Food became a source of comfort, and before long I put on 10 pounds. My mother admonished me: "If you gain even five pounds a year, in 10 years you'll have gained 50 pounds."

A whisper told me to apply that concept to my trysts with men. There weren't many, but thinking of the few I'd been with disgusted me. The futility made me ashamed, needy, and unable to sustain a relationship.

Nothing helped control the pain, and I wasn't at all convinced God cared.

Something needed to change. So, for a couple of years, I went to church every Sunday no matter how late I stayed out Saturday night or how hungover I was. Though I liked being with kind people, I still craved a man who could make me feel the way Jan did. Someone who cared about me but didn't travel and wasn't a playboy. Someone exciting who loved life and could make me laugh. Someone I could talk to about things that mattered. Someone who wouldn't leave me. I wanted Jan, but the Jan I wanted didn't really exist.

Agony washed over me in angry waves, pounding me. Drowning me. One night I called my sister, Suzie, begging for a life-preserver. "Patti, trust and believe. God can do anything. I have a poem that might help. I'll send it to you. A few days later, Grace Noll Crowell's poem "Promised Strength" arrived in the mail. After putting Josh to bed, I pulled it out of the envelope and started reading.

> One day when my burden seemed greater
> than my body and spirit could bear,
> weighed down by the load, I faltered
> beneath my worry and care. . . .
>
> From *Apples of Gold*, p. 65 c. 1960

The poem spoke to my aching heart. Trying to imagine my future without Jan, I was attempting to carry a burden far too heavy for me. Only the strength supplied by the living God could sustain me day by day.

Taking one step at a time, I began applying the poem's advice. Combined with Biblical truths like Matthew 11:28–30, I discovered how Jesus wanted to enfold me into His comforting arms:

> Come to Me, all who are weary and heavy-laden, and I will give you rest. Take My yoke upon you and learn from Me, for I am gentle and humble in heart, and YOU WILL FIND REST FOR YOUR SOULS. For My yoke is easy and My burden is light.

Soon after reading it, one unforgettable morning on my way to work, I stopped at the intersection of Mission Blvd. and Mountain Ave. In the length of time it took for the red light to turn green, I determined to never again suffer from my own self-inflicted misery. Talking to Jesus, I said, "That's it, I'm done. I'm finished trying to find a man, who can make me feel good about myself. And, I'm done attempting to manipulate circumstances that aren't within my control. From now on, I'll do my best to live your way instead of mine." Though Jesus had been my Savior for quite a while, that day, He became my Lord.

In that instant, I made a vow. "You are the Creator of the universe. You made me and love me. So, I'm not even going to question You when I don't understand." The Almighty God—with unlimited power, vision, and resources—might easily do things in ways I couldn't possibly comprehend with my limited perspective.

More Alive Than Ever

This vertical relationship with a Being far greater than myself, who held to constant standards, began transforming my life. My well-being started shifting away from dependency on ever-changing values and other people's perspectives. Because I had no doubt about how much Jesus loved me— enough to come to me on a cruise ship while I was in the midst of an affair—I embraced His values. His Holy Spirit had been with me that night I sat on the chaise lounge under the stars, whispering Truths that I needed to hear. And, when my heart was broken by Jan's and my human inability to sustain our relationship, Jesus picked up the broken pieces.

Over time, that decision began shifting my view of success. Obedience to God became my goal—in good times and bad. His approval and strength helped me stand firm against my mom's erroneous edicts. It set me free from craving her validation. At the same time, God's admonition to honor my mother and father gave me the freedom to listen with respect when she offered sound financial advice. In many ways, my mother was an intelligent woman and listening to her frequently prevented me from making costly mistakes.

Sometimes I wonder if insisting on having our own way, despite the harm it does to ourselves and others, might be the root of all sin. In the garden of Eden, Adam and Eve disobeyed God because they thought they knew better.

"My Way" by Frank Sinatra was my mother's favorite song. She wanted everyone from the sales clerk at Macy's to her bridge partners to the server at Marie Callender's to cater to *her* way. That lack of regard for others made her difficult to be around.

After having been raised so differently, Jesus taught me how genuine love requires self-denial, selfless acts of kindness, and self-sacrifice. At first after Jan left, I tried to find comfort by the same means my mother had—doing things my way to try and satisfy my soul. That meant frequently leaving my son with babysitters so I could go dancing. But this self-absorbed thinking made me irresponsible and led to increasing pain. While reading the Bible and attending church, the Holy Spirit (also called the Wonderful Counselor) helped me understand my own self-destructive patterns.

Freedom to Make Better Choices

Josh needed me to stay home at night, putting his needs ahead of my own. By the time he was four, I infuriated my mom by refusing to go on any more cruises. Although I wasn't permitted to use our family's beach cabin, a co-worker started renting me his condo for two weeks every year in San Clemente. By God's undeserved favor, that became our vacation spot. Friends and family who wanted to spend the night pitched in a small amount on the rent, which added up. They also brought groceries, making meals less work and more affordable. Staying in the truth about my son needing stability permitted me to discover the sheer joy of building sand castles and playing frisbee with him. That extended into other areas and I started staying home more.

By putting Josh's needs above my own, I wanted to show my mom a different, better way. I hoped she'd discover the freedom I'd found by living in the truth of my choices—forgiven for foolish ones and with a variety of tools that helped me make better ones.

Entrenched in Old Wounds

For her entire life, my mother kept past traumas buried deep inside where they dictated self-destructive behaviors. Trying to uncover the devastating circumstances of her childhood brought me a measure of understanding and compassion.

While driving home from dinner one night, I asked how she'd felt as a child when a judge awarded custody of her to her dad.

For a long while, my mom sat in the silent darkness while we sped down the freeway. Then her voice quivered as she spoke softly while looking straight ahead. "I was only about three when my mother drove me to my dad's parents and dropped me off. As she started to drive away, I grabbed the car door's handle, crying, begging her not to leave. But she did."

My heart ached for that sad little blonde girl who felt abandoned. My mom had probably never before spoken those words aloud. Maybe she didn't even understand how those memories had impacted her. Some experts say such a traumatic experience can lead to self-soothing techniques of manipulation, control, and superiority. High intelligence may also have contributed to the self-absorption that caused my mom a lifetime of pain.

Over the years, she convinced herself that her dad paid off the judge to gain custody. Yet, one day while preparing for her to move, as we sat on the floor of her spare bedroom sorting through old files, I found an envelope with the return address of "Pacific Colony," a mental institution. Opening it revealed a handwritten letter from a doctor to my grandmother. It described my mother's uncle explaining that there was no cure for his problems. "Mom, did Uncle Archie molest you when you both lived with Grandma? That would explain why Grandad got custody of you."

"No. It was nothing. Men are just like that. It was part of life."

Being a victim of sexual abuse as a child likely impacted her relationship with men including my dad. Though he had cheated on her, I knew firsthand, there could be powerful reasons behind infidelity. Her refusal to live in New Mexico must have contributed to my dad's loneliness and the emotional distance between them. Perhaps, in part, her issues had driven him into another woman's arms.

Self-absorption had obscured my mother's vision and sense of responsibility when it came to others, even her own family. For her, success was defined by wealth. That New Mexico job had likely paid better than local opportunities. Monetary gain may have been the main reason she married the man who molested Janet. He offered a pathway to financial security and social status. Unable to decipher the consequences of what he'd done, she sought the advice of our family doctor as well as a highly respected attorney. They convinced her that "the less you say about it, the better." Their advice validated her upbringing—men were just like that.

The decision to marry a pedophile destroyed something in my mom. His abuse and infidelity led to their divorce, and that's when we started going on our cruises. By then many people had embraced pleasure-seeking as a way of escape—especially women like my mom who were close to 40.

In the late '60s, early '70s, the cultural mantra became "if it feels good, do it." It was the epitome of self-indulgence. That's why my mother encouraged me to leave my son home while escaping into a fantasy world of luxury. And, why she thought I should have an affair. My pleasure should come first, without regard for my family or the consequences of my choices. Without any kind of stabilizer or standard for truth, I had believed her. It was only after starting to study the Bible, cultivating a relationship with Jesus, and learning from others, that it became increasingly clear how wrong she'd been to listen to society's lies.

Over time, her distorted thinking negated social responsibility to the point that it could have cost someone his life. While taking her to get groceries one day, a car sat in front of us, stalled at a stoplight. As the light turned green, I maneuvered around it and saw the driver slumped over the wheel. My heart started pumping hard. He needed help.

"You don't need to stop! Let someone else do it. I need my groceries," she badgered. Parking as quickly as I could with my mother screaming at me, I jumped out of the car to go offer assistance. Fortunately for all of us, before I could get involved, others had come to the driver's aid.

Now, such memories clouded our ability to offer a more traditional celebration of my mom's life.

A Difficult Afternoon

About 30 of us ordered lunch, then we tried to honor my mom the best we could. Though it was impossible to escape the reality of self-obsessed behavior, Diane recalled our mother being an excellent seamstress. My eldest sister had been so tiny in high school that rather than try to find clothes in her size, Mom adapted children's patterns to give Diane a fantastic wardrobe. She also made tailored shirts for my dad and sewed for me while I was in school. Though simple, the stylish evening gowns she made me when we went on the cruises exceeded many we found in stores.

Still, Janet and Valerie's memories of Mom involved constantly being chastised for eating more than she deemed appropriate. Or not scouring the sink right. Or . . .and on and on it went.

Janet couldn't think of one good thing to say. Not. One. Good. Thing. Hoping to bring a happy memory, I mentioned Mom buying Janet a horse. After school, Janet hopped on her bike riding downhill to where Blackie was kept. Then my mom picked her up on the way home from work.

Days later, Janet explained how I'd inadvertently perpetuated a lie. Although, for years, Mom had painted a sweeter picture, Janet described how after a long day at school, then caring for and riding Blackie, she'd been expected to ride her bike several miles uphill to get home. Such unrealistic expectations and differences in perspective exacerbated Janet's depression and thoughts of suicide.

Being newlyweds with challenges of our own, Val and I remained oblivious to the problems. That's when our dad sought custody and took Janet with him to Laos where they could hear bombs blasting in the not-too-far-off distance. Although it took years and a lot of conversation for Valerie and me to understand, Janet had felt safer there than at home. While our single mom dated and pursued her own interests, she'd been blind to Janet's loneliness and intense pain.

Val's son, Eric, spoke eloquently about the lack of generational connectedness. Summing up the feelings of all our boys, he said, "It made me sad that we never had a grandma." Our mom never attended their soccer games, took them to movies, read to them, or baked them cookies. Her way of saying "I love you," involved giving them gifts. That was the only way she knew.

Recognizing the importance of extended family relationships, Eric's lament turned into a lovely tribute to Valerie and how she was the kind of grandmother children need.

Challenged to find something good to say, Val spoke of finding a letter from our dad expressing his regrets for his affair and asking our mother's forgiveness. Her voice choked with emotion, my sister said, "I believe our mom was the love of his life, and we've always known he was hers. Now, maybe they are together in heaven." Though they had fought horribly in court, for many years, every Christmas our mother put a poinsettia on the evergreen tree our city had planted in his memory.

Being self-obsessed had ultimately made her life a living hell, yet the possibility of a relationship with Jesus gave us hope that in eternity God has healed our parents in ways that answered our childhood prayers for them to be together. Mom's peace-filled sleep without food or water for ten days was extraordinary, but it provided the time we needed to say things we couldn't say while she was lucid. Things like her need for forgiveness and our willingness to give it. We also talked about her need for Jesus as her Lord and Savior.

A chaplain had asked if we wanted her baptized, and though skeptical that it could make a difference, I said "yes." He had me answer his questions on her behalf and I wonder if perhaps somehow while she slept, she embraced a relationship with the living God. While alive, once in a while, she'd mention how she prayed for us every night. And I'd tell her to pray to Jesus because only He could help. There's no way to know what happens at the point of death, but that hope replaces our despair over her life.

As the luncheon came to a close, I hugged my sisters goodbye and emotional exhaustion settled in. Val and I were the last to leave. After chatting about the memorial being the best it could have been under the circumstances, I picked up the orchid and walked out to my car, carefully placing the plant back in its transport box. While getting behind the wheel and starting the car, I again wished Jan could have been with me. These days, being single, I thought of him often. Hearing his voice again and discovering how he felt about me had changed my life. Today, I had no doubt he'd not only comfort me, but also share my wonder as to whether the excavation team might finally discover what happened to my dad.

Chapter 11

Wonders Never Cease

Early the next morning, November 11, 2017, I took the Windblown Girl from the china closet and placed her carefully on the mantle above the red used-brick fireplace in the living room. Then I curled up in my favorite overstuffed blue denim chair, as I did every morning, to prepare for the day—mentally, spiritually, emotionally. Rubbing my hand across the chair's threadbare arm, the lovely Lladro figurine captured my attention. By far the most precious gift my mother ever gave me, she embodied a significance that had taken years for me to comprehend. Why hadn't I remembered to talk about this at her memorial?

The mysterious Christmas package that contained the beautiful porcelain girl had arrived in the middle of a life-changing year. Though more than three decades had passed since then, indelible events etched that time period into my memory. It started in the spring of 1986.

Foreshadowing a Visit

While sprinkling blue cleansing powder into the bathroom sink, a strange impression engulfed me—*Jan was outside.*

Thoughts whispered into my mind on a gentle breeze usually proved accurate. But never had I experienced any with such overwhelming clarity. Besides thumping hard in my chest, my heart began pounding in my temples. I wrung out the purple sponge and washed my hands. After more than a decade apart, he was there. Outside. Watching my house. Trying to decide whether to knock on my door. Anxiety prevented me from leaving the small bathroom to peek out the living-room drapes. I didn't need to look. He was there.

To steady myself I grabbed onto the white porcelain sink with both hands. There was zero doubt. Jan was outside. He mustn't see me like this. Overweight. Dressed in dark purple corduroy pants and a plaid gauze shirt. My long hair had been cut short.

Even worse, a pterygium had irritated my left eye so much I could no longer wear contacts. Despite a surgical procedure to remove its tip, this iceberg-like growth had forced me back into glasses. Wearing them took me straight back into fourth grade when putting on glasses made me feel like I was putting on an ugly face. Combined with an extra 25 pounds from quitting smoking, I'd almost stopped caring about my appearance.

That didn't matter to my second husband Tim. He liked my cooking. And, though I tried to be a good wife, our lack of emotional connectedness after five years of marriage added to the problems.

Before marrying him, I'd been so concerned about the possibility of Jan coming back that I'd talked with Jesus about whether I should be planning a wedding. While spading fertilizer granules into the ground around the roses one day, I silently asked, "What about Jan?"

In response, strong impressions murmured inside my mind. "You let me worry about Jan." The Guardian and Shepherd of my soul knew exactly how I felt. Attempting to hide my feelings from the One who made me would have been silly. He knew my longing for Jan had never eased. Heaving a sigh, I plucked a small weed from the cold dirt.

That soft breeze continued, "Patti, marriage to Tim will be very difficult. With an alcoholic dad, there are many issues, but if you marry him, you will learn much." This challenge felt necessary.

Tim was a good guy. He'd been kind. And, he loved Josh. My son needed a dad who'd be there for him. After that day in the garden, I asked two pastors, who didn't know each other but knew me well, for their advice. Each one indicated their approval. It was tough to be a woman alone. Though Tim and I didn't have much physical chemistry, I convinced myself that would come with time—after we married.

But I was wrong. Considering my first marriage, I should have known better. Being married to someone without that physical connection was tough. Nor did God resolve the problems in the way I expected. On the way home from our honeymoon, I began to realize that my new husband couldn't meet my emotional needs any more than I could figure out how to meet his.

For months I stayed angry at God and angry at Tim. This was exactly the type of situation I'd tried to avoid. Though Tim and I had much more in common than I'd had with my first husband, now I was in another difficult marriage—where once again, sex was a major issue.

Yet remembering my vow to trust the Lord, even when I didn't understand, finally stopped me from yelling at my husband. Instead, I started working on myself. During that time, I insisted we both get counseling. At the same time, I started reading self-help books like *Boundaries* by Cloud and Townsend. *Make Anger Your Ally* by Neil Clark Warren taught me how to cope, while giving voice to my concerns and dealing with my aggravation.

In addition, my good friend, Cynthia, showed me a "train diagram" that started helping me make better decisions. The engine pulling the train runs on *facts*. Next comes the coal car fueling those facts by *faith*. The caboose follows behind, carrying my *feelings*. Despite experiencing frustration, anger, and hurt, the fact was that I was married. This time, I realized it wasn't just a contract to be broken. Now, I understood how I'd made a covenant before God, and my responsibility was to do things His way, not my own.

So, rather than focusing on my emotions, I focused on my commitment to be the best wife I could be to Tim. I'd promised his mom that before the wedding. When my mom tried to convince me that I could get a divorce in six months if I wasn't happy, I'd promised her that God was big enough to make this marriage work. I'd promised Tim to care about his needs, and I'd promised myself that there would not be another divorce. By faith, I intended to uphold those promises.

Despite the grief and loneliness, or maybe because of it, I started learning some priceless character-building lessons. I learned to sacrifice my own desires to do the right thing and honor my word. Rather than shutting down and refusing to communicate as I had in my first marriage, I learned to express myself. At first shouting in anger, but over time as my inner strength grew, I learned to speak the truth in love with kindness.

Most important, I learned to choose love—even when I didn't feel like it. Within a year of our wedding, we had a son and together we chose his name. After much deliberation, we decided on Benjamin Joseph after the MASH characters on television: B. J. Hunnicutt and Benjamin Franklin Pierce. B. J. Thomas was my favorite singer, and my mom's initials were B. J., so she was thrilled. Rather than thinking of his nickname as initials, we called our son, BJ.

Although Tim equally participated in parenting both Josh and BJ, that certainly didn't resolve the problems between us. Rather our different perspectives on parenting often exacerbated them.

Jerry, a wise pastor/counselor, assured me that *doing* loving things was loving. So, after one particularly bad argument with no resolution, I chose to make Tim's favorite dinner. While stuffing those bell peppers and praying, my anger melted. Compassion replaced my frustration as I looked at the situation from my husband's point of view and remembered the way he'd been raised.

Still, no matter how much counseling we received, it didn't change the problems. As hard as I tried nothing changed my desire for Jan or prepared me to handle the idea of my former lover being outside my home. However, I realized that letting my emotions preside over the facts could do nothing but bring chaos and long-term suffering to my entire family. I had no desire to repeat the pain-filled lessons of years gone by, but that didn't change the reality that I craved Jan's gentle touch, his sweet kindness, and our ability to laugh and talk. The empty caverns of my soul yearned for him to fill them up.

But this was not the way I wanted him to see me. If he'd envisioned that younger version of me all these years, I couldn't destroy that image. Besides, if he still wanted me, how could I resist him? So, I stayed hidden in that tiny bathroom begging God to take him away.

More whispers impressed themselves on my mind: "He's been engaged twice, yet never married." "He has a child." "He wants you." "One day he'll contact you through your sister, Valerie." Diane would have made way more sense. The thought of Valerie was bizarre. He'd only met her briefly when we picked up Josh. I must be losing my mind.

After about 20 minutes, a sense of release came convincing me that Jan had left. Shaken to the core, I went and knelt by my bed.

Tears started to slip down my cheeks. "If he ever comes back, God, you'll have to get me on my knees because I won't want to pray. I'll want to be with him. And, you'll have to make me forget my promise that no man could keep me away from him. I'll also have to forget the first time we made love and how afterward when Jan saw my tears, he swiped them away with his thumb. The thought of forgetting those precious memories was incomprehensible.

By the time I finished cleaning house, I had dismissed that strange experience and moved back into the reality of work, marriage, and family. Shoving away the impulse to daydream, whenever my thoughts started to wander into dangerous territory, I prayed them out of my consciousness. Tim knew only the bare minimum about Jan, that he'd been my friend, one I'd slept with. I had no desire to complicate things with any more information than that.

December 25, 1986
An Unforgettable Christmas

The oblong box my mother handed me was too heavy for clothes. Wrapped in red foil and tied with the same soft pink sparkly bow my mom used every year on my special present, I couldn't imagine what was in it. Ripping off the paper exposed the Lladro name on a grey-blue carton, and my heart raced. Could it be the Windblown Girl, the one we'd seen in the Caribbean more than a decade ago?

Quickly I cut away the clear tape imprisoning the contents in Styrofoam. Finally, that simple porcelain girl was set free from her box. My mother had remembered. On a recent trip to Spain, she'd gone to the Lladro factory and bought my sisters and me the collectibles she thought best represented us.

In an instant, sweet memories brought back my inexplicable bond with the Windblown Girl. However, it took a few more years to comprehend her significance.

November 11, 2017
Not My Mother's Life

Nothing ever prepared me for the pain involved in the transformational process that Lladro figurine embodied. Yet the Windblown Girl often reminds me, as she did the morning after my mother's memorial, that life's brutal circumstances don't have to blow me around like a tumbleweed, plunging me into society's gutter. In the midst of the fiercest gale, I can stand strong, safe, and secure in the confidence of Christ.

Epitomizing the peace, love, unity, and respect that I'd longed for, even in my 20s, this young woman stands on a rock-solid foundation confident of being deeply loved. Projecting a unified spirit of wholeness, self-respect keeps her standing strong, and that assurance cultivates respect from others. Without denying my selfish forbidden desires, I never could have experienced such prized attributes.

Soon after receiving her, I had placed her on the fireplace mantle, but my mother informed me how stupid that was. She was too fragile. The Windblown Girl should be hidden away where my sons or husband couldn't break her. So, I put her back in the box and placed it high up in a kitchen cupboard.

Now, however, my mother was gone, and I hadn't played it safe in years. Dramatic escapades kept cropping up—unanticipated adventures beyond anything I could have imagined. The Windblown Girl belonged where everyone could see her.

My next adventure, after my mom's estate settled, might be a cruise to Norway. I'd always thought that if I had the money, I'd go. That also seemed a fitting tribute to my mother in memory of the voyages we'd shared. But a cruise like that was expensive.

Looking at my shredding pansy-adorned drapes with the fuchsia-and-white plaid ruffle reminded me that they needed replacing before I did anything else. My denim chair and its ottoman needed recovering too. Everything in the house needed updating. Imagining all that work was overwhelming.

Still, thoughts of a trip to Norway brought Jan near. His phone call, only a few months after I received the Windblown Girl, continued to play like an unforgettable melody in my mind.

Thursday, March 26, 1987
A Phone Call Changes Everything

After going to the store, I picked up BJ from kindergarten. In the pouring rain, I juggled an umbrella and grocery bags while trying to unlock the front door and usher him inside. The urgent ringing of the telephone rushed me into the kitchen where I spilled cereal boxes, a jar of peanut butter, and canned goods onto the table while grabbing the receiver.

"Hello?"

"Patti, you'd better sit down." Val sounded serious. I thought people only said that in movies.

"What's the matter?"

"You'd better prepare yourself. Jan is going to call you in one hour."

"How do you know?"

"It was the strangest thing—maybe even a miracle." Valerie never used that word. My heart throbbed in my temples. Jan was going to call? How could that be?

"I had just come into the lab after delivering x-rays and our new receptionist was about to hang up the phone. When she saw me, she hesitated and said, 'Wait, she just came in. Let me ask her. Val, do you know someone named Patti Townley?'

'That's our maiden name. Patti's my sister.'

'This woman is trying to find her.'

"So, I took the phone, and a lady said she was a colleague of Jan's in Los Angeles. He's here on business. When she asked why he never married, he told her about you. She asked if he'd call if she found your number, and he said 'yes.' Somehow, he remembered the name of my lab. If I'd been one minute later, I would have missed her! Evidently, he went to lunch but before leaving, he told her to say he'd call you at 1:00. I gave her your number. In an hour, he's going to call!"

Numb, I said good-bye and hung up the phone. "Oh God, what am I going to do?"

Spreading peanut butter and jelly on a slice of white bread, I considered my options. Maybe I just won't answer the phone. But then he might come over. The only thing that might dissuade him from trying to see me was to insist on having my husband present. After handing BJ his sandwich, I stuffed down all emotion and called Tim—only because it was the right thing to do. "Jan's in Los Angeles and is going to call me. If he wants to get together, is it OK if I ask him to come over?"

"Do what you want. I'll be there," Tim said coldly.

Closing the bedroom door after putting BJ down for a nap, pain in my chest began radiating outward toward my arms. It burned in my throat until I couldn't breathe. Walking into the living room, I fell to my knees and started to pray. "Oh my God, I'm having a heart attack!" If I die, BJ will be left alone. Please God help me! Because I wasn't thinking straight, the idea of calling 911 never entered my mind.

"I want him, Lord. I want him so badly I can't bear it. What will I say? I can't do this. There's no way I can even talk to him. He'll know. And if he knows, he won't go away. I'll never be able to resist him. This hurts too bad. You be my voice. Be my strength. Jesus you'll have to do this by your Holy Spirit, because I just can't!"

Over the years, Christ had done other things I couldn't—magnificent things that demonstrated His care and proved I could trust Him. He even came near in August of 1984 when I was on television with the whole world watching. Would He meet me again as He did then?

Chapter 12

A Really Big Deal

Stepping back on the grass, I looked down at the multicolored sign. "I put on a BRIGHT new look for the 'All New Let's Make a Deal.'" Sprinkling glitter all over the television show's name had been a flash of extraordinary brilliance. With such a sparkly sign, Monty Hall couldn't resist choosing me.

Years before, Suzie and Valerie had each won the big deal of the day— Suzie, a shiny black Triumph Spitfire sportscar. A couple of years later, Val, a full-sized pool table. But when I'd gone, my insecurities got the better of me. Whereas my sisters were bubbly and fun; I clammed up. No one even noticed me.

This time would be different. Wearing a bright turquoise jacket, a fuchsia-colored blouse and spraying my hair red, I'd sparkle like the sign.

August 1984
Making the Right Choice

Exuberant anticipation made me bounce up and down while Tim and I stood in line. Sure enough, the show's producer handed us that special ticket for the trading floor. Moments later Monty Hall chose us to make a deal.

"Do you want to go for the car or trade for what's behind curtain #1," he asked, after we nervously priced some grocery items. Though Tim worked for a beer distributor and was pretty good at pricing, if we were even a little off we'd lose everything. After a whispered conference with my husband, I shouted, "Let's take the curtain."

As the draperies opened, they revealed our prize: a wall-sized picture of a sunny beach signifying an all-expense paid trip to Hawaii. Tim was ecstatic. He'd always wanted to go there.

But all I could envision were the hidden costs. Meals. Taxes. Our limited budget was already stretched too far. After BJ was born, I became a stay-at-home mom, and we could barely make ends meet. Leaving my job at FMC had been a huge risk, but when our trusted babysitter quit, we believed it was an indicator that I should stay home to raise Josh, now 10, and BJ, now 2.

Once again convinced that God would guide us, I couldn't escape the facts. Money had been so tight, we needed everything. An extravagant trip to Hawaii would only make matters worse.

So, when Monty came back and asked if we wanted to go for the big deal of the day—I was ready. A whisper inside my mind had convinced me to take the risk, but Tim wanted that trip to Hawaii. Unless he agreed, I couldn't trade it away. After a brief consultation, when Monty pressed for an answer, Tim said, "Let's go for it."

Our curtain opened to reveal the big deal of the day! And, I almost burst into tears. How could this happen? It contained nothing we needed.

The announcer described our prize. "Direct from Beverly Hills, a white satin-finished couch, ultra-modern chairs, brass-and-glass tables and the ugliest console television imaginable." Those weren't his actual words, but perhaps better descriptors than the ones he used. Designer furniture worth over $11,000.00. If we took it home, we'd have to pay taxes on that amount. That couch wouldn't survive an hour with our two rambunctious boys. Even I'd be afraid to sit on it. Tim thought he could sell the showcase and make a profit, so we approved delivery hoping to come out ahead.

When it arrived, we piled everything into our little den and shut the doors, making that room off-limits. At the time, winning such stuff seemed senseless. Yet, months later, right before April 15th, Tim sold everything. After taxes, enough money remained to buy a nice television and my first computer. That took my stay-at-home business to the next level. Typing and editing doctoral dissertations supplied an ongoing way to increase our income, something a trip to Hawaii could never have done. Lesson learned: Our Creator's purposes far exceed our limited perspectives. Sometimes we just have to trust Him while waiting to discover His plans.

March 1987
Higher Stakes

This time, I was gambling with my integrity. My character and my family were at risk. Jan's best good, too. He needed Jesus as much as I did. Would I allow my feelings to guide my choices and choose to be unfaithful again? That was an overwhelming temptation. How I longed for his strong arms to hold me close against his chest. Or could I risk everything for the deal of a lifetime, winning back proven character against all odds? Demonstrating faithfulness despite incredibly alluring memories?

My marriage had been tough for six years. Only by applying biblical principles, especially those in Philippians 2:3–4, could I keep my family together. Although I'm lousy at memorizing anything, Jesus engraved those Bible verses into my soul. Daily they reminded me to

> Do nothing from selfishness or empty conceit, but with humility of mind regard one another as more important than yourselves; do not *merely* look out for your own personal interests, but also for the interests of others.

Certainly not what I'd been taught by my mom or many of the most prominent voices of my generation. "Do what's right for you" was a constant message. "You deserve to be happy." Even many so-called Christians made that their supreme goal. And yet, happiness *my way* meant certain trauma for others. Cheating on my husband meant taking away my sons' stability. My parents' divorce devastated me, and that insecurity had set the stage for both my marriages. I hadn't wanted someone like Jan to hurt me the way my dad hurt my mom.

Remembering My Figurine

The refrigerator humming in our dining room reminded me of my Savior's goodness when I chose to walk by faith and trust Him with the outcome. The kitchen, recently gutted, was ready for new cabinets including a pantry and a china closet. Our major remodel would not only give me office space, but soon everyone would be able to see the Windblown Girl.

Now I knew that precious porcelain figurine was a "type" of *who* I wanted to become. Confidently standing on a rock, she looked off into the distance toward the future. A book clutched behind her back lent support.

That certainly hadn't been my identity when I got involved with Jan. Trying to live by cultural standards, I experimented with sex, thinking I could walk away from him without regrets. Trying to be different things to different people—an employee, a mom, a wife, and a daughter (none of whom ever measured up)—had enslaved me to my feelings. Acting on them had tossed my life into turmoil.

Without a binding relationship, I'd intended to use Jan to satisfy my "self." However, that didn't work. Our relationship started as a fairy tale but was doomed from the beginning. While we ate dinner that night before he left, I'd known. An unfathomable flash of insight convinced me that if he tried to give up his dream of being a captain, he would have hated me. And, I would have grown to hate him—his drinking, his flirting, his lack of ability to settle down. The only way to protect what we'd had was to end our relationship before we destroyed it.

Neither of us was a commodity. Trying to separate our minds from our bodies didn't work. Now more than 11 years later, we continued paying an agonizing price.

Trying similar behavior with others, I not only dehumanized them but myself as well. I couldn't pretend not to feel the shame of being an individual who used others. Kind people like Ron, who had taken what belonged to his wife to comfort me. Regardless of cultural standards, I never wanted to be that person again. Ignoring potential consequences, my behavior could have contributed to unimaginable suffering.

Discovering that my Creator formed my identity while I was in my mother's womb changed the way I looked at myself and those around me. Studying the Bible convinced me that each individual is made in the image of God, created for relationship with Him. That reality never changes. It's rock-solid truth worth standing on, the same today as it was 2,000 years ago.

Regardless of who might think otherwise, my resemblance to my heavenly Father gives me worth. My identity doesn't depend on what I can do, who cares about me, or how popular I am. Value as a human being is intrinsic, given by God. My relationship with Christ had been built on a strong foundation—immovable, unshakable regardless of the winds of change or of circumstances. Whether in my mother's womb or when I'm 100 years old, that truth remains the same. Jesus is the Rock of my salvation.

Undeserved Compassion and Goodness

Though I still had much to learn about marriage, Jesus knew I still craved Jan's touch. Nothing compared to the emotional and physical connection we'd had. Our Creator had made human sexuality and saturated genuine intimacy with pleasure. Jan and I had deliberately disregarded boundaries set in place for our own good. And, now I paid a tremendous price.

But that only set the stage for unparalleled grace. Despite knowing my feelings and temptations, Jesus continually provided tangible evidence of how much He cares about the things I long for. Our home renovation proved He could be trusted with my desires.

Frustrated by trying to work at the dining room table while our tiny den housed that white satin couch and glass tables, I had longed for an office. When mortgage interest rates went down, we started wondering about refinancing and taking some equity to add on. When we got a bid from a contractor to turn the den into office space and add a large family room, it was $50,000! Way beyond our means. But one astonishing event after another between 1986 and 1987 allowed us to almost double the size of our home.

Although my mother was furious, we couldn't afford not to take advantage of the lower rates. That reduced our house payment substantially. She thought we were crazy to take out enough equity for a $15,000 remodel. Yet Diane's husband, a general contractor, offered to advise me as I oversaw the project. By hiring contractor friends, Bruce thought we could do what we wanted within our budget. Still, it was a huge financial risk.

Beyond My Capability

For weeks I looked at magazines and stewed about the architectural design. Convinced divine authority had brought us this far, I prayed for the Creator's creativity. But, on the day Diane and Suzie's stepfather, Del, was coming to draft the plans, I still had no clue how to lay out what we wanted—until I took a nap.

Exhausted from formatting dissertations, taking care of the kids, and trying to make such challenging decisions, I put BJ down for a nap, then went and laid on the living room couch. Somehow after closing my eyes, whether in a dream or a vision I'm not sure, I saw the exact layout. By the time Del arrived, I could describe exactly what I wanted.

A few weeks later when I took the plans to the city for a building permit, the officials were astonished. Incorporating a short wall around my office space permitted just enough light to filter into the room to meet building code requirements. They couldn't believe I'd thought of it. Neither could I.

Construction started right after the first of the year. BJ climbed up on a stool to watch out the back-door window as a small bulldozer demolished the cement patio so the slab for the room addition could be poured. Years of memories had taken place on that patio—impromptu soccer celebrations, barbeques with friends, and birthday bashes. In October, we'd held the last and best party ever—a GI Joe extravaganza complete with dog-tag invitations for BJ's fifth birthday. Girls dressed as army nurses. Boys in camouflage. After a flag-waving military parade, and an obstacle course, I scooped baked beans and wieners into metal pie tins for the chow line. Counting parents and siblings, as well as some of Josh's friends, about 40 people came. I'd sure miss all that outdoor family fun.

Yet now I could envision a home beyond anything I'd ever imagined—one perfect for indoor celebrations. By taking one step of faith at a time, it would be completed on budget. The wall between the kitchen and former den opened into Tim's new office creating an island with bar stools and enough space for a foosball table. The den's sliding glass door had been removed and framing for my new office with a four-foot wall around it expanded outward from there.

That anomaly not only provided the necessary light, it would also allow for some privacy while still permitting me to monitor the kids as they watched television in our large family room. A laundry area had already been framed in across from my office. No more trips to the garage to use the dryer. Only a master planner could have pulled all those details together in such a functional way. And, that planner sure wasn't me.

Agonizing Dreams

Our family life seemed fairly normal. Though Tim and I had no emotional closeness, when we disagreed, we didn't usually argue. He'd ignore the problem, and I'd try to remain quiet or kind until I could get over my frustration. We lived simply, and I did my best to be respectful—even when I wasn't happy with the choices he made. In turn, he didn't get upset with me when the house was a mess, or I needed him to make a grocery store run. Despite our lack of emotional intimacy, I chose to love my husband, and I adored my kids.

Although I didn't permit myself to think of Jan very often, I had no power to stop the dreams. When I told my best friend, Sharon, she advised me to pray, putting Jan in God's hands, then let it go. Usually that worked. But occasionally, an intense dream left me deeply distraught with an almost physical ache. After one such dream, I wrote a poem to express my anguish.

When I am sad, are you?

If you are, I'm sorry. It seems as though it's a constant sadness—uncontrollable, yet occasionally lessened by a momentary diversion—and then back again just as strong or perhaps even more so than before.

When I'm in pain, are you?

If you are, I'm sorry. It seems the pain is always there, like a fire that smolders, then bursts into open flame, as white hot as those which melt metal—growing hotter and hotter until my heart melts within me, becoming like molten lead until the agony becomes unbearable. Then the fuel lessens, the embers intensely glow; and sleep is the only escape. That's when the dreams come.

When I dream, do you?

If you do, I'm glad. The intimacy, the gentleness in your voice, seeing your face; o' that we might live in the dream. It's so glorious until the dawn. Then reality sets in, along with the awareness that I must live another day without you.

And now, I no longer had to wonder if he ever thought about me. Once we spoke on the phone, I'd know the truth about his feelings. He was in Los Angeles, only an hour away.

1987—A Pivotal Year

Only a few days earlier, my friend, Cynthia, and I had wrapped dishes in newspaper and packed them in boxes for storage until the new cabinets arrived. After taking the Lladro box off the top shelf, I started describing how 1986–1987 was a year like no other.

"It's unbelievable all that's happening," I said, showing the Windblown Girl to my friend, then carefully tucking her back into her box. "We hadn't seen our grandad in decades. He'd never met either of my sons, and Josh is 13. Our trip to visit him in Canada meant so much to all of us. Well, maybe not my mom. I don't think she really wanted to go, but Val, her two sons, Josh, BJ, and I had an unforgettable time.

"In May all my sisters including Diane and Suzie, plus our husbands, will go to the Air America reunion in Dallas. I'll see my stepmother for the first time since my dad disappeared. Though it's been 16 years, I still can't stand her. She stole everything of my dad's, even our family pictures. The only thing she can't touch is the money from our family's beach house. Whenever it's sold and that could be any time, we'll inherit his portion."

"Regardless, it will be fascinating to meet some of the men my dad worked with. And, it makes me proud to know they are putting his name on the memorial at the University of Dallas. And now the remodel. I can't believe we're actually doing this!"

Later as Cynthia was leaving, I mentioned that "once things get back to normal," we'd have to get together for lunch.

Her gentle reply struck like a lightning bolt. "Patti, face it. This is your normal."

She was right. Nothing about my life had been boring the way I'd feared before becoming a Christian. High highs and low lows. Vibrant. Real life, abundant life, where I never knew what might happen next.

And, now Jan was going to call. This was crazy. Hearing from him for the first time in more than 11 years. House torn up. Life torn up. Constant challenges with life-altering decisions.

Thoughts of Cynthia and the train imagery as well as the stability that had brought into my life, even during chaotic times, started calming my emotions. Deciding to call her, I got up off my knees and went to dial her number. She'd understand my prayer request to run on facts, not feelings, better than anyone. Sharon was out of town so I couldn't even talk to her, and I needed strong support and accountability. By the time I explained what was happening to Cynthia, only five minutes remained until Jan's call.

He'd call at 1:00. Not 1:15 or 1:20. I didn't doubt it would be 1:00 p.m. sharp. For a few minutes I paced the floor. My marriage, my sons. "Oh God, even though it would destroy lives I can imagine leaving everything to be with Jan. If he has any idea of how I feel, nothing can keep us apart. Please stand in my shoes and help me."

The phone's piercing ring startled me. Taking a deep breath to calm my racing heart, I picked up the receiver as an inexplicable river of peace began to flow inside my soul.

Chapter 13

The Phone Call

"Pat-ti, Pat-ti. It is Jan. Do you remember me?" A sense of command, yet a hint of uncertainty—his accent as though I'd heard it yesterday.

My heart thumped wildly. Taking a deep breath, I deliberately kept my tone quiet and calm. "Jan. How good to hear your voice. Of course, I remember." Do I remember? Oh, how could I ever forget?

Instant intimacy erased time as once again we came together.

"How did you find me?"

"I remembered going to the dental lab."

Of course. I'd taken him there to inquire about getting braces to close the small gap between his front teeth. I hoped he hadn't done it.

"But how did you remember my last name? It was different when I knew you. I didn't even know you knew my maiden name."

"I remember everything."

Resurrected Memories

His voice brought back a multitude of dormant images long relegated to the shadows of my mind. Jan's attention to detail left no doubt that he had treasured thoughts of me even beyond my recollections of him.

"How is Joash?" Jan's rich warm accent bathed me in tenderness. I wanted to inhale every word, every detail, each inflection—every word of this conversation. Gulping air like a fish out of water, I replied, "Josh is fine—Oh Jan, he is so very smart."

"Good thing he wasn't so smart to crawl out of his bed when I was there."

If he'd been anyone else, his words might have sounded crass but combined with his affectionate chuckle, they drew me deep into our fearless openness, a place where we could speak our hearts and minds. Nothing was off limits. We'd often laughed about how Josh had better not creep into my bedroom. Cherished details poured forth as Jan opened the long-forbidden closet in my mind where they'd been stored.

"He must be shaving by now," Jan continued, remembering, drawing me back into the moment they came out of the bathroom with shaving-cream lathered faces. Jan so tall, lean, tan, a lock of graham-colored hair falling across his forehead. Josh, still in his cotton PJ's, a tiny guy with golden curly locks, grinning from ear to ear. How could so much time have stood still? Basking in the warmth of familiarity, the same smoldering desire lay just beneath the surface of our easy banter.

"Pat-ti, I want to see you."

Calm beyond comprehension, my voice stayed soft and low. I took another long drink of air in through my mouth, pursing my lips and breathing out slower. "I'm married, Jan."

"How long?" he questioned as though it somehow mattered.

"Six years. In fact, I have another son. He is five years old. He's taking a nap right now."

"What is his name?"

"It's Benjamin Joseph, but we call him BJ."

"I am JB!" Jan's voice still contained that crackle of surprise.

Did he think I named my son after him? That hadn't even been a thought. How had this happened? "Yes, Jan. I remember. Did you ever get the shirt I sent?"

"Yes. Yes. I got it when I returned to Spain. And I still wear it."

For more than a decade! How could that be possible?

"You do? Still?"

"Yes," he said quietly. "Often." His tender tone smeared healing salve over the years of wondering whether he still cared. He'd continued wearing my shirt—the shirt I'd embroidered, every stitch laden with deep sentiment.

"You've been married six years." Why did his voice sound so odd? Why does it matter? I can't see you. I can't have you. My soul wept silent tears as he continued.

"I never married. I've been engaged twice, but I couldn't marry. I could never forget you. It didn't seem fair because no one could compare with you."

"But you can't do that!"

"I can't help it. I remember everything about when we were together. Especially the first time you cried."

Misplaced Moments

Jumbled thoughts mixed together like pieces of a jigsaw puzzle dumped out of the box. Some right side up. Others upside down with none of the picture showing. The first time I cried. It must have been important. Why couldn't I remember? "You mean when I left the ship?" "When I spilled the drink?" "At the beach?"

"No," he responded after each question, the weight of heavy sorrow increasing with each reply. A memory he treasured, lost to me. How could that be?

With his voice cracking, Jan continued. "Pat-ti, I must ask you, will you forgive me?"

"For what?"

"For never coming back. I am so sorry."

"But Jan, I never expected you to. Of course, I forgive you. There's nothing to forgive."

He heaved a deep sigh and was that a tremble in his voice? "You don't know what that means to me. It is as though a huge weight has lifted off of my shoulders. I have carried it all these years, like an anchor around my neck. All I could think was: 'Jan. You stupid.'"

"I'm so sorry, Jan. How could I be angry with you? I never expected you to come back." Oh Jan, I didn't expect you to come, but somehow, someway I knew one day we'd have this conversation.

He interrupted my thoughts. "Do you still have that picture from Barbados?"

"Yes," I responded not knowing what he was talking about. What picture? I have everything—what picture is he talking about? From Barbados? I'd have to think about it later, but I couldn't remember a picture from Barbados. Did I have it? It seemed as though a puzzle piece was missing, but there wasn't time to look for it now.

"Did you ever become a captain?"

"Yes. I had my own ship sailing around Singapore, Bali, and other places. Until one of those blue-haired ladies decided I should share my bed with her. She was one of the owners, and I would not do it, so I am no longer with the cruise ships."

"What kind of work do you do?"

"I work for the ministry of Norway."

The ministry? Could he be a Christian? At first my heart soared. Then, my mind shifted. No, he said of Norway—that must be the government. "What do you do?"

"It is sales involving electronics. I have all of North and South America for my territory. I come to L.A. at least twice a year. I have wanted to call you but, just didn't. I didn't know if you lived in the same place. But now I want to see you."

Jan's next words stunned me into silence.

"I have everything and none of it means anything to me. I finally bought a car and a sailboat. I have a mansion in Norway, and all I want is for you to come and fill it up."

How could he say that? He hasn't even seen me in years. Oh, how I would fill his mansion. Even in the midst of the remodel, the lilacs on my dining room table infused the air with their sweet fragrance. His home should be filled with beautiful bouquets, laughter, music, and love. I took another deep breath, inhaling air like it was cigarette smoke, deep into my lungs and blowing it out slowly.

Clinging to Reality

"Jan, I'm not the same person anymore. I'm different. Much stronger. I'm a Christian, now."

Stronger? Stronger how? Why did I say that when I felt weak as a day-old bluebird about to be eaten by a cat?

"I know about your Christianity, Pat-ti, and I don't share your faith." He sounded bitter. "Your Jim and Tammy Bakker have been all over the news."

"They don't know the meaning of the word, 'Christian!'" I spat out the words. Bakker was a criminal who had stolen millions from their congregation. He cheated people who trusted them. And, from what I could tell, she didn't uphold biblical values either. Their scandal had been all over the news giving people like Jan the wrong impression of Christians. They don't know the meaning of loving You, Jesus, and now because I do, I can't have the one man I want more than anything in the world. Too many people who trust me would be hurt. I can't do that. Please God help him know there's a difference between their brand of Christianity and mine.

Jan continued. "I've been to Guatemala, Nicaragua, and El Salvador—that is where I work. And, I cannot understand a God who would let people live in that kind of poverty. I do not understand why some have so much and some so little."

A knock on my front door threatened to interrupt our conversation. Seeing Jerry through the window, I remembered that he was coming to pick up the weekly church bulletin I typed for him. Without saying anything to Jan, I opened the door to my pastor/counselor/friend, motioning him to come inside. Grabbing a paper and pencil on the kitchen table, I wrote, "This is a man I haven't talked to in 11 years. It's important. Can you come back tomorrow?" He nodded, then left without saying a word.

"Oh Jan, you are so smart. How can you not believe? Have you ever tried reading the Bible?"

"Yes. And I don't understand it."

"Read 1 John and ask God to help you. Ask Him to show you who He is."

"Don't preach at me Pat-ti. Just talk to me."

"I never thought I'd see the day you were afraid."

"I'm not afraid. But, please don't tell anyone this: one year ago, I came to your house and parked across the street. I sat there for about 20 minutes, but for some reason I could not come to the door. Then I drove to the bar where we used to go. What was it called?"

"The Boarshead?"

"Yes. I drove there and sat wishing you would come in. Pat-ti, I want to see you. I've already postponed my flight. I was supposed to leave tomorrow, but now I am not to leave for the next three days." For a moment he sounded expectant, sure of himself, cocky.

Words came without thinking. "The only way I can see you is if my husband comes with me." That was a calculated risk. What would I do if he agreed? Even if I was with Tim, I'd never be able to hide the fact that I was still crazy about Jan. Besides if he saw me now, he'd be so disappointed. I looked down at the same ugly purple corduroy pants and plaid gauze blouse I'd worn the year before when Jan had been outside my house—the day I'd prayed until he left.

The urgency in his voice rattled me. "I don't want to see your husband. I only want to see you." What could I say that would make a difference?

Trying to Ease the Pain

"I'm not the same any more, Jan. I don't have long hair. It is short. I'm fat and ugly. Please just remember me the way I was." If this was killing me, it must be even harder on him. I wanted to make it easier, to take away his agony.

The tone of his voice grew softer, and that's when I knew the truth. My looks didn't matter. He loved me just as I was.

His tender response enfolded me in an embrace so real I could feel it. "I'm still the same. I still have the same body." He was reminding me of the night I'd told him I loved—his body. I remembered.

"I still have the same beard, too." That beard had felt like sandpaper. I could almost feel his cheek scrape mine as he kissed me. Sometimes he'd shave for me in the evening despite having shaved in the morning. "My friends say I look the same."

I didn't. But Jan didn't care. I could hear it in his voice. There was no mistaking the deep affection and longing.

"Do you still smoke?" he asked.

"No. I quit a few years ago." By the sheer grace of God everyone in my office had decided to quit, except me. My coworkers told me I couldn't smoke at work. That lasted for two weeks. Then, one by one they all admitted to starting again. I was the only one who succeeded. "That's when I put on 25 pounds, and I can't get rid of it."

"Do you still drink?"

"Well yes, but not like I used to."

I couldn't think. His voice hadn't changed. Nothing had changed. We were as close now as we were then. Yet, some things had changed. I had changed. Heaving another deep sigh, I attempted a shift to the mundane: "We're remodeling our house. You ought to see it." Jan wouldn't be dissuaded.

"I don't want to talk about your house. Do you remember when you got upset with me when we were driving home from the beach?"

I didn't. Not really. But I should. Maybe later after I got off the phone and replayed our conversation in my mind. "Yes." I couldn't have forgotten. "Jan, is your birthday November 20th?"

"Yes." He sounded surprised that I remembered. Every year on that date I let myself think of him. And, I prayed.

"And, yours is in September?"

"Yes. The eighteenth."

"How old are you?"

"Thirty-six. One year younger than you," I said softly. He heard the reference to our conversation on the ship as we lounged on his bed. Though the words remained unspoken this time, we heard them in our minds: "Perfect for each other."

"I'm so tired of younger women Pat-ti. I want someone my own age to talk to. Someone to sit with me in a rocker on the porch of the old folks' home. I want to see you. Alone. I do not want to see your husband. I want you to think about that. I know this conversation is shock for you. I am going to hang up now—for one-half hour. I know you are surprised at me calling, and you need time to think. Please remember Pat-ti, I will not be in Los Angeles again for very long time. Think about seeing me, and I will call you back."

Numb, I looked around at all the dirt from the remodel. What if he used those 30 minutes to just show up? He could be here in less than an hour. Knowing I had a husband might not deter him. Dirt from the construction was everywhere. It wouldn't matter. Jan loved me. He didn't have to say the words; I could hear it. His voice was saturated with emotion. He remembered every detail; some I'd long forgotten. For years I'd asked God to bring someone who could tell him about Jesus. That someone was me. But seeing him in person might destroy the impetus for him to receive that message. He'd have what he wanted. Me. If I saw him, Jan might never realize how much he needed his Creator, the one who knew him far better than I did. The only one with enough power and wisdom to actually fix this mess.

No Escape From Reality

Moments before Jan called back, BJ came out of his room, thumb in his mouth, dragging his scruffy yellow blanket. My heart sank. He wouldn't stay quiet long. My youngest son always wanted my attention, especially while I was on the phone. When it rang, I picked up the receiver and explained why I only had a few more minutes.

Jan's gentle tone didn't disguise his authoritative words. "Let me talk to him."

"BJ someone wants to talk to you." After I handed him the receiver, he listened intently responding in his small shy voice. "OK. OK." He didn't say what Jan told him, but handed the receiver back to me, then went and turned on the TV. Not once in the half hour that followed did he interrupt me. Jan must have talked to him the way he'd talked to Josh—man to man.

When I came back on the line, Jan said, "Have you thought about it, Pat-ti?"

"Yes, and I cannot come. I respect my husband too much to do that." Respect? Did I respect Tim? Saying the words made them real.

"Don't you remember your promise?" Jan sounded almost desperate.

"I'm sorry, Jan—I don't. Do you want to remind me?" How could there be a promise, so important to him, yet lost to me? What was it?

"No," he said flatly, hurt. "Just keep in mind, I'm here only three days more. Then I leave for Canada. I'm hoping to be home by Easter." That was only a couple of weeks away.

"Yes, that would be nice for you." How hard to travel so much.

"I want to see, you, Pat-ti, I am in L.A. You could come to my hotel. It is . . ." I didn't listen as he named it because I didn't want to know.

"I'm so sorry, Jan. You should have had children. You'd make such a good daddy."

He started to speak, then hesitated, but only for a moment. His voice softened. "I have a little girl."

"Oh, Jan. I'm so glad." His happiness meant more than my own. I sucked in my breath, held it for a moment, then let it out slowly. My joy for him far surpassed my heartache that someone else bore his child. "Do you see her?"

"Of course!" His voice weighed heavy with annoyance at my question. "But not enough. She's a great little girl—just eighteen months and so smart." He sounded like the proud father I knew he'd be. "She lives about an hour from me, but with travel, it is difficult."

I took another deep swig of air. Hearing his voice made it hard to breathe.

"Tell me, did they find your dad?"

"No. There's a picture that Diane and some others think is him in a POW camp. But I can't bear to think he's still alive over there. In a few weeks my sisters and I are going to a memorial service in Dallas for him and the other Air America personnel who were lost."

Mundane Intrusions

Josh came home from school, went into his room, and shut the door. Tim could come in at any moment. Though I wanted it to continue forever, our conversation naturally came to an end.

Jan repeated the name of his hotel. "Please think about it some more, Pat-ti. I don't get here often. I want to see you, and I'm less than an hour away. I'll be here. Waiting. Just come."

He knew. So did I. If we saw each other again, nothing could keep us apart.

"Don't wait for me, Jan. I won't come. But I do want your home address." What for? I hadn't a clue. Why had I asked for it? He gave it to me, along with his phone number, then asked for mine.

The turbulence of regret permeated our good-byes.

My heart was broken, but I couldn't cry. My sons must not see me upset. Silently I begged God for strength and stuffed all the feelings deep inside into a separate closet of my mind—one where the door could be slammed shut. At least until I was alone.

I called Cynthia to thank her for praying. After I told her how loved I felt during the call, I mentioned that neither of us had ever said the words, "I love you."

"Patti, you need to write Jan a letter to tell him how you feel." How could she tell me to do that? She was a missionary and wouldn't advise me to do something wrong. I was stunned. That idea needed prayer. Was that why I'd asked for his address?

Later, when Tim walked in the door, he didn't say a word but headed to the bedroom to change clothes. As he reached the doorway, I walked up behind him and hugged him from the back—"I love you, Tim, and nothing can change that." Words born on a deliberate choice, not a feeling.

His voice hardened: "F . . . off."

Numb, I pulled back. "You might like to know; Jan didn't want to get together. He won't be coming over." Then I turned and walked away, furious.

The next morning, after everyone was gone, I went into our bedroom, stretched out on the bed, and let the tears come. Giant wracking sobs tore through my shredded soul. "Oh God, this hurts so bad." The boo-hoo sobbing continued off-and-on all day. When Jerry came to pick up his bulletin in the afternoon, he noticed my swollen eyes.

"Did your conversation go OK yesterday?" he asked in his calm concerned way.

As our marriage and family counselor, Jerry knew my situation well. And, he knew how hard I was trying to be a good wife. For a couple of years, we'd chatted every week. Tim and I had been to him many times—together and separately. Briefly I described my affair with Jan, the cruise, Jan's living with me, and his phone call.

Empathetic tears welled in Jerry's clear blue eyes convincing me he understood the depths of my pain. With gentle compassion, he said, "It must have seemed as though not one moment of time has passed."

"How did you know?"

"Because in real love, there is a spiritual concept. God is love, and God is eternal. Therefore, real love is eternal. Time changes nothing."

It hadn't. Jan and I were as intimate on the phone as we'd once been in bed. And, yet, Jerry's words were a stunning revelation. Why had it taken me years to comprehend the depth and reality of our feelings? I loved him. Despite all my intentions, despite knowing the impossibilities, the reality of genuine love was stunning. Jan loved me, and I loved him.

Shaking my head, I looked at my wise friend. "I had no idea. We never said the words, maybe thinking if they weren't said they wouldn't be true. I was so determined *not* to love him. But you're right. Not a moment of time had passed."

"You have to write and tell him how you feel."

"Oh Jerry, how can I?"

"I don't know but you must. You need to write him a letter. Soon. That's only fair. He has a right to know." In all our counseling sessions, Jerry never told me what to do. Rather he gently led me to figure out the answers. But this time, he was adamant. Certain. No hesitation whatsoever. And, he was a godly man—a pastor I trusted.

It was the strangest advice I could imagine. The same as Cynthia. Two people, who didn't know each other and who adhered to biblical teachings. How could they advise me to write a former lover?

The next day was Saturday. While Jan waited in L.A., I asked Tim if he minded if I went shopping.

"Get the hell out of *my* house."

Before leaving in despair, I made one thing clear. "I will never give you this house. If you don't like the way things are, you can get out! I am through taking care of you." Slamming the door on my way out, I got in the car and silently vented, *Since I was six years old, I've lived in this house. We bought it from my mother for less than we could have otherwise. She'd charged less interest than the going rate. And, we'd saved realtor's fees. Though my dad had not been officially declared dead, when the life insurance policy my mother had paid on for years settled, it made our down payment.*

As I pulled out of the driveway, I thought about how much I hated my husband and wondered where I should go.

Chapter 14

If I Can Live A Year

Driving away that Saturday morning, two things were crystal clear. As much as I wanted to go to him, I could not see Jan. Though I longed for his comforting embrace, if I went to his hotel, with one kiss we'd be carried away into forbidden places.

Defiance of my marriage vows would turn me back into an unfaithful liar and cheat. Once again, I'd be untrustworthy. And, worst of all I'd step back into the darkness of lies instead of enjoying the freedom I'd found in Christ. Freedom to be more me than I'd ever been before, even with Jan. Now, although sometimes I wanted to escape reality, the price of denial was simply too high. The wrong decisions would impact far too many people.

Love's Critical Components

Aside from my commitments, my marriage vows, my love and desire for my sons to be raised in a stable home—Jan offered intimate companionship, a mansion, a yacht, travel, and adventure. Yet, the only thing he could not satisfy was his desire for me. If I went to him, he'd likely never recognize his need for a Savior. And, that could impact his well-being for eternity. In my humanness, there was no way I could solve his problems or fill that empty space in his soul.

For years, I'd prayed God would take Jan to the pits of the earth, if necessary, to get his attention. Because I genuinely loved him, even if it meant we couldn't be together, I wanted him to know the vibrancy of life without an alcohol addiction.

Freedom from sin, shame, and guilt. A moral compass. The confidence and wholeness that came with unchanging values. Until he surrendered to Christ and put Jesus in control of his life, Jan could never know true peace, wisdom, comfort, and joy. Without Christ, all the problems we'd faced years earlier would only be multiplied.

The other thing I knew with certainty was that Tim would never throw me out of my beloved childhood home. I needed to go home before enough time had elapsed for me to go to L.A. and back. My husband must not have any reason to distrust me.

Even so, I doubted that things could ever again be the same between us. Those words "get the hell out," encased my feelings in a block of ice—one far too thick to ever thaw.

For a little while, I just needed time alone. Keeping up a façade of being OK took more energy than I could muster. Driving a few blocks to a department store, I got out of the car and wandered through the aisles.

There was no one to talk to, but the One who was always with me. Sharon was out of town until Sunday. Jerry and Cynthia were with their families. If my sisters knew how bad I was hurting, they might try to convince me to go see Jan. They might not encourage me to stay with Tim if they knew how bad our problems were. It was already enough of a challenge to do the right thing. No matter how much it hurt, I intended to keep my vow to do things God's way. Not to do so was certain to be even more excruciating to myself and others.

A salesgirl stopped me as I absent-mindedly picked up a purse. "May I help you?"

"No. I'm just looking." Setting the black leather handbag back, I continued wandering as words from an old poem by Mary Carolyn Davies came to mind:

> I love you,
> Not only for what you are,
> But for what I am

When I am with you. . . .
I love you because you
Are helping me to make
Of the lumber of my life
Not a tavern
But a temple;
Out of the works
Of my every day
Not a reproach
But a song. . .

Long forgotten, I'd memorized the poem in college because it described the kind of love I longed for. Although I didn't realize until his phone call, how much I loved Jan, he had put his "hand into my heaped-up heart" and passed over my "foolish weak things." And, he'd brought out "beautiful belongings" no one else had ever noticed. Reflected in his eyes I'd been smart, sexy, and capable. Yet he hadn't been able to make me good or to take my life and build "not a tavern, but a temple" or "out of the works of my every day, not a reproach but a song." What Jan couldn't do, Jesus had done.

Damned if I Did and Damned if I Didn't

There was no way out. Whatever direction I chose involved pain, and the only man who could help me through it was Jesus—the Way, the Truth, and the Life that is the light of men. So often, as I sought my Savior, His Holy Spirit guided me. Comforted me. Taught me. And, gave me peace. Such goodness was worth the agony. So was the hope that Jan might experience the peace I'd found—a peace independent of circumstances.

Still, that one phone call had changed everything. It could never be undone. I could *never* unknow that Jan genuinely loved me. After all these years, even though I'd told him I was fat and ugly, he loved me. The unspoken words had floated on the breeze of his tender voice recalling precious memories and longing to make more. If a man like Jan could love me all these years, then I must be of considerable value. And, if he had called once, someday I might see him again. If that ever happened, I wanted him to be proud of me.

Why God orchestrated that call remains a stunning mystery. Part of it was a test I'd expected and needed. Would the same temptation that had carried me into the captivity of my own selfish pleasure—no matter who it hurt—ensnare me again? Or, in Christ could it be different this time?

Yet there was so much more I couldn't comprehend. Depths of love, both divine and human, made me start caring about my appearance again. Thoughts of comfort food, even chocolate, almost made me sick. Rather I wanted to be worthy of a man loving me from the distance of an unforgettable past. His love reinforced my desire to be trustworthy, honest, fearless, and compassionate while possessing enough courage to make right choices even though they cost us our relationship. Nevertheless, that exquisite pain was torturous enough that I wasn't convinced I'd live.

My sons and husband must not see me break down. If I fell apart, I might not ever be able to pull myself back together. Meandering into the housewares section, I paused here and there, looking at kitchen utensils but seeing nothing. Numb.

As I walked, the promise I'd made to Jan penetrated my thoughts. "No man will ever keep me from you." How could I forget that solemn vow?

My lapse must have hurt him terribly. I'd also forgotten my tears, the night we first made love, and how he'd swiped them away with his thumb. How could I have forgotten that look on his face as though he cherished what happened between us? It still meant something only because I hadn't slept around. What if he'd been the only one, I'd ever given my body to? Only a living God could have erased that moment from my mind—even for an instant.

Jan had been outside my house the year before and a divine hand had restrained him from getting out of his car. I dared not look anywhere but at that all-powerful Being, who knew me better than I knew myself. There was too much at stake.

When I returned home, as expected, my husband acted like nothing had happened. That was the way he coped with conflict. As usual, we both pretended to be fine.

Emotion-weary, I took a nap. Later we drove an hour to Dana Point for dinner with Tim's family at the Wind and Sea, one of my favorite restaurants. Though I pasted a smile on my face and made polite conversation, the food tasted like cardboard. With every beat of my heart, I knew Jan waited in his hotel room, hoping to hear my knock on his door.

Tomorrow would be the third day, and he'd be leaving while I was at church with my family.

After the service, I ran into Sharon. "I'm so glad you're back! I need to talk to you as soon as possible."

"Come over right after church, I'll be home."

Confirmed Guidance

Seeing me at her front door, Sharon grabbed my hand and led me straight into her bedroom. She shut the door, then sat on the bed, while I started pacing back and forth. "Jan called."

"I knew it. As soon as I saw your face, I knew. One minute you looked ecstatic and the next like you were in torment. It couldn't have been anything else. What are you going to do?"

"I told him I can't see him."

"Oh Patti," she said with a sigh leaning back against the pillows. Sitting back up slowly, she said, "I figured I was going to have to tie you to the bedframe to keep you from going to him."

"Sharon, he loves me. I could hear it in every word he spoke. He really loves me. And, he offered me everything I could ever dream of. I've never even imagined having all he offered." She knew how hard my marriage was. So many times, she'd listened and offered wise counsel as I struggled to keep my family together. "How am I going to live through this?"

"You have to tell him how you feel. It's only right. You have to write him a letter."

Stunned, I could barely speak. "Sharon, you are the third person to tell me that. Cynthia and Jerry, the counselor/pastor I type for, said the same thing. And, they don't even know each other! Now you."

"Then it must be the Lord," her wise gravelly voice stated with confidence.

"What will I say?"

"You'll know. Just tell him how you feel. God will help you. And, put my phone number in there in case he wants to talk."

"Jan won't call you. I know he won't. He'd be too proud."

"Do it, anyway. It might be important."

The twilight zone—how was this happening to me? This was crazy. Three people, who I looked to for spiritual guidance, had strongly advised me to write a former lover a letter telling him my feelings. And, all three knew the extreme challenges in my marriage, especially Sharon.

Heaving a sigh, I started to sit down next to her on the bed but instead rose again and started pacing. "Yesterday while I was out shopping, I went to the Christian bookstore and picked up a copy of the only tract I like. This little orange booklet gives a simple description of how man stands on the edge of a cliff with a great gulf separating him from God, who is on the other side. The cross of Christ forms a bridge across the gap enabling man and God to have a relationship. It's 'The Bridge' written by the Navigators. Isn't that ironic? Jan was a navigator."

"I also bought two identical wallet-sized cards. Printed with Isaiah 40:31 'But they that wait upon the Lord shall renew their strength, they shall mount up with wings as eagles; they shall run, and not be weary; and they shall walk, and not faint.' While standing there wondering whether to buy them, I told Jesus—'if one more person says, I need to write Jan, I'll believe it's You.' Now, you make the third. I don't understand why and don't know what I'll say, but I guess I have to do it."

A Letter of Love

The next morning Tim left at 3:00 for a grocery store reset. Waiting until I heard his key turn in the deadbolt lock, I got out of bed and went into the kitchen. After hearing his car start and drive away, I turned on the light. Pulling blank 8½" x 11" sheets of paper from my printer, I sat down at the kitchen table to write. Words poured onto the page:

My dearest Jan,

It was so good to hear your voice on Thursday. You were right, I was in shock when you called, so there was much I could not think of to say. Some of this might be better for you not to know, but I can't bear to keep these things inside of me any longer. I hope you will forgive me, but even more than that, I hope you will understand.

I love you, Jan. I loved you then. I love you now. And, I will love you forever. I've loved you during the good times and during the times I've thought might be bad. I am still the same person I was when you were here. I still feel the same feelings. And I, too, still remember. I remember the first time I cried—it's one of my most treasured memories. You can't imagine how many nights I've lain in your arms. You cannot know how many times I've felt you loving me. No man has ever possessed me the way you did.

Jan, I do remember my promise to you. When you were outside that day a year before you called, I knew. So, I hid in the bathroom and pleaded with God not to let you come to the door. I also prayed that if you ever contacted me, I'd forget my promise. And, I did. No mere man could ever keep me away from you. Not even my sons could have kept me from coming to you. I would have left, even them, but I cannot leave my God.

After you left my house all those years ago, I fell into an abyss. I didn't care if I lived or died. But I needed to live for Josh's sake. And the one who pulled me out of that pit of despair was Jesus Christ. He is the one who has helped me. He is the one who makes me strong. I want you to know him, Jan. He is the one who has been with me all these years. And, if we can't be together in this life, I want us to be together for all eternity.

I, too, have seen the poverty in this world. I've been to Egypt, and I remember what it was like in Haiti. It is only the Lord who makes me care about these things and helps me do what I can about them. We even have street people here in Ontario. When Josh was not being challenged enough in school, I took him to the homeless shelter. There, he worked with the drug addicts, prostitutes, and drunks. I don't know why things are the way they are, but I do know Jesus cares. That makes me care, too.

The little booklet I'm enclosing tells about knowing Jesus. Please read it, Jan. People spend a lot of money to buy life insurance to protect their loved ones after they die. And, yet they won't take the time to consider whether the Bible is true, so that they can ensure eternity. And if you do come to know the Lord, please send the little book back to me, so I'll know that we'll be in eternity together.

Please carry the enclosed card in your wallet. I will keep one like it with me, too, to remind us that Jesus can help. And Jan, if you need someone to talk to about these things, I want you to have my best friend Sharon's phone number. Even if you don't want to talk to her, would you please give her number to someone you can trust. I've always been afraid something would happen to you, and I wouldn't even know. This way someone could notify her, so she could tell me.

Oh Jan, I long to beg you to never marry. Who knows what will happen? But I cannot do that. I want you to be happy. Yet if you should decide to get married, please ask God what to do as He is the only one who can show you.

I'm entrusting these things to you, Jan. Because I loved you, I could not take you away from the sea. I didn't want to try to change you.

Please don't ever try to come and see me, Jan, because I couldn't resist the temptation, and I would end up hating you if you came between me and my God. Even if I were with my husband, I could not resist you. But I won't tell you not to ever call me. That's OK if you want to talk. I can't bear the thought of never hearing your voice again.

You are my precious love,

Several pages of those white sheets of paper quickly filled with words of love. My soul exposed. Naked. Vulnerable. Tears smeared and blotched the ink as I signed my name. But if I tried to rewrite the words, the same thing would happen. Never again would I wonder if Jan knew how much I loved him. What would he think of me? How could I ever speak to him again after being so open with the feelings I'd hidden, even from myself, for so long? Yet after his phone call, I believed he felt the same. Never had I expected to trust him with so much of my heart. Yet, there was no doubt in my mind that he'd respect my wishes.

There's something worse than getting a sexually transmitted disease from sex. Something worse than getting pregnant without being married. I'd never understood until now. During that cosmic moment, when we were together, Jan and I had become one flesh. The pain of not being with him would linger as long as I lived. Without him, part of me was missing.

There is a huge difference with cheap sex. Some people claim that each sexual partner takes a piece of you. But after experimenting with casual sex, I'm convinced those people don't know what they're talking about. You don't really give pieces of yourself away. It's way worse. To give something of yourself, there has to be someone to receive it. Sex between two people who only want physical pleasure has no real giver, no real taker, of the most precious part of your being. The only thing given or received might be a moment's pleasure, but that's even questionable, despite what Hollywood portrays. Instead, that lack of connectedness creates an emotional void, an abiding shame, a loss of dignity and self-respect that leaves a gaping wound—at least that's what it did in me.

But Jan had given himself to me, and I to him. All of me. All of him. And as we became one flesh, that meant each of us became part of the other. Our union couldn't be undone no matter how disastrous it was or how hard we tried to forget. That kind of unity only belongs within the covenant of marriage.

After placing the pages of my missive to Jan in the envelope, I licked the flap and sealed it. Looking at the blank left-hand corner, I realized I couldn't include a return address. If, for any reason, the letter came back and Tim found it—well, I couldn't take that risk. So, I'd have to trust that if it was meant to be, the letter would reach Jan. If it got lost in the mail, maybe he'd be better off not knowing the contents. So, that's how I prayed. If it was wrong for me to tell him how I felt, that the letter would never reach him. But it did.

By the week before Easter, I no longer had to wonder.

Home Alone

With 13 thesis papers to type, I couldn't go to the Colorado River with Tim, the boys, and a couple dozen of our friends for spring break. Usually, I loved this first river trip of the year. The sun beating down while the girls sat on beach chairs dangling our legs in the water. Playing cards for hours on a cut-down table while gambling for dimes and sipping wine coolers. Boat rides. Jet skis. Lots of fun and good food. Laughter. But this year, my family needed the money I could make by staying home. This time, they'd be going without me.

I was relieved. Not only would I have time to work, but I'd also have time to grieve. The loss of what might have been haunted me. Every day since Jan had called—after Tim left for work, Josh and BJ for school—I laid on our bed and boo-hoo bawled. Deep. Wracking. Sobs. By the time everyone came home, I helped with homework, cooked dinner, and did my best to maintain normalcy and be present in the moment for my family. Finally, I'd have the time and space necessary to process everything that had happened.

The guys had been gone several days when the phone jangled, startling me. With intense focus on a dissertation, it took a few minutes after I picked up the receiver to comprehend what Sharon was saying. "Patti, you'd better sit down."

Gripping the phone tighter, I wondered what had happened. Leaning back in my office chair, I asked, "What is it?"

"A couple of minutes ago, I hung up from talking to Jan. He said he'd just finished reading your letter about 15 times!"

Shocked, propping my elbow on my desk, I leaned my forehead into my left hand. It took a moment for her words to register. "I can't believe he called you."

"Jan must love you very much, Patti. He asked me to take care of you for him. He said he'd come home early from his trip, and your letter was there waiting for him. He read it over and over again, and I guess he just needed to talk with someone. He said you have no ballast and asked if I knew what that meant. When I said 'yes,' he said you have 'no stabilizer.'"

"So, I told him, 'Yes, she does. His name is Jesus.' He also said he couldn't do what the little book said, but that he was going to send it back to you. I told him, 'No,' that you only suggested that so you'd know if he became a Christian. He shouldn't send it unless he enters into a relationship with Christ."

After we hung up, Jan's words rang in my head. "Take care of her for me." No one but my mother had ever wanted to take care of me. He loved me. Fresh tears replaced the ones I'd already cried.

A Battle for My Mind

Aware of Jan's love and knowing he'd never married because of me, I typed. And typed. And typed—taking handwritten drafts of undergrad papers and turning them into formatted footnoted papers ready for academic advisors. Hour after hour, I worked. My fingers typed while my mind wrestled with an unseen enemy. Internal voices chastised me. Ridiculing me. Claiming that Jan would never become a Christian. That I was stupid for thinking he might. Breaks meant going to lay on my bed and sob, broken-hearted.

Late the night of Maundy Thursday, bone weary, I lay flat on the floor between Tim's and my new offices. Face down, on my stomach, I stretched out my arms from my sides in a "t" shape as the darkness closed in. Every muscle ached from sitting long hours at the computer, sometimes from 3:00 a.m. until 9:00 p.m. Hour upon hour of futile thoughts tortured my soul as I entered my own Garden of Gethsemane.

"Oh Lord, I can't bear this. No one can help me. No one but you can understand. Only You realize what this is costing me. Oh God, take this cup from me, and don't make me drink it. I can't handle knowing he loves me, and I have to turn away from him. This is my cross to bear."

Long minutes passed. It may have been 5 or 10 or 60. Images of Christ sweating blood brought me to the conclusion of "not my will, but Yours be done."

Getting up from the floor, I went back to work while the war with unseen spiritual forces and the lies of the evil one raged most of the night.

Voices inside my mind badgered me for hours as I pushed to finish a student's paper.

Yet, during this internal battle, there was a certainty that to listen to the lies and go to Jan would mean descending into spiritual death and a hell of my own making. There would no longer be the possibility of redemption. No light. No hope. The darkness of denial would close in and destroy me.

Long after midnight, my Bible drew me as though by some irresistible force. At random I opened it to Hebrews 11:1. "Now faith is the assurance of *things* hoped for, the conviction of things not seen."

Comfort came as I continued reading about "the people of old" who had believed against all odds: Noah, Abraham and his wife Sarah. Jacob, Moses, the prostitute Rahab. To her, I could relate. Yet God's Word listed her among the righteous.

On my own I certainly couldn't claim that character trait. I'd cheated on my first husband—had an affair, then divorced him. And, worst of all, I still didn't feel guilty. Not even about loving a man who wasn't my husband. Still God's righteousness through Christ's blood covered *all* my sins, every single one I'd ever committed or ever would commit. Jesus had set me free from sin and shame. James 5:16 assured me that "the effective prayer of a righteous man can accomplish much." So, the more I made good choices, the more effective my prayers would be. That appealed to me. Besides, I'd rather die from heartache than reclaim the instability and chaos of that old version of me. Taking one day at a time, I decided that if I could survive for a year, I might live.

The next day, I took time off to attend a Good Friday luncheon with Sharon. Upon discovering the text for our speaker's message, I was convinced God was speaking to me. Betty Rose spoke on the faith Hall of Fame in Hebrews 11. These historical figures, flawed individuals like me, who trusted God with the future, reminded me that faith is being convinced of the things I couldn't see. As much as I hurt, I could choose to believe that God had greater purposes for me and for Jan than I could think or imagine.

Finding Hope

After the guys returned, I started rising each morning at 5:00 a.m. while they were still asleep. Developing that habit prevented me from deceiving myself. The truth was my heart could not be trusted. Going to Jan would be disastrous. To be honest with myself and keep that clear in my mind required strength and courage beyond my own.

Only Jesus had the answers I needed. He knew exactly how I felt. Trying to pretend with Him would be foolish. So, I prayed asking for the Holy Spirit's help day by day. Sometimes moment by moment. That and reading the Bible gave me the tools I needed to keep going, one step at a time. Still, every day, when no one was home but me, I cried.

Our remodel diverted my attention and provided tangible evidence of God's care. By summer, the work was completed within budget. Despite having to opt for the cheapest Formica counters and linoleum for the kitchen floor, every morning I marveled at the difference the remodel made in our home.

Early one bright blue-sky morning, I carefully lifted the Windblown Girl out of her rectangle box and placed her on the shelf of the china cabinet. Though behind glass, she stood in plain sight, where I could see her any time I wanted. Now, others could see her too.

No longer hidden away, she stood on a rock. A hymn I learned at Bible Study Fellowship sang its message into my mind: "On Christ the Solid Rock I stand, all other ground is sinking sand." With those words came the realization of why she signified so much—long before I'd had any clue of her connection to me or of what was to come.

Throughout the Bible, Jesus is described as the Solid Rock. And, Psalm 139:13–16 convinced me that He had determined my true identity before I was even born.

> For You formed my inward parts;
> You wove me in my mother's womb.
> I will give thanks to You, for I am fearfully
> and wonderfully made;

Wonderful are Your works,
And my soul knows it very well.
My frame was not hidden from You,
When I was made in secret,
And skillfully formed in the depths of the earth;
Your eyes have seen my unformed substance;
And in Your book were written
All the days that were ordained *for me*
When as yet there was not one of them.

He knew my past, my every thought, yet loved me anyway. He understood my tears and cared about them so much that, according to scripture, He stored them up in a bottle. Unlike the beautiful figurine, I might lay crumpled on that Rock, unsure of myself, unable to stand tall, but I'd keep following Him no matter what. Jesus had already brought me through one trial after another—step by step. The book behind my back was the Bible. That's what gave me the confidence to withstand life's hurricane-force winds.

They continued blowing fierce while the Holy Spirit's machete, God's Word, strengthened me enough to clear away the undergrowth of connections between Jan, my dad, and Eugene Hasenfus—the soldier of fortune at the epicenter of the Iran-Contra affair.

Chapter 15

Hidden Enemies

When the Sandinista government in Nicaragua shot down his C-123 cargo supply plane on October 5, 1986, former Marine Eugene Hasenfus was the sole survivor. The rest of the crew died.

Against protocol, Hasenfus had borrowed a parachute from his brother before leaving his Wisconsin hometown. While trying to make his way out of the jungle, Sandinista soldiers captured him. According to a *New York Times* article by Richard Halloran on October 8th, Hasenfus's plane took off from El Salvador to assist rebels who planned "to open a southern front against the Sandinista government in Managua." At the time, the State Department, CIA, and Department of Defense emphatically denied claims of the U.S. government's involvement.

Their denials resonated with disclaimers about the United States not having men in Laos. Yet, my family knew the truth. Our dad lived as a civilian in Vientiane while flying "resupply" missions. He worried about the "Red Chinese" and Russian MIGs near the Laotian border. And, like Hasenfus, he flew a C-123. Convicted on terrorism-related charges, Hasenfus had been sentenced to 30 years in a Nicaraguan prison. Unlike our family, at least Hasenfus's children knew their father's fate.

While asking God for the wisdom He promised in his word, a remarkable "coincidence" began unfolding. Jan, too, worked for his government in Nicaragua, El Salvador, and Guatemala. What was he doing there? Was he in harm's way?

Like my dad and Hasenfus, Jan wasn't often home and didn't have much time for his daughter. If we'd stayed together, not only would I have had to put up with his being gone months at a time, I'd be in constant fear for his life.

Nonetheless, I was proud of my dad for the work he'd done and understood why he joined the fight against communism in Vietnam. If we didn't fight authoritative regimes overseas, we'd have to fight them in America. I'd read enough history to understand that tyranny must be stopped or its evil spreads. The men who risked their lives to keep us free—whether in Laos or Nicaragua—paid a tremendous price.

War is hell for their families too. Afraid for her husband, Sally Hasenfus used the media to raise awareness of her husband's plight. She made three trips to Nicaragua, the last with Senator Christopher Dodd (D., Conn). In part, due to Dodd's influence, Hasenfus was pardoned and returned home with his wife to their three children. These dramatic events kept me glued to the television news as though they involved my own family. It was a tremendous relief to see Hausenfus released. Yet, that was only the beginning of a tremendous ordeal regarding America's involvement in Nicaragua.

The same day as the Iran-Contra hearings began, May 5, 1987, President Ronald Reagan wrote a letter to convey his greetings to all of us, who would attend Air America Club's 1987 reunion at the end of the month.

Ready for Take Off

Amidst excited chatter, my sisters and I, along with our husbands, stood in line waiting to check in for our flight to Dallas.

"If we weren't going for Daddy, there's no way I'd get on that plane. I hate to fly!" Suzie fidgeted with her suitcase until Bob playfully shoved it out of reach, and we all laughed. Sometimes Suzie reminded me of Lucille Ball with the way she amused us just by being herself. No doubt my sisters would make this trip fun, despite our stepmother being there.

"I just wish we didn't have to see Vergie. This will be the first time I've been around her in years. I can forgive, but I don't trust her at all." She was my least favorite person on Earth. Not only had I seen her be sweet to Diane's face, then talk bad behind her back, but due to Vergie's greed, I had nothing of my dad's. Maybe she was good to Janet, but I dreaded having to be nice to her.

That started us all talking over each other until Janet's excitement redirected our conversation. "I can't wait to see Jim Ryan. He's such a sweet man. There are so many wonderful people from Air America that I haven't seen since moving back from Laos."

"Is Jim the one who lost his leg after being shot at as his plane searched for Daddy?"

Janet nodded her somber reply.

"Will Ann Mills-Griffiths be there," I wondered aloud.

"No," Diane responded. "Her brother was Navy, not with Air America so this doesn't involve her. She's been the Executive Director of the National League of POW/MIA Families almost from the beginning," Diane told Valerie. "A couple of years ago, she even arranged some high-level negotiations between the U.S. and Vietnam." James disappeared about 20 years ago, and she's kept the pressure on the government all this time to find out what happened." Diane and Bruce gathered their things and moved toward the counter.

After we all checked in and regathered, Diane mentioned that the CIA must have covered about half the cost of our rooms. "They couldn't possibly be that inexpensive."

We found our gate, then while waiting to board, Val and I browsed in a gift shop. "Why are you wearing your glasses? I noticed that when we went to see Grandad but didn't realize you wear them all the time now."

"My contacts are no longer an option. Even though I had part of that pterygium removed, the doctor said it's like an iceberg. The part that remains still irritates my eye. I wish Vergie hadn't taken all of Daddy's money. If we'd received an inheritance, I'd have that surgery to fix my vision. Maybe someday, when the beach house sells."

I pulled a card from the rack. Its powerful sentiment reminded me of Jan. Showing it to Val, she saw its relevance. "You should buy this. I'll keep it for you in case you ever want it."

A Raucous Reunion

The Hyatt Regency Dallas rolled out the red carpet for more than 500 former members of Air America and their families. Entering the lobby, raised voices permeated the atmosphere with anger. "What do you mean, we can't use the downstairs bar? Do you understand that this is the convention for the NFL coaches? We must be given access to the lounge immediately!"

The hotel manager remained calm but firm. "I'm sorry sir, but it is closed to all but Air America members and guests. A hospitality room has been set up for you upstairs."

The high-level priority of our reunion astounded me. Glancing toward the main hotel bar, it was obviously overflowing with men hoisting drinks— a couple even stood in the doorway.

We all headed for our rooms to drop off the luggage. Taking a few minutes to hang up my clothes, I quickly unpacked, not wanting anything to wrinkle. Then Tim and I headed back out to meet the others. Before opening the door, I noticed a sign on the back of it with the room rate. Diane was right. It was double what we'd paid. After years of public contempt, anti-war protests, and neglect from the government, the respect and appreciation for our men began putting me at ease.

We'd agreed to reconvene near the bar, so Tim and I started walking in the direction of someone loudly reciting Air America's motto: "We were first in, last out." Coming closer we saw a group of men raise their glasses in a toast to the final helicopter plucking the last American civilians off the roof in Saigon. "That was us," one of the men announced to anyone within hearing range.

Diane stood and waved Tim and me over to a table where she and the others had already gathered. Hearing rowdy laughter made us wish Daddy could be with us, swapping stories and singing bawdy songs with his compadres. Stories about transporting explosives. Carrying refugees and a pig out of harm's way. A woman giving birth on the plane. Longing to hear my dad's voice, I wondered about all the escapades we had missed.

Tim and I ordered drinks as men I didn't know stopped to chat with Diane and Janet.

Looking around, I spotted Hasenfus. Ever since hearing he'd be at the reunion, I'd been hoping to meet him. Scooting back my chair, I got up and made my way through a throng of people to the crowd gathered around him. When he glanced my way, I introduced myself as Roy Townley's daughter. "I'm curious, did you know my dad?"

"Know him?" Leaning against a railing, Hasenfus's eyes flamed with memories. "We flew some missions together. I was young—the kicker on his plane." Just as he'd done in Nicaragua, he'd shoved supplies out the tail end of their C-123.

It had been more than a decade and so much had happened in the meantime. Realizing he didn't have much else to say about my dad, I asked about his recent ordeal. "Your captivity must have been horrible for your family." I could almost hear a familiar voice as Hasenfus spoke. "Sally and my kids faced so many challenges because of my job." Deep sorrow darkened his eyes. As he pasted a smile on his face and rejoined the group of men, I turned away.

May 30, 1987
An Indelible Tribute

After breakfast the next day, a bus took many of us from the hotel to the University of Texas. My sisters, our husbands, and I walked into the Mc-Dermott Library and found seats on folding metal chairs as the dedication ceremony for the memorial was about to begin.

Our hearts swelled with pride at the descriptions of how Air America had recruited the best of the best: adventurous highly skilled pilots and cargo-kickers. Said to be "sheep-dipped" by some, these patriotic civilians (many who were former military) flew secret missions rarely acknowledged or appreciated. Yet today, they were honored, even by President Reagan. As his letter dated May 5, 1987 was read, years of pent-up tears began streaming down our cheeks. His gratitude for the sacrifices our families had made touched us deeply.

> Although free people everywhere owe you more than we
> can hope to repay, our greatest debt is to your companions
> who gave their last full measure of devotion. Just as their
> names are inscribed on this memorial, so their memories
> are inscribed in our hearts. We will never forget them or
> their families, some of whom still seek answers.

Hearing that he pledged to seek the "fullest possible accounting" of our MIAs gave us hope that one day we'd have answers. Each of us received a signed copy of the president's letter.

The governor of Texas, William P. Clements, Jr., also sent greetings to the Air America Club. He described how these men had answered the call of duty to risk their lives for our country's preservation. His sweet words smoothed healing balm on our wounded souls:

> It is with thanks and gratefulness that I offer my best wishes
> to the surviving members of their families. It is high time
> that these brave individuals be honored, and there is no
> better place than the McDermott Library's aviation section.

Former director of the CIA, William E. Colby gave the dedication address, titled "Courage in Civilian Clothes." Visions of my dad's civilian clothes—white Levis, plaid cowboy shirts with snaps instead of buttons and cowboy boots—brought back childhood memories of how much I'd wanted to be like him. As a little girl some of my favorite Christmas gifts contained white Levis and cowboy shirts with snaps—oh how I missed my dad and appreciated this commemoration. My sisters and I had never really been given the chance to grieve.

Yet after taps was played by the bugler and we went to see the name Roy F. Townley on the bronze memorial, the reality remained that MIA was listed after his name. We still didn't know what had happened to our dad.

Being at the reunion reminded me of how little control we have. These men loved their families, but that didn't stop the bullets from striking and killing some of them. Some were tortured. Some died in captivity far from family and friends.

Like my dad and Hasenfus, Jan was only a man. He couldn't control our circumstances. He worked in foreign countries and left his little girl for long periods of time. Like my dad, he drank a lot but rarely showed signs of drinking too much. While at the beach one time, my Aunt Eileen expressed her concerns for my dad not wanting to eat much because he'd rather drink. That had been true for Jan as well, and by now I realized that some alcoholics can drink a lot and not show any signs of inebriation.

Although I adored them both, my dad and Jan were only men. Not invincible. Nor above temptation. Yet Jesus, though 100 percent man, was also 100 percent God. He created the cosmos. He saw all of time from eternity past to eternity future. My Savior always had my best interests at heart and by His Holy Spirit gave me enough courage to face my fears and do His will instead of my own. It was far easier to trust Him than to try living life on my own terms by putting all my hopes and dreams into a mere man.

Entering A War Zone

Returning home, the lack of regard for my need to grieve escalated our marital battles. Measurements for a new refrigerator hadn't been made as I'd asked, so when the cabinets arrived the only frig that fit was smaller than our old one. That oversight resulted in an explosive argument. Struggling to control my anger, I prayed for God to help me love my husband without destroying myself in the process. At times I hated him, and I suspected there were plenty of times he hated me, too.

Reading Bible verses gave me wise advice, especially Proverbs 15:6. Memorizing its words, "a gentle answer turns away wrath. But a harsh word stirs up anger" started helping me gain enough self-control to stand up for myself without flying into a rage the way my mother had. So did asking the Holy Spirit to replace my weaknesses with His strength. A few close friends gave me the emotional support I so desperately needed. God's word also helped me learn to choose love even when I didn't feel like it.

The important thing was staying in the truth so I didn't make self-destructive choices. Or allow someone else's behavior to dictate mine. It was a tricky balancing act, but I was all too familiar with the pain of divorce for children. In a counseling session with Jerry, I became determined to break the cycle of divorce that had plagued my family for generations. I also realized that the grass is not necessarily greener on the other side of the fence. Hard lessons like these would have been necessary, regardless of who I was married to.

Though I believe that in his own way my husband tried, maybe as hard as I did, he couldn't figure out the solutions to our lack of emotional bonds any more than I could. As tension escalated, our physical relationship deteriorated even further. Sex became less frequent and more difficult. Since early in our marriage, I'd held scripture to my throat like a knife *feeling* like I had to submit to him despite the problems—at least until an unimaginable breach happened—one I didn't ask for or want.

Chapter 16

Better than 20/20 Vision

A couple of weeks after Air America's reunion, I took Josh and BJ to San Clemente to ride the waves and celebrate summer. Being out in the bright sun all day on their boogie boards wore them out, so they slept on the way home. Trying to keep myself awake, I had a rather absurd conversation with Jesus.

"If you ever want me to have that surgery on my eyes, somehow you'd have to convince me it's you, or I'd be too scared." Radial keratotomies to correct near-sightedness were fairly new, but the day before, I'd checked out the possibilities to find out if that might be an option for me.

After examining my eyes, Dr. Fabricant leaned back on his stool. "You'd be an ideal candidate. I think we'd have excellent results."

"You mean I wouldn't have to wear glasses anymore."

"I don't think so." He sounded fairly certain—no more glasses.

Although it would likely be years, if ever, before I'd have enough money—on my way out, I asked the cost. Besides, I wouldn't want the surgery unless it was successful. Only an all-knowing deity could see the end result beforehand, so I put my longing in Christ's hands and asked for His will instead of my own.

That night after the boys went to bed, Tim and I watched a movie so I was up later than usual. Around 10:00, the phone's shrill ring startled me. No one ever called this late. With my heart pumping hard, I picked up the phone's receiver and said, "Hello."

Valerie got right to the point. "I know it's late, but I couldn't wait. Patti, how much is that surgery for your eyes?"

What on earth? Breathing a sigh of relief, I said, "$1800. $900 per eye if I pay cash. It's a lot, but I'd do it if I ever have the money."

"If you'll do it now, I'll pay for it," she said with conviction. Like a brightly colored beachball, that afternoon's conversation with Jesus bounced back into my mind. This was the confirmation I'd asked for. Whatever the results, he'd inspired Val with incredible generosity. Tears of sheer joy streamed down my cheeks.

"I'll do it on one condition. That when I get the money, I'll pay you back. It has to be a loan." That hadn't been her plan, but she agreed. We both knew it might take years.

Sight for the Blind

Within weeks, the operation was performed. First, my right eye; the following week, the left. A whispery breeze played in my soul convincing me of good results, making me fearless. Oh, I didn't like thinking about slits being put into my eyes, but after having had a shot for the pterygium I knew the surgery wouldn't be painful. Nor was I surprised afterward by feeling like there was gravel in my eye. But the results astonished me.

As I sat in the big leather chair waiting for Dr. Fabricant to remove the bandage, I wondered, Would I experience the miracle of clear vision? Coming in, he slid a stool over in front of me and sat down. Then he pulled off the tape and removed the gauze. I could see! For the first time without the correction of contacts or glasses, I could see. Reading the vision chart all the way to the smallest print, my vision tested better than 20/20.

Forever I'd be grateful for Val's thoughtfulness. She'd given me a precious gift long before I could have had it otherwise.

A Panoramic Perspective

A few months later, over Labor Day weekend, my sisters and our families all went to the Townley beach house for one last visit before it was sold. Late one night, I looked out the big picture windows to see the moonlight illuminate silhouettes of Josh and his teen-aged cousins running across the wet sand at low tide.

Precious memories rushed back as my sisters and I reminisced about late night grunion hunts. Taking long walks as children so the Easter bunny could hide eggs. Playing solitaire at the huge kitchen bar where a dozen aunts, uncles, and cousins played off of each other's piles accompanied by shrieks of laughter.

How glad I was to have special memories of Jan in this cherished place. At least, he got to see it before it was sold.

The next afternoon, the five of us sisters took rubber rafts out to ride the waves the way we had while growing up. Squealing with delight, we raced toward shore. For the first time ever, I could recognize people on the beach. Though I hated that our beloved beach house was being sold, soon I'd be able to pay Valerie back.

Every day my corrected vision produced sheer joy. Being set free from wearing contacts or glasses increased my determination to take better care of myself. I started going to Jazzercize and trying to eat better. If Jan ever happened to see me, I didn't want him to be disappointed. Discovering how much he'd cared about me—thought of me—longed for me—made me care too.

Astounding Revelations

Over time, developing a biblical worldview started correcting my spiritual vision in ways that changed me even more than the eye surgery. Clarity came as I attended an international Bible study (Bible Study Fellowship) where each week I learned to apply eternal truths. Seeing the big picture from the time of creation throughout history improved my view of reality as I watched one truth after another come alive.

For years, pop culture had obscured my perspective by bombarding my sisters and me with lies. Self-worth depended on being pretty enough, smart enough, good enough. Until we broke free from those misguided concepts, our mother's voice had been the loudest—*she* had to be the prettiest, the smartest, the best at everything. But that meant none of us ever measured up to her standard. All that did was make her and everyone around her miserable.

Studying Scripture explained man's goodness and wretchedness like no other belief system. That goodness gives us inherent worth and makes our lives valuable. However, without a Savior, because of sin, we often deceive ourselves like my mom had. Engaging in self-destructive behaviors, we try to satisfy ourselves while longing for more. Unable to find satisfaction, those behaviors can turn into compulsions that lead us into a struggle for the power to use and control others. That can happen with sex, too.

While I was a teenager during the 1960s, the free-love spirit of the age (zeitgeist) had started promoting the idea that the mind and emotions are separate from the physical body. As many people, including my mom, bought into that concept, my values became so at odds with the culture, that I accepted the lie that the problem was me. Then, learning the hard way, I experienced the torment involved with trying to disconnect my mind from my body. That detachment fractured and distorted my identity with far-reaching consequences for myself and others. Especially when I disrespected marital vows and became unfaithful. A liar. And, a deceiver.

That brought about an incredible loneliness until I almost despaired of life itself. Disassociating mind and body devalued my life and the lives of others until we became merely commodities using each other to satisfy whatever whim seemed important at the time.

Learning about the problems with the prevailing "personhood" theory—the separating of mind from the body—validated my experiences. And, now I can see how that low view of personhood (relentlessly promoted by media, education, and government) has consequences that extend into all of society. This low view has not only made sex cheap but also life itself. When the mind and body aren't united in a holistic way as intended by our Creator, an unwanted body can be killed. Such erroneous thinking legitimizes infanticide as random human beings determine when a baby becomes a person.

If an unborn child is wanted, he lives. If unwanted, she dies. In many cultures, that is exactly the way it is—girls are unimportant and unwanted, so many more of them are aborted. Boys are considered more desirable.

Viewed by abortion proponents as inferior, minorities also suffer the impact. Honored to interview a young Hispanic woman for a newspaper feature, I listened to her describe in poignant terms how minorities are often pressured into abortions they don't really want. Then, they're left alone to struggle with the intense guilt and shame. Injustice. Minorities. Personhood defined not as our Creator intended but as a relational construct defined and administered by sin-filled individuals.

I'm convinced this perspective of relational personhood lies at the heart of injustice. Slavery, the old Jim Crow laws, and ongoing civil unrest. It's how Germany decided to get rid of the Jews. Why Asians were interned. And, if human decisions regarding the value of life continue to escalate in my lifetime, those claiming superiority and exerting power over the poor or minorities or those with physical or mental challenges or the elderly or those who are LGBTQ or of a particular belief system may decide to exterminate those they consider less than human. Despite appearances of concern for the disadvantaged, the current administration is setting that course as funding for abortions is extended, here and abroad.

My heart breaks for foster children indoctrinated with the viewpoint that unwanted children are expendable. Perhaps they'll decide the world is better off without their bodies in it. A low view of personhood leaves no room for growth or change or medical breakthroughs.

For me, Jan's phone call annihilated this concept of the mind/body separation. It did not work for me, and it didn't work for him either. Rather, he treasured the oneness we shared—a unity of bodies, minds, emotions, and souls. A unity that remained in place throughout time and distance even though our relationship had been outside the covenant God had instituted for our protection.

A Story Worth Writing

The choice to go my own way, doing all I could to please my "self," or to die to self and live unto God was mine to make. It was all about me—*who* did I want to be? Self-absorbed, a narcissist who put my agenda ahead of everyone and everything else. Or more like Jesus, who loved me enough to sacrifice Himself. I wanted others to know that by embracing the pain of dying to self, we're set free from the selfish baggage that prevents vibrant fulfilling lives.

Not long after Jan called in 1987, my new friend, Wendy, told me about a writer's conference. Knowing my story, she told me, "You should go. If you'll go, I'll pay for it."

After thinking and praying about it for a few days, I agreed to attend the five-day event at a nearby university. Recalling my childhood dream, long set aside, convinced me that God might be providing this incredible opportunity. If I took a chance, who knew where I might be in five years or even 10.

From morning until evening, I sat in seminars led by established authors and editors. For the first time in a long time, I felt like I belonged. At least until a break when I had an appointment with a literary agent who gave me feedback on a writing sample. While sitting on a cement block wall under tall trees on that college campus, his words slammed into my psyche like a fist.

"You have no style," he said. Crushed, tears filled my eyes. However, before they could spill over and run down my cheeks, his next sentence offered hope: "But you can learn." I was good at learning and became determined to follow his advice.

Early morning devotional times by Wightman Weese, an editor from Tyndale House, inspired me so much that I came home and wrote a short piece about the impact of his kind encouragement. Without judgment, he'd listened to my sordid tale about Jan and my difficult marriage. Soon after the conference, Wightman surprised me with a phone call, offering to mentor me. I didn't mention submitting my devotion involving him to be considered for publication in a compilation.

That piece, "Don't Touch Me!," was published in a book alongside Edith Schaeffer, an author who had been one of my earliest role models. The following year another one was published in a second compilation along with another favorite author, Elisabeth Elliot. Married to a man martyred by the Auca Indians in Ecuador, she raised her little girl among them—loving her enemies and powerfully impacting my life. A year later, the third book featured Corrie ten Boom, a woman who survived internment in Ravensbrück, then forgave one of her cruelest guards in a face-to-face encounter. Through their books, these women made a deep impression on me. They gave me glimpses of the woman I wanted to become—not only as a writer, but even more as a woman who believed in the mighty God who loved me.

Over and over again Wightman had me rewrite my first full-length article. He still thought it needed more work when I submitted it to a contest and won third prize against authors who had written numerous books. Another article was soon published in an international magazine with hundreds of thousands, if not millions, of readers. When that editor bought it, he told me they only published 1 percent of what they received. Years later he published that piece in a parenting book. Those few successes paled in comparison to all the rejections I received. God knew how much I had needed strong affirmation to persevere in such a difficult process, especially during such trying times.

Increasing Clarity

My marriage was in big trouble. Despite my desperate desire to be a good wife and to cultivate a healthy family, I couldn't deny that certain things weren't right. Although I tried my best to love my husband every day and create a secure home life for my sons, Jesus forced me to take a fresh look at truths I would have preferred to ignore. The Bible had taught me that sometimes genuine love requires risking a relationship to speak painful truths in an attempt to stop destructive behaviors. As I learned to stop being codependent and set boundaries, I had no choice but to do what I could to stand against what I considered egregious behaviors, even if it cost me my family.

Our years of problems culminated one afternoon after an unfortunate incident, the details of which don't belong in this book. They're just too complex. Suffice it to say that truth could no longer be denied, and as a result of that forceful catalyst, words came out of my mouth that not only shocked my husband but me as well.

"From here on out, we're separated. Because of our financial situation and the need to maintain stability for the boys, we'll live in the same house and sleep in the same bed, but that's it. On an emotional level, we're separated until things change."

We'd been to marriage counseling—together and separate. I'd read every self-help book I could find, yet as I kept learning, the trouble and turmoil intensified.

In a surprising twist, circumstances completely beyond my control finally resulted in an actual physical separation—at least until our emotional connection grew. Sadly, for my family, it never did. Some might fault me for that, but those who knew what was involved didn't.

Apparently and more importantly, neither did Jesus. By his amazing grace I learned that for a woman, lack of an emotional connection can make sex *feel* horrible, even within marriage. No longer was it necessary to pretend a desire I didn't feel. An honest assessment helped me understand that according to scripture, Tim and I didn't have much of a marriage— no matter how much either of us wanted it to be different.

This wasn't easy for him either. He said that kissing me was like kissing his sister. Despite being married, our emotional disconnect destroyed physical intimacy. I hadn't planned that. Although I wanted to deny it, the reality is that two people must work together to develop a strong marriage, and as hard as we tried my husband and I could not reconcile our perspectives.

In my first marriage, I'd tried to submit to my husband despite our problems. In the process, I lost my "self." Excluding my feelings and trying to do what he wanted diminished me until I became less than nothing. The only way to recover my identity was to flee the relationship—at first mentally, then physically.

During my second marriage, our problems were much more subtle and complicated. They had to do with our upbringing, our belief systems, and the way we were raising our sons. Yet, because my identity was already secure in Christ, I could remain in the marriage without losing my sense of self, even as our relationship deteriorated. Though I still don't fully understand my actions, as I learned to create and maintain healthy boundaries—something I'd never been able to do before—I gained peace and self-respect. And, I started developing a sense of wholeness.

For purposes of self, sexuality, and social issues—our Creator designed a phenomenal unity between our minds and our bodies. This wholeness embraces a much higher view of sex than that promoted in our hypersexualized culture. Vibrant sex happens when two individuals become one flesh preferably in the context of a committed marriage covenant. That powerful unity brings deep healing to a person's concept of self.

Though I may never understand it this side of heaven, perhaps in some measure that's why God allowed me to know how much Jan loved me. Despite being emotionally beat down, despite my sins, as I trusted Christ with my feelings, I could see how He took my worst and used it to bring about an astonishing sense of healing—healing that led to internal wholeness and peace. Dying to my "self" had made me more than I'd ever been. And, I knew beyond any doubt that I was loved—not only by Jan, but far more by the God who died on the cross to pay for my sins.

There was no way I wanted to jeopardize my relationship with Jesus by trying to replace Him with a mere mortal, regardless of how much I was tempted. But then, Jan called again on my 40th birthday.

Chapter 17

A Phone Call at Forty

"Why don't I give you a birthday party?" Val asked.

"Please don't." Though I appreciated my sister's offer, I rapidly shut down the idea because I didn't feel like celebrating. My relationship with Tim had continued on a downward spiral, and I had no idea of how to handle what I perceived to be destructive behaviors. Yet, Tim insisted I was the problem.

Our marriage was in serious trouble, and I couldn't pretend otherwise. After all I'd suffered, I'd hoped God would heal my marriage, but it wasn't happening. Other than asking for God's will, I didn't even know what to pray. Though I was sticking to my vows, even the one not to question God, I couldn't figure out the answer. Still, I was determined to keep doing things God's way by taking one step at a time and waiting to see what unfolded. We needed a miracle.

Josh's youth group was hosting a back-to-school dance on my birthday, and I didn't want to miss it. Almost a year earlier, when the youth pastor had asked me to be the coordinator for the adult small group leaders, Josh had been all for it. It was sheer joy to be around him and about 200 of his friends. That's where I belonged on my birthday. These young people, and the special volunteers who interacted with them, would take my mind off the pain, at least for a little while.

September 17, 1990
My Birthday Eve

While driving home from running errands, a quiet breeze whispered, "Jan's going to call for your birthday." Sometimes silly ideas popped into my thoughts, but this one couldn't be easily dismissed. It penetrated my mind in the same way as when Jan was outside my home. Was the Holy Spirit preparing me, again, the way He had before? Strange thoughts. Maybe I was just weird. Or maybe, just maybe—could it be possible? The gulf that existed in my marriage made my heart heavy. And it deepened my yearning for the closeness I'd experienced with Jan.

"Please Jesus, if Jan calls, do the talking for me. I've got more than enough trouble already." Longing to hear his voice, I'd have no idea of what to say. Especially after pouring out all my feelings in that letter three-and-a-half years ago. How could I talk to him without being embarrassed?

Whether Jan called or not, the thought of him made me smile. If he could only see how all those teens hugged me and vied for my attention. They made me feel so loved. I could imagine Jan watching our interactions, then his warm brown eyes devouring me the way they used to. He'd love those kids, too, I had no doubt.

Occasionally, when I was in the depths of despair over my marriage, I'd think of Jan. Perhaps that's all this was, a little relief from the recent emotional upheaval. For a moment I could almost hear him say, "Pat-ti, I'm so proud of you." He would be—my writing, my friends, my character—I valued honesty, kindness, and my family. My friends trusted me. These things made me feel good about myself. By not walking away from a difficult marriage, I'd proved that I honored my commitments no matter how difficult. By not giving into temptation, I'd become worthy of the kind of love and respect I longed for.

Pulling into my driveway, the garage door rose on reality. Thoughts of Jan dissipated as I lugged the groceries out of the trunk and into the house. Quickly my mind started shifting toward work and dinner. Balancing two brown paper bags plus the cleaning I'd picked up, I pushed open the back door. Tim and BJ sat in the family room watching a rerun of Mash. "Tacos tonight," I said, heading for the kitchen. "I'll fix them in about half an hour. I need to email a client first." After putting things away, I walked into my office just as the phone rang.

A Birthday Surprise

When I picked up the receiver, a woman said something garbled then asked for Patti Covert.

"This is Patti," I responded thinking it must be a new client.

"Go ahead, please," she said.

"Pat-ti, Pat-ti, it's me. Jan.

"I'm in shock," I said quietly, realizing that the woman was a long-distance operator and that I'd already prayed for this conversation. Unmistakable peace engulfed me.

"I know. I know," he laughed. "Sit down and talk to me. There is much to say, but on the phone . . ." his words trailed off. I could almost hear him remembering my letter. "Just talk to me Pat-ti. Let me hear your voice."

"There *is* something I want you to know, Jan. I'm writing now. I've actually been published in a book and in a magazine." He wasn't surprised. All along, he'd believed in me.

"You'll never guess what I am doing now," he sounded bitter. "I am in fisherman ministry in Colombia."

My heart thumped hard. Due to his accent, I must have misunderstood. What was he talking about?

"And, I am at rock bottom."

Too many thoughts tumbled as though in an old-fashioned flour sifter. Something was terribly wrong. What was it?

"I am in big trouble, Pat-ti. I live in Medellin. Do you know Medellin, Colombia?"

"No, I don't know anything about it," I said slowly, wondering if Tim was listening from the family room. My office wall was shy of the ceiling by several feet. Usually I liked hearing what was going on with my family, but now . . .

"It's the drug capital of the world. I work for the Finance Ministry." This time his words cut through his accent. "The government of Norway has been pouring aid into that country. For the past year and a half, I've lived there. And, my friends, we party together—they never say what they do, but

I know." He heaved an ominous sigh . . . were they drug lords?

"I see about 10 murders every day," he continued. "It is terrible place. But you don't have to worry about me," he laughed cynically. "I'm still so skinny, they can't shoot me. I came home to Norway for a month to think about things. Please make a prayer for me, Pat-ti."

Jan's sorrow broke my heart.

"I do pray for you—almost every day."

"You do!" He sounded stunned. "You still think of me?"

"Every day." It was true. He never left me. He was part of me. The only way to keep memories of him from interfering in my marriage was to pray, every morning. Only that kept me focused on reality and conquered the thoughts that could otherwise entice me to sin.

"I've been looking at pictures from Barbados. They're spread out all over my bed. You said you were fat and ugly, but—I just want to turn back the clock."

"Jan, you can't do that! The only one who has the answers for all of this is Jesus." For years my prayer had been that God would take Jan to the pits of the earth if need be—Medellin, Colombia. My heart ached as I imagined the horrors he'd seen.

A Precious Gift

"I don't have to be sorry for the way I feel. In fact . . ." he hesitated as though wrestling with a decision. "There is a song. Do you know of Leonard Cohen?"

"No. I've never heard of him."

"He is singer from Canada. Well, forget it . . . no, you should know. There is a song you should hear."

I grabbed a piece of paper while trying to decipher his accent and keep up with what he was saying. Listening intently yet unable to wrap my mind around his every word, I was afraid I'd forget the name. And, the tone of his voice left no doubt that these lyrics made him feel something for me.

"It's right after, "First We Take Manhattan, . . . ""

"Spell his name for me." I'd no more than written the letters down, and Jan spoke again.

"I'm a terrible alcoholic, Pat-ti. Nothing has been able to help, not even the Minnesota Program."

Putting the pen down, I asked, "What's that?" hoping my voice conveyed all the gentleness, kindness, and compassion I felt.

"It's the last hope for an alcoholic. It costs $10,000, and even that did not help."

"Have you tried AA?"

"Yes. I went for a time, but it does not work."

"Oh Jan," I sighed. "You need Jesus. How can you be so smart and not know there is a God?"

"I know there has to be a God. A woman gets her period every 28 days. The cycle of the moon is every 28 days. This is not coincidence. But there is something I have to do first."

"Have you read the Bible?" I asked.

"I've tried, but I don't understand it."

"Jan, I never thought I'd see you afraid."

"I'm not afraid of anything. I was not afraid to call you at home right at dinnertime, when your husband and sons are there."

"It seems to me you're afraid to ask God to show you that He is real. If He isn't real, He can't do anything. But if He is, you need to know."

"I don't want to hear any more Christian stuff. Just talk to me Pat-ti. Let me hear your voice."

"Did you know tomorrow is my birthday?" I asked.

"Yes, Happy Birthday, Pat-ti. You must be having a big party."

"No." I said. "My friends are scattered in so many places, and some are far away. It wouldn't feel right to have a party without them."

"Oh. Well, I guess you wouldn't party any more. You probably just wear sackcloth and ashes," he said with a sarcastic chuckle.

He still could make me laugh. "Jan, I just went to a party in Mexico with 38 people. It was so much fun! We caravanned down and laughed all the way while talking over CB radios. Then we stayed in two houses right on the beach."

"Good. I'm glad you still know how to have a good time. His voice resonated with warm affection. How is Joash?"

"He is so smart and a good leader! I'm very proud of him. He'll be in college next year.

"Yes. My daughter, she is smart too." A heavy silence closed the distance between us. "We should have had a child together," his tone so quiet, I almost didn't hear the words.

O God, he'd wanted me to have his baby. Neither of my husbands had been excited about the idea of me getting pregnant; I'd had to convince them both. The longing in Jan's voice matched the longing in my heart. He'd thought about me having his child. A purr welled up from deep inside my soul and escaped with the slightest sound. It didn't escape Jan's notice.

"I know that sound."

He'd heard that indescribable satisfaction before, in bed. Once again time didn't exist. A moment could be a year or many years but a moment. Fat and ugly or a terrible alcoholic, it didn't matter—our love remained.

Deep Grief

"Pat-ti, my grandfather died two days ago. We bury him tomorrow."

From the time I met Jan, he'd spoken of his grandparents with great affection. "Oh, Jan, I'm so sorry."

"After that, I am leaving." An eerie timbre pervaded his words. He wasn't talking about South America.

"Where are you going, Jan?" I asked insistent, wanting to know. At the same time hoping not to hear what I thought he was saying.

A caustic chuckle clarified an unspoken message; he wanted to leave this world.

"I'd better go now," he said. "I'm calling from Norway, you know."

"You can't end this like that. Promise me you won't go anywhere without calling me."

"I'll call you if I am going anywhere good."

"No, Jan, you can't do this to me! Promise you will call, no matter where you're going."

People had told me alcoholics are liars, but promises had been sacred between us. I believed they still were. Even as we hung up, I was convinced Jan wouldn't go back on his word. And, more than ever I knew I'd made the right decision not to go to him. As I'd suspected he'd become an alcoholic, and no earthly program could change it. Only Christ. Even though he was miserable, he'd been too proud to surrender his life to the living God. Maybe now, he'd finally recognize his need for a Savior.

Celebration Worthy

After his promise, we said good-bye. With a heavy heart, I hung up the phone just as Tim walked into his office.

Turning to look at him, I asked, "Do you know who that was?"

"Must have been your lover," he said, his tone low enough that his words couldn't be heard by our son. "As soon as I heard your voice, I knew and started getting tied in knots. That's how you *always* sound when you talk with him."

"Funny, I haven't talked with him except once in about 15 years. And, you weren't even here that day. In my opinion, today, Jan sounded suicidal."

Tim rarely apologized but this time his heartfelt words came instantly. "I'm sorry. I am really sorry. I just got jealous."

During both the conversations with Jan and the one with Tim, peace prevailed. This was peace in the midst of a raging storm, a turbulent tsunami of emotion. Hidden in Christ, I felt safe and secure, calm and confident. Going into the kitchen to cook dinner, I walked by the china cabinet and behind the glass could see the Windblown Girl. She stood tall, proud, and composed despite the desperation of a former lover. A jealous husband. Life's fury roaring fierce.

The corn tortilla in my cast-iron skillet started to sizzle in the hot oil as Tim came into the kitchen. "There is one thing I know now. He never was a threat to me." My husband had no idea of how much Jan meant to me, yet he was right. Jan had not been a threat because Christ had kept me in the truth of reality. Life with Jan would have had extreme highs and lows. My children would have suffered and whatever had been good between us would have been destroyed. Tim and I didn't have the marriage I wanted, but Jesus had taught me to be faithful. He had taught me how to choose love for my husband, even when it was difficult. He had taught me to do everything in my power to keep my family together.

Jan had called close to 5:00 p.m. on the 17th. With a nine-hour time difference between the U.S. and Norway, that made it about 2:00 a.m. on the 18th, his time. He was probably drunk. Yet, he'd remembered my birthday and saved my phone number all this time. And pictures from Barbados with me in them. Where did those come from and why hadn't I seen them? We hadn't taken any. Some pieces to this puzzle seemed to be missing, but one thing I knew—he loved me. I could still hear it in his voice.

September 18, 1990
Feeling Valued

Waking to the sound and smell of coffee brewing surprised me. My old pot had broken the day before. I hadn't had time to get a new one. While pouring a cup, I considered Tim's thoughtfulness. He was trying, that was clear. But it was always the same. The deep wounds of a crisis. Though he wouldn't apologize, he'd do something kind, convinced he'd done nothing wrong. For a while I'd go along to get along. Then, the tension would start building, again. Each time, the divide between us got wider until now, a simple gesture could no longer bridge the gap.

Taking my coffee into my office, I picked up a note sitting on my computer keyboard. From Josh, it described "A Mother's Love," warming me more than the coffee. BJ's first words that morning had been "Happy Birthday, Mom," delivered with a hug. "Mom." The sweetest word I knew. No sacrifice was too great to keep my sons secure.

That night, the music blared as I rushed up the walkway toward the back-to-school dance. Tim had insisted on taking me to dinner, so I was late. As fit our pattern, he was trying to build bridges between us, but it felt phony, forced, and I did not enjoy my meal. My mind was reeling. We'd had little to say to each other.

Momentary thoughtfulness didn't change the reality of serious issues. No matter how much I wanted to, I couldn't pretend them away. Despite years of counseling, the gulf between us continued to grow. Now, for at least a few hours, I'd be transported into a world filled with teens—their highs and lows, their need for hugs and compassion as great as my own. Though some of them weren't really wanted at home, they knew I loved them.

While I was still outside, Mike, a big guy I'd grown quite fond of, walked over opening his arms for a bear hug. "Happy birthday, Patti!"

How did he know? I wondered continuing on toward the door. A couple of girls standing around on the patio greeted me with giggles and a "Happy Birthday! greeting." Strange, I thought, but maybe not so much. Josh had probably mentioned it. He'd come early to help decorate. But as soon as I walked inside the door, I saw it—a huge bright-colored banner hung from the ceiling wishing me a happy birthday. The back-to-school dance had been turned into a special celebration for me. I was deeply touched.

Called up on stage so everyone could sing to me, the youth pastor presented me with a gold Cross pen and a giant card signed with sweet sentiments written by the kids. Group dancing with them flooded my heart with joy.

When the band took a break, I headed out into the cool night air. Gail, an adult volunteer who had become a good friend, caught up with me. Because she already knew my story, after her birthday wishes, I mentioned Jan's surprise call.

Finding the Melody

"I wish I knew where to get that song by Leonard Cohen, but none of the music stores I called carry anything by him. I guess he's from Canada."

Gail grabbed my arm, her eyes wide, a stunned expression on her face.

"Patti, you're not going to believe this, but I leave Friday for Quebec! If I see a music store, I'll try to find it for you."

No one but God could have orchestrated all the details. So many times, Gail and I didn't even get a chance to talk. Only a handful of people even knew about Jan. Her trip, at just-the-right time. But why would He do that? "Lord, only let her find that song, if my having it is your will. If I shouldn't have it, please let her forget about it." After that night, I deliberately put it out of my mind.

Two weeks later, I was talking with students when Gail walked up behind me, putting her hand on my shoulder. As I turned around, she held out a small package. Her green eyes sparkled and so did her grin. "Happy birthday, a little late."

Tears welled up in my eyes. I didn't need to unwrap the gift to know it contained a cassette. She'd found the song.

The next morning, after Tim and the boys left, I got the tape out of my purse and scrutinized the list of songs. Jan hadn't actually mentioned the name of the one he wanted me to hear, but he'd told me it was right after another song—What was it? Why hadn't I written it down? Was it the one about Manhattan? I wondered if I'd even recognize which one reminded him of me. But when I heard Leonard Cohen's deep gravelly voice speaking-sing the lyrics to "Ain't No Cure for Love," I knew.

How could he love me that much? He'd even repeated one of the lyrics on the phone about not needing to be forgiven for the way he feels. The reality of his love exploded as memories flooded into my consciousness—Jan's face when I left the ship. His watching me at odd moments as though memorizing my features. His wanting me to write his mom and having her initiate our correspondence. While staring at my face one night, he even noticed something about me that no one else had—not even me. "You have a dimple. Only one." Touching the left side of my cheek softly, he'd smiled.

The stricken look on his face that last day at my front door still hurt my heart. I hadn't thought about it in years. We knew we'd be apart for a long period of time but never imagined this constant bittersweet agony.

More than ever before, I understood why the commitment of marriage is so important. And, the high price we'd paid to become one flesh outside of it.

In that, I was much better off than Jan. Bringing my broken heart to Jesus, He poured comfort into it—healing me and setting me free. Though there were challenges, I could even choose love for another. No wonder Jan was so miserable. Without turning to the one who heals broken hearts, his remained shattered. I wondered if I'd ever find out what happened to him.

Chapter 18

A Complete Failure

By 1998, my marital problems had escalated beyond what I thought possible. My husband of 18 years and I had come to the place where there was no alternative but for him to move out. Losing his job due to medical issues meant losing his company car. Starting work for a different company necessitated transportation, so, during the week, he drove mine. We were still making payments on it to my mother. For the first time since I was 16, I was without my own car. Once a week I "borrowed" it to run errands.

Jesus hadn't worked according to my expectations or answered my prayers the way I'd hoped. Resolution seemed impossible. Then, Tim called with life-changing news.

He came straight to the point: "I want a divorce."

Gripping the receiver tighter, I asked him to repeat the words I only half-hoped to hear, words that would devastate my family with ongoing consequences. Part of me had thought that if I did the right things, God would do the miracles necessary to heal my second marriage. But that didn't happen. Instead, He had taught me about unconditional love, and now it appeared I was being set free.

Deep down, I really didn't want another divorce. What I wanted most was a right relationship between my husband and me. Now that hope was crushed. The resulting turmoil drove my youngest son to go live with Valerie. With Josh living in Berkeley, I was alone.

Losing Everything

Was the failure of my second marriage my fault? Maybe. I don't know. How had I achieved oneness outside of marriage with Jan—a unity of body, mind, and emotions? Yet, not with my husband? Had that been a factor in its failure? Only God knows the answer to that.

All I know is that I tried as hard as I knew how to make my marriage work, and by God's grace and mercy, Jesus gave me peace and strength throughout the difficulties. He'd taught me so many things I needed to learn. Still, failure the second time around broke my heart. All I'd ever wanted was a family, and now mine was shattered.

Whatever complications we struggled with, suffice it to say, it was my understanding that Tim believed I was at fault, and he'd had enough.

So, he filed for divorce, then came while I was gone to take the king-sized bed his friend had built and our television. Tugging a twin bed mattress from the guest room into my bedroom, I left it on the floor until someone stronger could move the frame. My mom gave me her little 17" black-and-white TV with rabbit ears.

After my computer crashed, I used Tim's for my business, but then he took that too. Though I borrowed money from Valerie for a new one, the income from editing dissertations didn't stretch far enough to sustain a household, so I went deeper into debt.

Our friends had gone to high school with my husband, so they, too, vanished.

Tim wanted his half of the house as soon as possible. Having refinanced for the remodel, we didn't have much equity. But he genuinely needed whatever he could get. For months, we haggled over the property settlement. It was a terrible time for us both.

Thoughts of losing my childhood home devastated me. No more lilac bouquets like the dozens I filled church with one unforgettable Easter morning. The joy that filled my heart giving them away to friends and family would be gone. An inheritance from my grandmother had put the wood-burning stove in our family room. This was my family home, and the idea of selling it and moving elsewhere was crushing. Heartbroken, I grieved for the loss of everything I held dear. I'd already discovered that the best source of comfort and hope during times of tremendous pain was the Guardian and Shepherd of my soul, so I clung to Jesus.

Starting Over

Until we could secure the property settlement, my mom paid the house payments and put the car loan on hold. She thought I should agree to sell the house. Frequently she took me out to lunch and dinner. Though I had no money to spend, our shopping trips brought a little relief from the pain. Within weeks of Tim's leaving, my mom also gave me some sound advice.

"Patti, you need to get a job—any job. One that will give you something to do and a little income at least temporarily."

She was right. The tenderness in her voice expressed concern for my well-being. Selfishly she enjoyed my unrestricted weekend visits, but this time she put my welfare above her own. My problems went far beyond money. Something needed to keep my mind busy while my life got sorted out. So, I decided to be strategic in my job search.

Even though my dissertation business was in a slump, I still sat at the computer for hours at a time. When I wasn't editing, I worked on a draft of Jan's and my story. A second job meant I wouldn't have time for the gym except on my days off, and even then, I'd probably visit my mom. Seeing the hustle and bustle of a copy center near my home, I applied and was instantly hired. That would give me exercise as well as some income.

Not wanting to leave Friday and Saturday nights open to temptation, I requested weekend nights and that ingratiated me with my coworkers. It also gave me the goodwill I needed to insist on Sunday mornings off, so I could attend church. Soon my boss promoted me to full-time copy-center manager—a position I didn't want but took because I needed the medical insurance that came with it.

Every time I put on the uniform's red polo shirt, I felt like a complete failure. Most of my coworkers were teenagers. At almost 50 years old, I was going through a second divorce. As soon as BJ graduated high school, he went to live with Josh in Berkeley so now both my sons lived too far for visits other than holidays. They were busy and rarely called. My stay-at-home business declined even further as my business partner and I parted ways. With barely enough money to pay the bills, cultivating friendships became almost impossible. And, the sale of my beloved home could be forced any day.

Though I felt unwanted by almost everyone, Jesus gave me hope and sometimes even joy. The people in my Sunday school class made me laugh and encouraged my heart. As I revealed the need for a suitable career opportunity, they prayed for me. Their respect and kindness reminded me that I had value and purpose. My Creator continued strengthening me enough to embrace the pain and continue learning about the depth of His love, care, and compassion. Dependence on Him kept me from going after men who might use me then toss me aside. Not having sex was hard but not as tough as giving myself to men who didn't care about me.

Jan may have been an alcoholic, but knowing he loved me was enough. However, there was no temptation to try and contact him. I had enough trouble of my own without adding fantasy thinking to the problems.

Never Really Alone

Sometimes while at my lowest, the Creator surprised me with flowers—beautiful blooms from my garden reminding me of his abundant provision and care. A breathtaking sunrise revealed His unlimited power—big enough to take care of my problems. The moon, illuminating the darkness, lit the way for hope.

The only gift I could give in return was my trust and praise, even as my lawyer said the unthinkable "For Sale" sign would soon be placed in my front yard. Whatever the outcome, I had confidence that I'd be OK. Despite being devastated by the disintegration of my family, I had no doubt that the One who placed the stars in the sky was bigger than my problems. He continually spoke to me through His word, and His faithfulness exceeded all my expectations.

During this time, due to some unreasonable expectations, my boss demoted me and started cutting my hours. Because of the inappropriate way he handled things, my medical/dental insurance remained in place. By then my dissertation business had picked up again, which allowed me to resume paying my bills. For almost two years, I worked one day a week at the copy center and received full benefits. The day those benefits ended, I quit.

And, before that "For Sale" sign was stuck in my front lawn, something astonishing happened that only the living God could have orchestrated.

The Proverbial Rich Uncle

My dad's brother had no children. His wife, my Aunt Fern, had preceded him in death. A few months after Uncle Omar passed away in December of 1999, my cousins, sisters, and I gathered for lunch to honor him. Then we went into a lawyer's office to be informed that we had inherited his estate. By many standards, the individual amount wasn't huge, but it was to me. My share would be enough to pay Tim for his portion of the house, *if* he accepted my offer.

Before calling him, during a morning quiet time, I heard the Holy Spirit's whisper telling me I needed to apologize for all the things I'd done wrong. That familiar breeze also specified the amount to offer my now ex-husband.

After humbling myself to admit my own wrongdoing, which included a good cry, I swallowed hard and called Tim. "Can you come over?" I asked. "I have something I want to talk to you about."

My hands shook as we sat adjacent to one another in straight-backed chairs at the heavy wooden dining room table I'd had long before we married. "Tim, I am so sorry for all the hurtful things I've said." His eyebrows raised as he heard the conciliatory tone in my voice and saw genuine tears of sorrow in my eyes.

Reminding him that this was the only home our sons had known, I spoke about how although they no longer lived nearby, there had been too many changes for them not to know they could return. Reminding him that this was my childhood home, I also spoke of my grandmother's lilacs, the wood-burning stove, and our down payment—all because of my family's heritage. This was practically the only home I'd ever known. Then I suggested buying him out and asked for mercy.

Only Jesus made any of that possible. While waiting for Tim's response, I held my breath. Considering his share of the two years of house payments we owed my mom, the amount was fair, probably even generous, but I was pretty sure it wasn't what he hoped for. I told him he could take time to think it over. To talk to his lawyer, who was also his best friend. To be sure he was making the right decision.

Instead, to my amazement, he agreed to accept the offer saying he had never wanted to force me to sell.

I'll always be grateful for his agreement—and incredulous that my elderly uncle died at the "just-right" time for me to have the "just-right" amount. Although Tim didn't want to stay married, it was evident that he trusted and respected me. Within days we agreed to do everything we could to make this transition as easy as possible for our sons.

A Generous Surprise

Several months later, Valerie threw me a 50th birthday party. During the evening, my cousin Nancy called me aside and handed me an envelope. Opening it, I found a check for $47,500.

The next day I totaled the amounts I owed people: The payment to Tim, my mom (for the house and car payments), and Val (for the computer). Altogether I owed $47,000. With $500 left over, I opened a savings account. Only a gracious loving God could have orchestrated such an incredible surprise for my birthday. Now I was debt free.

Soon after, I decided to complete my college degree and applied for an accelerated program. Though I would have preferred a good job, that search seemed futile. My dear friend, Lois, who faithfully prayed for me, suggested we ask Jesus to bring me the right job. In the meantime, I quit looking and focused on rebuilding my dissertation business. Yet, nothing prepared me for the way God would answer our prayers.

Chapter 19

Under the Stars, Again

While editing dozens of organizational leadership dissertations, I became fascinated by the topic. Reading the most frequently mentioned books intrigued me even more, so with a no-interest loan from a local charity and a $1,000 scholarship, I arranged to start BIOLA's Organizational Leadership program. With a degree, I hoped to find a career in communications. But in an instant, a phone call radically changed my plans.

Expecting a doctoral student, I was surprised when the caller identified himself as the vice president of a science-faith think tank. He wanted to know if I'd be interested in a job as an editor. After describing the position, Dave (a brilliant NASA scientist) mentioned a salary higher than I could have imagined, even with a college degree. I'd receive full medical benefits, a 401K and after a year, three-weeks of vacation. Though I believed my skills were worth it, I wasn't at all convinced I wanted to work with scientists.

"You need to understand, I don't know anything about science." It had always seemed so boring. I'd even failed astronomy in college. Because my professor was horribly dull, I'd skip class, going to the beach instead. But the money and benefits of this position might be worth whatever it took.

"We don't see that as a problem," Dave said. "In fact, we think it may be a good thing because we need someone who can make the writing of our scientists easier to understand. You've written magazine articles, haven't you? And edited doctoral dissertations? So, you must be used to academia."

"How do you know all that? Who gave you my name?"

It was the kind biochemist in my Sunday School class. Wanting an experienced editor, Dr. Fazale Rana had been urging them to hire me.

Dave invited me to come for an interview, and I remembered that Lois had been praying for the right job to come to me. Even though I wasn't convinced I could meet their expectations and science seemed boring, I agreed to come in the very next day.

Beyond My Ability

As the two-hour interview involving several people wound down, I was asked to start right away. Although the responsibilities were a bit terrifying, the money and benefits were too good to pass up. The thought of editing the writing of an astronomer, a biochemist, and a philosopher/theologian as well as other scientists intimidated me, but the least I could do was try.

While driving to work that first day, on the interchange between the 10 and 57 freeways, I envisioned a worst-case scenario. Once they discovered my lack of skill, I'd be fired. Yet, if that happened after two weeks, two months, or two years—Jesus would still love me, and I'd be OK. Just as I'd been OK after Jan left. And OK without my family. My success was no longer dependent on other people's perspectives. Doing my best was all I could expect of myself.

A bright pink, yellow, and orange bouquet of Gerber daisies on my desk welcomed me into my private office. However, my first assignment made me put my head down on my desk in despair. Even the scholars I worked with admitted their struggle to understand a series of articles by a Distinguished Professor of Philosophy on the complexities of the mind/body problem. I had about a week to bring clarity to his third and final piece. Not knowing whether to cry or pray, I walked outside and leaned against the second-floor black wrought-iron railing, silently asking the Holy Spirit to help me understand. This was way over my head.

My mom called that night to see how it went. Her first question was: "Can you do that job?" Her tone made it clear, she didn't think I could. All I could say was, "I don't know, but I'm going to try."

The next night, on my way home, I stopped at the grocery store. While waiting to check out, I glanced at the magazines. On the cover of *Self* magazine was a picture of a brown-haired beauty, naked. While marveling at how the photographer had captured her by strategically placing her arms and legs, the revelation that she was *not* just a body illuminated some of the complex principles in J. P. Moreland's article. This model wasn't an empty shell.

For most of my life, encouraged by cultural lies, I had perceived the body as being its own entity. But this momentary flash of insight changed my thinking. Perhaps this cover girl was uncomfortable posing naked but needed the job. Maybe she was proud of her body and wanted to show it off. She was someone's daughter. Perhaps her mom's physical attributes contributed to her beauty. But maybe her real passion was engineering. Working hard to keep her body slender enough to snag photo shoots, she'd use her mind to decide what to do with her pay. She could buy designer shoes and purses. Or use the money to study for an advanced degree.

In that moment, a sense of self—the mind and body—became inextricably intertwined. That understanding illuminated the article's principles and empowered me to edit it so readers could more easily understand them. The scholars deeply appreciated my work. Later, although I never saw the communication Dave received from him, I heard enough to suspect that the article's author did too.

Becoming a Lifelong Learner

That incident started building my confidence. With help from the Holy Spirit, I could somewhat bridge the gap between the academic and popular thinking. Somewhere along the way my job turned into a career, and I grew to love its challenges. They exercised my mind and stretched me to reach far beyond my own limited perspective. If I hadn't been in such dire straits, I never would have taken that position and realized my potential.

How sad it was that my mom refused to try any new technology, insisting on keeping her VCR long after DVDs became popular. Though only in her 60s, she was determined *not* to learn anything new. How different my new working environment was, where everybody was anxious to embrace new discoveries.

Learning how credible science supports belief in God fascinated me as much as the possibilities for applying the leadership techniques I'd learned. Equally satisfying, I sometimes made biblical applications in the articles I worked on with the scholars. To see the astronomical details for how our Creator put the universe in place kept me eager to find out more.

The body was equally fascinating as I discovered how cells even have a proofreading/editing process. Such complex brilliance had to be the result of intentional design.

My position opened up opportunities to network with distinguished scientists and communications professionals across the nation—and on one occasion even a high-ranking government official in Beijing! Never would I have thought myself capable of such a career.

Within a short time, I was promoted to an executive-level position. All those dissertations I'd edited had taught me how to develop the teamwork our communications department needed. Because we could see effective results, my supervisor encouraged me to continue learning those principles, which I did. Developing rapport with the astronomer, biochemist, philosopher/theologian, and staff that I supervised started easing the agony of missing my family.

My career fascinated me so much, I came to love Monday mornings and being around the people I worked with. Never had I ever thought scientists could be so creative! In addition, our profound philosopher made me think with more depth too. Always eager to get to work, I'd wonder what new discovery might arise. Sometimes I learned something scientific. Sometimes the lesson involved building character. Opportunities often arose to encourage my team and others. On several occasions I also had to hold people accountable while building trust.

Under my direction, our magazine won the top Evangelical Press Association award. But as we stood at the convention in Colorado waiting to find out the results, our team knew it was too expensive to continue the publication. Together, we remained flexible, changing strategies, and refocusing on book development. While visiting my sons, who had moved to Hawaii,

I made a strategic connection that led me to approach a literary agent on behalf of the scholars. He accepted our proposal and we put together a 12-book contract for our publisher. I was honored to be the liaison. At times, the company I worked for generously paid for me to travel with the exec team to promote the work we were doing and participate in fundraising events.

A Night to Remember

On August 28, 2004, my personal satisfaction from this dream job's opportunities culminated during "An Evening Under the Stars" gala.

Walking into the eastern courtyard of the Beckman Institute at the California Institute of Technology (Caltech), I looked around to see what still needed to be done. In about an hour, 150 guests would arrive. The set-up crew had called, while I was on my way, to say they were still at dinner and would be late.

Good thing I decided not to go with them but came straight to the venue instead. The amount of work still to be done was staggering. Our caterer was already unfolding a long table soon to be loaded with crème puffs, blueberry tarts, lemon cake, and more. However, the round table tops remained stacked against the wall and the chairs stood in rows, lecture style. All of them had to be moved.

The exquisite floral centerpieces I'd ordered sat on the floor behind a glass door. It was locked. Boxes of our newly released books also needed to be opened and readied for signing.

Grabbing my cell phone, I called the number for maintenance, explaining the need for him to hurry. As the chair of this event, tonight's celebration may have had even greater significance for me than for my employer. I wanted everything perfect. Quickly pulling chairs around the table bases, my mind wandered to another night under the stars.

The balmy evening air carried me back almost 30 years to when I sat on the chaise lounge by the Sun Viking's pool after that devastating phone call from my first husband. Feeling incredibly small, I had looked up at the stars and figured there would have to be someone big enough to hang them in the sky to fix my problems. Now, I gazed up at a vast array of radiant celestial bodies, marveling to think that their Creator and mine had given me an extraordinary career filled with evidence for His existence.

Bringing Order Out of Chaos

The Big Bang had been a misnomer. It hadn't been a chaotic explosion at all. Rather, the brilliant scientists I worked with had explained how this exquisitely orchestrated event of fine-tuning displays God's authority and control. Each astronomical body hand-placed by a Grand Designer established the order that makes life possible on Earth.

Considering such power made my problems miniscule by comparison. The almighty God's power had brought order out of my chaos and led to an incredible life where it was possible to become my best self. Dying to that old version of me—an individual steeped in self-destructive choices—had been excruciating. However, over time, as I learned to live according to the truths of the One who made me, I had discovered the abilities that led me here. It never could have happened if I'd taken matters into my own hands.

And, in an instant, if the Lord of all heaven and earth was so inclined, He could even reunite Jan and me. Having no idea what dignitaries might show up tonight, I couldn't help but wonder if this might be the occasion where I'd see him again.

This Magic Moment

Unlike any ordinary day, this one had already revealed delightful serendipity. While a high-end stylist gave me a Hollywood cut, we started getting to know one another. Lyda mentioned having gone to school in southeast Asia. So, I told her about my dad and sister living in Vientiane.

Stunned, she said, "That's where I lived!"

"My dad worked for Air America. Why were you there?"

"My dad worked for Air America, too!"

Connecting the timeframe, we marveled at how small the world was. Here we were clear across the earth in Southern California discovering how our dads had worked together in Laos during the Vietnam war. That God-orchestrated moment made me wonder what other astonishing surprises might await.

The gala testified as to how far I'd come. Juggling all the responsibilities of my career had required a multitude of tough lessons—setting boundaries, staying in the truth, being trustworthy, along with getting "self" out of the way to choose love and forgiveness on the job.

God's plans exceeded anything I could have imagined. Opportunities like tonight presented unique challenges, stretching me as an individual and giving me the chance to exercise my creativity outside the office. If Jan knew, he'd be proud. The thought made me smile.

Seeing the maintenance man arrive brought me back to the present. While he unlocked the door giving me access to our flowers and books; Dave and his wife, Diane, entered the Mediterranean-style courtyard. Though I hadn't expected them, help had arrived. Breathing a sigh of relief, I knew that Dave, the brilliant scientist who once led the NASA team that helped save the Galileo mission to Jupiter from antenna failure, would gladly pitch in with whatever mundane tasks needed doing.

As he started setting up the sound system, Diane pulled the remaining chairs around the tables. The aroma of strong coffee wafted through the air, while I finished putting the stunning centerpieces in place. Indirect lighting glimmered through the trees and reflected off the water in Caltech's iconic Gene Pool that displayed strands of DNA. That stunning setting made my soft black-and-white polka-dot tea-length dress feel glamorous. Quickly changing my shoes before anyone else arrived made me stand a little taller.

Shaded by lush greenery, three wooden tables with maroon umbrellas were soon piled high with stacks of books ready for signing. When their authors (Hugh Ross, an astronomer; Fazale Rana, a biochemist; and Kenneth Samples, a philosopher/theologian) arrived, we chatted with excited anticipation.

For months, I'd worked hard editing *The Origins of Life: Biblical and Evolutionary Models Face Off* by Fuz and Hugh, which explained scientifically credible evidence for the Creator. He'd not only hung the stars in the sky, but also designed the intricacies of each individual life including mine. Kenneth's *Without A Doubt: Answering the 20 Toughest Faith Questions* tackled objections to the Christian faith, showing me how a good God can allow evil. It supplied intellectually satisfying reasons for my biblical world-view. It also addressed the issue of why I don't have the right to do what I want with my own body. In the process of working with Ken, I continued to grow in my understanding about why I'd made the right choice to no longer turn sex into a mindless commodity.

A string trio began playing softly as guests clad in cocktail dresses and suits started wandering toward the book tables. My dear friends Dr. Gary and Lois Voorman arrived and waved. He looked dapper in his tuxedo, and she glowed in a lovely periwinkle evening gown. Everything was in place, and we were ready to begin.

Taking the microphone, Hugh's wife and my immediate supervisor, Kathy, welcomed everyone, then introduced me thanking me as the chair for tonight's event. Various distinguished guests congratulated me on an exceptional job of making the books more readable as well as for the incredible evening. Yet, I was ever aware of the teamwork involved and that the unparalleled living God deserved the credit not only for the content of the books but also for the night's success.

Again and again I'd stopped to ask the Wonderful Counselor to help me comprehend the technical jargon. And, if I'd gone to dinner as planned, tonight could have been a disaster. Whether anyone recognized it or not, in every aspect of success the Holy Spirit had guided me, taught me, and cared for my needs. My heart swelled with gratitude for God's lovingkindness.

Better Than Good

This night celebrated my hope for the future—one, where anything might happen. Although Jan didn't magically appear, perhaps even more satisfying, I realized that the triune God had made my life a thrill ride despite unanswered hopes and dreams. Or maybe it was because of them.

This celebration of a personal and professional victory brought incredible contentment. My well-being didn't depend on circumstances, another person, or sex. It was based on my character—my identity in Christ—and His great love for me. He was molding and shaping me in His image, and had given me enough courage to experience life's grand adventure. Sometimes troubles might whirl with tornado-force winds, but that night under the stars, life was good—and I was at peace.

Still, it wasn't long before the winds of change, once again, blew fierce.

Chapter 20

Fired!

While sitting at my desk after lunch, that perceptive whisper spoke to me once again. "If you ever want to write about your romance with Jan, you'll have to leave here."

Agreeing to take my current job had required me to set aside my original desire to write about Jan and how God's love exceeded that idyllic experience. Trying to write while working in such a demanding position was simply too difficult. Now, I loved my work and coworkers too much to ever leave on my own.

Frequently I put in 50-to-60-hour weeks because the work was so satisfying and stimulating. Seeing the difference my efforts made caused my career to be my happy place. At home, I didn't have time or energy to dwell on the past because my mind was constantly engaged trying to further the efforts of my colleagues. They had become dear friends, a family of sorts.

A couple of weeks later, one afternoon while in Ken's office, he stopped discussing book edits and leaned back in his chair. Then, he folded his hands and looked me in the eye: "You should be involved with justice issues." How odd for him to mention that out of the blue. Because it was so odd, almost like a quiet shout, it registered deep inside my mind. Several months later I realized that God had been hinting at a new direction—once again not one of my choosing.

A Stunning Verdict

In November 2009, a sense of foreboding followed the phone call asking me to come into an exec team meeting. For almost a year, a coworker had been harassing me, and my supervisor had told me to keep a record of it. Almost weekly I sent her an email describing ridiculous stunts designed to torment me. However, when I walked into Hugh's office and sat down at the table, I looked at the stern faces of three people I considered good friends. The words Hugh spoke made me sit back in my chair and take a deep breath. In essence, he said, "You're fired."

My response surprised me almost as much as the words he spoke—I had nothing to say.

Although my supervisor assured me she didn't have a single complaint about my work, without any warning whatsoever, she claimed I was negative and divisive. The executive team then told me to go home for a week with pay to think about their decision.

Though outwardly I remained calm and didn't cry, my thoughts raced. Perhaps they'd reconsider if I apologized and promised to change. Yet, as I asked God for wisdom, I couldn't escape the reality that good teamwork must be based on trust. To build trust, problems must be resolved. The only way to do that was to identify them, then work together to find solutions. I'd learned the hard way that trying to ignore conflict only makes it worse, and I couldn't pretend otherwise. My attempts at problem-solving may have been perceived as negative and divisive by my supervisor, but I knew they were based on principles designed to build teamwork on a foundation of trust. God knew the truth, and so did almost everyone who knew me.

My team would attest to the fact that I'd frequently called them to remain positive and to work with the woman who harassed me. She'd also undermined them. Remembering the Holy Spirit's whispers convinced me that Jesus was in control. Although I was about to lose my livelihood and the work I loved, I decided not to apologize or try to defend myself.

My mom, however, didn't sit idly by. A staunch ally, she wrote a letter telling my supervisor that she got it wrong. Making such a bold move was so uncharacteristic for my mother that when she gave me a copy, it made me smile. But her note didn't make any difference.

Overnight, I lost my income, treasured relationships, and professional satisfaction. Social activities too. Convinced of their allegations, the exec team insisted that coworkers avoid all contact with me. Despite that, several stood with me at my unemployment hearing. With no valid evidence against me and plenty of documentation, my benefits were issued. From my perspective that adjudication vindicated me. Due to an economic downturn, those benefits were extended for two full years. Although it wasn't much to live on, with my home's mortgage paid off, I had just enough to scrape by.

Returning to the Unknown

Once again, the same all-powerful Creator brought order out of the chaos in my life. As usual, He didn't just go "poof" and make everything all right. I had to trust Him and pray and wait. And, wait. For almost a year, I didn't know what to do with myself, except to make online applications for jobs all over the country. In between, I played video games and volunteered to write for a Christian newspaper.

Crafting feature articles involved me with stories about the poor, foster children, and the many Hispanic women traumatized by abortion. Understanding a biblical identity that instills dignity and meaning into every human life from conception to the grave—regardless of ethnicity, income level, or choices—began cultivating my sense of responsibility to do whatever I could to make a difference in the cultural issues that plague our society.

This was quite a contrast with my mother's narcissistic tendencies. Despite her having been my champion at times, money was her criteria for success. She reminded me of that one morning while vehemently explaining how I wasn't worth much because I didn't have much. Her financial resources meant she was worth much more.

Exchanging Cultural Lies for Rock-Solid Truth

Although in our society, it's often claimed "He who has the most toys wins," wealth didn't define my success. Nor did the approval of others. Rather than envy the material possessions of others like my mom and sister, biblical principles challenged me to focus on developing my character to be more like Jesus. That grew my concern for those less fortunate. Comparing my life to my mom's made me realize how incredibly rich I was.

Shifting my focus from what I didn't have to gratitude for a roof over my head and food on the table gave me a peace independent of circumstances. Nothing could have been worth more than exchanging discontent for an attitude of gratitude. Appreciation for the Creator's most exquisite gifts—peace, grace, mercy, love, and joy—set me free from jealousy and bitterness.

Countercultural values gave me determination to fight injustice in every way possible. The more I learned, especially about the underlying causes of human trafficking (poverty, greed, foster care, and broken families), the more determined I became to raise awareness of this travesty.

A feature article assignment covering a global forum on modern-day slavery made me realize how vulnerable I'd been when I met Jan. He'd validated me, called me beautiful, and gave me a sense of worth.

While attending that global human trafficking symposium, speakers described how today's traffickers target girls trying to escape life's pain and groom them using a similar methodology. The tremendous injustice of one of the largest criminal activities in the world (second only to drugs) led me to help start two anti-trafficking groups: one at the city level, another in Los Angeles County.

Many of America's young people (some girls and boys younger than 12) forced into sex slavery come from broken families with absent fathers. The COVID-19 pandemic, while encouraging self-isolation and social distancing, exacerbated the problems by creating greater demand for Internet porn. In turn, that increased demand for younger children and escalated violence against them. Traffickers easily ensnare throw-away kids in the foster care system who are craving love. Pimps promise to be their daddy—offering to take care of them. Instead, these children are exploited and raped until many die or are scarred for life.

How fortunate I was to escape the dangers of a hypersexualized culture that grooms young people to use sex for physical pleasure without being in a committed relationship. The lies of music, television, movies, and books encourage girls and young women, boys and young men, to make sex their god. Inability to disconnect their emotions from a physical experience enslaves individuals to self-destructive behaviors such as alcoholism, eating disorders, drug use, cutting, and suicide.

Reality's Dark Side

At many human trafficking conferences, I met young women who longed for a family, much like I did. Although my father was absent at critical points in my life, these victims walked a far more painful and self-destructive path. Many of those I encountered experienced God's grace rescuing them from devastating circumstances. Recovery took time and a multitude of resources.

The more I learned about biblical principles, the more I realized that justice is not a matter of politics. It's a matter of identity. Right behavior grows within individuals, who understand that every single person is made in the image of the living God.

Gross injustice occurs whenever a human being rebels against God and determines that "a body" (any body that's not convenient) is expendable. Black, white, brown, rich or poor, gay or straight, loved or not, Jesus instills in *every single human being* a sense of worth. Embracing biblical values taught me that every human life deserves respect and dignity—the homeless, the elderly, prisoners, teens on drugs, an individual struggling with mental illness or the veteran who lost his legs in combat.

For another human being to determine a person's value makes life or death dependent upon that individual meeting the criteria bestowed by someone in power. This mode of thinking reflects a low view of humanity—one that results in injustice.

Letting in the Light

A high (or biblical) view of life changes that low view. Each life is created in the image of the living God, and if there are what some may consider deficiencies, the Creator can use them for good. Finding out that Andrea

Bocelli's and Tim Tebow's moms were each advised to abort their babies due to potential birth defects validated these beliefs. Rather than listen to a particular human voice, these moms valued life and brought forth one of my favorite singers and a much-admired humanitarian who has made an incredible difference in our world.

Like these mothers, learning to embrace inconvenient truths transformed my life to the point where external circumstances or other people's opinions lost their power to control or derail me. So, after I lost the job that had given me so much, I embraced the future and began telling the stories of those on the front lines of injustice, those who fight for the well-being of others.

In the amazing twists and turns of Divine Providence, my love story took on meaning and purpose far beyond anything I'd ever imagined. The greatest love of all came about because of dying to self and giving up my original hopes and dreams. It hurt like hell, but I wouldn't change a thing. In the process of embracing the pain and being willing to explore the unknown, I've developed relationships with people all over the globe who are brothers and sisters in Christ—they are family.

Even more, I've grown beyond that young woman who took risks like climbing a rope ladder into a ship's hold or swimming to a far-off sailboat in the Caribbean. As I surrendered my "self" to Jesus, He developed that daring spirit in ways that have led to unimaginable places requiring leadership and teamwork. Every day, I'm excited to get out of bed, because I never know what might come my way. This vibrant lifestyle with its constant potential for adventure has also caused me to make some audacious decisions about sex.

Chapter 21

Sex, Strength, and Self

There's no doubt in my mind that regardless of how difficult my marriage was, my affair with Jan was morally wrong. Yet, even though it's been more than 40 years since I last saw him, I still miss the physical and emotional intimacy we experienced. Since my mother passed away, I often wonder what happened to him and long for his comforting embrace. Perhaps that's part of becoming one flesh. No matter how much I change, he's never stopped being part of me. That's why God designed sex for a lifelong commitment. It's supposed to unite two individuals as one flesh in a reflection of the way God the Father, the Son, and the Holy Spirit are three distinct persons, yet one entity. Complete Oneness. Wholeness. Splendor.

After suffering the inevitable loss of an unsustainable relationship, I never want to walk that path again. Sex is not a game to be played. When I tried, I lost—more than I ever imagined. My sense of worth disappeared along with my Norwegian navigator. Trying to find it again by seeking physical pleasure, I lost respect for myself and that impacted respect from others.

But once Jesus began transforming me into someone who values truth, He gave me a sense of self-worth that has built solid relationships. With my identity in Christ, over time, I've seen how I am becoming more like the Windblown Girl standing on solid rock while life's winds blow, fierce at times. Riots, a pandemic, and a government and media that villainizes biblical beliefs cannot shake the truths I've learned from the book I hold in my hands. By God's grace, I pray I never waver.

Facing Reality

Not once have I regretted my decision to abstain from a physical relationship outside of marriage with Jan or anyone else. The timeless truths in the Bible about sex belonging within the marriage covenant guard those who adhere to them against heartbreak. Human beings weren't given a list of rules but rather a gift of the deepest love designed to protect and care for the individuals who choose to embrace it.

That does not mean celibacy is easy. It isn't. Not even at my age. Without Christ, I wouldn't have had the strength to make good choices. Perhaps that's one reason why so many people turn to addictive behaviors, compulsive behaviors they hope will satisfy their souls.

There have been a few times when I've come close to falling off a precipice. Temptations on cruises with my mom tested my character and helped me understand that only the power of the Holy Spirit at work in my life keeps me from a catastrophe. The one I most need to be saved from is my "self."

Even now, I'm still vulnerable. Staying celibate unless I marry again requires me to continually disregard the constant bombardment of deception perpetuated through music, television, movies, and books. Any time I compromise truth and start believing the lies of our culture, I'll start making poor choices. Sometimes that temptation is greater than others, but it's clear to me that the consequences would be devastating. That's why I pray often for Jesus to keep me in the truth. Reading the Bible every day keeps me standing on solid ground. Rather than being limited by a list of dos and don'ts, I celebrate the freedom of a divine plan that promotes intimacy while preventing extensive pain.

The goodness of this plan helped me decide not to even date unless I'm convinced there's potential for a future. Never again do I want to attempt to disassociate my body from my mind with meaningless encounters that lead nowhere except to self-loathing. Rather the journey of truth has developed a sense of wholeness despite (or perhaps because of) requiring me to make sacrifices.

Superior Stability

In each of the phone calls I had with Jan, I claimed to be stronger now. At the time I had no clue *why* those words popped out of my mouth. In my own strength, I certainly couldn't have resisted him. Only the Holy Spirit giving me supernatural fortitude could empower me to make healthy choices, then adhere to them.

After years of reflection, I've come to realize that the living God has made me more resolute in several ways. I'm stronger in my

- *identity*—Now, I live in the awareness of *who* I was created to be and *who* I choose to be, day by day. My relationship with Jesus Christ has taught me what genuine love looks like. That love keeps me secure, and now I'm able to extend the same kind of love to others. For those who don't know how to live in that truth, I have far more compassion because for much of my life neither did I.

- *ability to sacrifice.* Real love wants someone else's best good even when it requires personal loss. Jesus set the example by giving His life on the cross for sinners like me, so we could live with Him forever. He demonstrated how to forgive the unforgiveable. How to speak truth with gentle kindness and stand on that truth even when the other person denies it and engages in self-destructive behaviors. Or rejects our relationship in ways that hurt like hell.

- *ability to do loving things when I don't feel like it.* Even when I'm furious I can choose to love someone by fixing a special dinner, being kind in the face of their anger, giving a gift without expecting one in return, refusing to be jealous of someone who has what I want. Instead, I can choose to be glad for them. That kind of love takes extraordinary strength—the kind that's imparted by the Holy Spirit while trusting a loving God. In the process it releases a priceless sense of freedom from bitterness, harsh feelings, and/or superior attitudes.

- *willingness to face my fears.* Discovering the courage to explore the unknown has been a life-changing gift. Learning to live alone and appreciate silence has helped me become more comfortable in my own skin. Working with those scientists despite my concerns and leading a team grew me as a person beyond anything I could fathom. Getting to know trafficking victims developed my compassion and increased my awareness of injustice. Taking vacations by myself has taught me that strangers are simply friends I've yet to meet.

Now, if something unimaginable happened that required me to move to a freezing climate where I didn't know anyone, I could do it but only if I was convinced God was guiding me there. A dream trip to Norway in 2018 gave me a brief glimpse of what living in a country like that might involve. It also caused me to wonder if I might see Jan again.

Traveling Solo

Waiting to board the flight from Ontario to Phoenix on my way to London made me nervous. Would they accept my carry-on? It weighed almost as much as my suitcase. Going on a 15-day cruise with only one 50-pound suitcase plus a carry-on meant maximizing every inch of space. When I went on those Caribbean cruises, I always took two large suitcases plus my carry on. And, the clothes for that hot climate were nowhere near as heavy as those necessary for the Arctic Circle—even in the summer. My tote-style purse and backpack were also stuffed full.

Hearing the announcement that gate attendants would check all bags, I breathed a sigh of relief. Getting ready for this trip had already been an inconceivable challenge.

Completing a Renovation

The day after my mother passed away, I looked around my living room. My shredding drapes needed replacing as soon as possible. So did my favorite overstuffed chair. It was threadbare. Though the living room easily held my mom's huge glass- and-gold coffee table, it looked out of place with my casual denim-checkered couch. By having the furniture reupholstered, I could re-decorate however I wanted. Even though it had made me happy for 20 years, it was time to let go of the past and embrace a new future. But spending enough money to make it happen was not easy after pinching pennies for so many years.

My friend Lynda shopped with me for fabrics that would complement the paintings I wanted to keep. A print of the Lady of Shalott hung over the couch reminding me that going after a lover could be deadly. Though he may not have been aware of its significance, my son Josh had brought me the print from London. Another print hung over my chair. In it, a homeless mother stands in the rain clutching the hands of her two children while staring into a brightly lit café window as well-dressed people rushed by—the plight of so many single moms. Over another chair hung two tapestries my mother had brought me from France.

After several hours choosing fabrics, I took Lynda to lunch on San Clemente pier. Over fish and chips, she gently said, "While your drapes are down, you might want to paint." Although I wanted to deny the need, I couldn't. She was right. The interior hadn't been done in too many years to count. And, that wasn't all. My cheap linoleum floor had torn to the point I worried about cutting my foot. My counters were still the low-grade Formica we'd installed during the remodel of 1987.

The thought of all that work was overwhelming. Yet step by step much of it had been completed about a month before my trip. The paint and furniture in the living room were stunning. Heavier brocade drapes complemented the artwork and the 50-year-old coffee table, yet their golden wheat color gave the room a soft glow that kept it from being uncomfortably formal.

Several friends suggested I upgrade my 50's style lights so I bought six $20.00 fixtures to replace those in my kitchen and hallway. However, by the time a repairman installed the first three, he refused to do anymore. Hand-ing me a burnt wire, he said, "Smell it." The stench convinced me that the entire electrical system needed an overhaul.

If my mom had lived even one more year, and I'd been aware of the potential electrical danger, I'd have sold my home. Even more likely the wiring would have started a fire, and I could have died.

Spending such an exorbitant amount of money to replace the entire electrical system took courage and strength beyond myself. I'd been advised to hire the best to do the work and Lynda knew just who to recommend. When Brian from BJ's Electrical came to give me a bid, he stopped on the front porch to pull booties on over his shoes. That alone almost convinced me he was the one for the job.

After discussing the details, I asked, "How soon can you start?"

"The end of June. And you might want to consider this—many people like to go on vacation while I'm doing the bulk of the work."

Stunned, I told him it "just happened" that my Norwegian cruise, the longest vacation I'd ever taken, started the end of June." After 15 days on the ship, I'd spend a day in Bergen before taking the train to Oslo—touted as the most beautiful train ride in the world. With travel time, I'd be gone a total of 19 days.

Running into Brian's dad at church, then later that same day his in-laws in the grocery store, confirmed that I'd chosen the right guy to trust with my home. The timing couldn't have been more perfect, way beyond human ability to plan. So, he'd start on the electrical first thing tomorrow morning.

You're Worth It

Brian's suggestions had made me almost as excited as getting on the plane. Updates like recessed lighting. A video doorbell. Automatic porch lights. Fans in the laundry area and the bathroom. He also advised me to hang a new chandelier in the dining room. That wasn't on my list of repairs, but after more than 40 years, he said the old one was dangerous.

What boggled my mind the most was how after years of making do with other people's cast offs, God's grace gave me the courage to spend the money necessary to be delighted with the results. Instead of a negative voice in my head telling me "you can't do that," a positive whisper urged me to get what I wanted. Once the electrical work was finished, the quality flooring and countertops I'd wanted ever since the 1987 remodel would be installed.

The same was true for this cruise. Spending enough to do it right had been a major factor in my decision-making. Traveling solo meant double the cost. Unexpectedly, one morning as I prayed about going, Scripture reminded me that my security doesn't lie in a bank. For years I'd seen how a good God had always taken care of me. Supernatural peace while booking the trip convinced me to consider it an extravagant gift intended for me to enjoy.

Such indulgence reminded me of the luxurious East Coast fall color cruise my mom took me on years before. She'd splurged on unforgettable excursions. The seaplane flight over the Laurentian mountains to a chalet with one of the finest wine cellars in the world had been astonishing.

Disappointed at being instructed to step into two separate planes, for once my mom kept silent. She'd wanted us to share the experience. Yet, for each of us the thrill of being seated in front next to the pilot eclipsed that desire. Rising into the clear blue sky, we watched the lush panorama unfold beneath us—a magnificent forest of autumn colors stretching to the horizon. Too soon we landed, skimming across a glorious lake that reflected the majesty of orange, gold, rust, and red woodlands.

Coming together again, we chatted like excited schoolgirls expressing our delight as we walked the short distance to an alpine chateau. Tasting robust red wines along with warm bread fresh from the oven, various cheeses, and the pièce de résistance—dark chocolate—a culinary fantasy wove its way into reality.

So, in honor of my mom, I booked extravagant adventures on my Norwegian trip instead of the free bus tours. A King Crab Safari. A Husky Hike. Kayaking in the fjords as well as the fabulous train ride. Working out at the gym almost daily had prepared me for whatever physical challenges I might encounter.

Nervous energy accompanied me as I boarded the plane heading toward the trip of a lifetime.

Beyond the Fjords

After a quick flight from Ontario to Phoenix and checking in for the trip to London, I began to relax. While trying to cram my overstuffed backpack and purse under the seat in front of me, my travel anxiety dissipated, and I started imagining the days and nights ahead. My young-adult fantasy of seeing the Norwegian fjords was about to begin.

Would I see Jan? A frequent traveler, he could even be on this plane.

Settling into my seat, I marveled at the possibilities. My sisters had asked whether I'd try to find him. But as hard as it was to understand, Jan wasn't the reason I decided to go. The land of the midnight sun had intrigued me ever since my first Caribbean cruise when I saw pictures of it projected onto the nightclub's walls.

Besides, I wasn't sure I wanted to know if Jan was married or still drinking or no longer alive. If we didn't share the same beliefs, our relationship could never work. And, I'd never really wanted to change him. He was his own man and the necessary transformation could only be accomplished by a great God who was absolutely capable of bringing us together again. He didn't need my help.

Without Jesus, Jan would have remained on a self-destructive path, and I didn't want to share that journey. Being crazy about him didn't make our problems magically disappear. Trust issues and value differences posed huge challenges. They might be far worse now. And, that could be heartbreaking.

How such truths had been so deeply impressed upon me from the beginning never ceases to be a source of wonder. Even though the way forward included deep suffering, I never cease being grateful for the way Christ kept me in the truth and provided a constant source of comfort.

Besides, there was another reason I didn't want to look for Jan. God's surprises never cease to astonish me. If a miracle of grace beyond fathoming had happened and Jan had embraced a relationship with Christ, I wanted our reunion to be as spectacular as the cruise where we first met. Or as stunning as his unexpected phone calls. Imposing my puny perspective on the situation could either get me into another agonizing situation or eliminate the possibility of something magnificent. Like most women, even at my age, I still longed to be pursued and cherished with tender romance delighting my heart. The results of waiting on God's plan might spare me additional pain or could perhaps lead me into an adventure more breathtaking than the stunning scenery I'd soon experience.

Viking staff met all of us going on the cruise at London's Heathrow airport. They took our luggage and shepherded us onto a bus that drove us to the Greenwich pier on the Thames River. After finding my cabin and unpacking, I stopped for a margarita in the atrium then headed into the dining room. It was late.

"Could I please be seated at a table with others?" I asked the maître d'.

"I'm so sorry, but most of the passengers have already eaten. I will make sure you are placed at a nice table with a view. Seated by a window, I looked out over the river.

Here I was in Europe with a fabulous dinner set before me. Alone. With a sigh, I realized it certainly wasn't the way I might have envisioned. But at least I was comfortable in my own skin, and the view was breathtaking. Even if I met no one, for the next 15 days I'd embrace the luxurious trip. Tomorrow, I'd explore the Tower of London with a tour. Toward evening we'd set sail for Edinburgh, the Orkney and Shetland Islands, then up the coast of Norway to the Arctic Circle. My fantasy vacation was beginning and, whether alone or in a group, I determined to savor every moment.

Into the Midnight Sun

Though this smaller ship lacked many of the glamorous features I'd appreciated on past cruises, my one goal was to see Norway and this vessel could get into the fjords where many of the larger ones couldn't. Without my mother to rush me, I began reveling in new adventures and listening to the stories of my traveling companions over meals or in the lounges while at sea. Hearing about my love affair with a Norwegian, Mark and Kim became instant friends especially after being serendipitously seated together at dinner three times.

At one of those meals, while enjoying our camaraderie, I left my comfort zone to try reindeer meatballs!

During the bus tour of Edinburgh, Queen Elizabeth and her entourage along with dreary rain prohibited a decent view of the Holyrood palace, however, jet lag made me glad to return to the ship for a long nap before cocktails in the foyer. A good night's sleep and leisurely morning the next day prepared me to see the green grasses of the Orkney and Shetland Islands. Imagining harsh long winters in the rugged environment, I watched ocean waves crash against rocky cliffs. Homes grouped together provided community where neighbors must have relied upon one another without the luxury of quick trips to the market or fast-food establishments. Though the scenery seemed peaceful enough in the summertime, it would be a stark place to live for a family, much less for a single woman in the winter.

Yet, sometimes along with the loneliness of being single, a sense of liberty comes with not having to accommodate anyone else. Selfish perhaps, but this lifestyle certainly hadn't been my choice. Somehow the single life had chosen me despite my intense desire for a family of my own. But rather than waste the years hoping for something that might not ever happen, the decision to be content gave me true freedom.

In some ways, perhaps the freedom of choice had caused me to love Tim even more than Jan—because our marriage required choosing love, day by day. Because I did not want a second divorce, it had been extremely difficult. For two years I'd grieved that loss and how our inabilities tore my family apart.

Now, watching couples on the ship reminded me of that grief and yet, I appreciated that sometimes we are better off alone. Regardless, I didn't really have to be lonesome, ever. Whenever I stood on my balcony, whether in the bright sunshine at noon or the twilight at 3:00 a.m., Christ's presence made itself known through the splendor of His creation.

July's weather was frigid in Honningsvag (Norway's northernmost city). Zipping ourselves into bright yellow and black cold-weather suits for the King Crab Safari, we boarded an open-air rigid inflatable boat and mounted pommel-horse-type seats. Sitting single file, I chose to be in front honoring my passion for flying across the water at high speed. I hadn't been on a small boat in years and never one like this. After gliding across the waterway, we cruised to a brief stop so our guides could empty the crab pots that yielded our lunch.

Continuing to our destination, we arrived at the dock where I stepped out onto the pier with the others. Laughing with sheer joy, someone handed me a writhing crustacean that stretched from the top of my head almost to my knees. After a demonstration on how to prepare these delicacies for cooking, our guides led us into a Sami teepee. Wooden benches covered with furry white-and-brown reindeer skins surrounded an open fire with a huge kettle containing the crabs hanging over it. My fellow travelers and I found places to sit, then soon feasted on sweet crabmeat boiled in saltwater from the sea and served with a plain aioli. After our scrumptious lunch, we exited the teepee to encounter a herd of reindeer on the nearby hillside.

The Husky Hike in Tromsø made me grateful for all the squats and lunges I'd been doing at the gym. After donning tall black rubber boots, our guide cinched a leather belt around my waist attaching me to a "husky." This exuberant canine was in summer training for the Iditarod.

Unlike the Siberian huskies I'd envisioned, Jack looked more like a small golden lab with a comical smile. He probably wore that grin in his determination to pull me face down into the thick black sludge through which we trekked. But by demonstrating my authority over him, I stayed on my feet. After the hike, our group cuddled sweet Siberian pups more in keeping with the images of the huskies I'd seen on television.

At an opulent farm near Lofoten, our host confirmed what Jan had mentioned years earlier—exorbitant taxes can require as much as 70 percent of a person's income. Perhaps the scrumptious tea the landowner and his daughters prepared for us helped offset some of their expenses. Another day I visited a thrift shop that catered to the homeless proving that suffering exists around the world regardless of government intervention.

Shadows of Jan's presence remained with me everywhere I went, especially while wandering through the seaside fish market in Bergen. Food vendors hawked their wares while stirring huge pans of paella, its steam mingling with the crowds. Display cases featured king crab along with many other fragrant morsels unrecognizable to me. If we were in our younger years, and Jan were with me, I'd delight in listening to him speak Norwegian and ordering delectable food and fruity sangria. After a scrumptious lunch where I might taste foods foreign to me, we'd likely return to our hotel room for dessert.

As enticing as that reverie was, I wouldn't have traded my life for that illusion. Romanticizing the possibilities didn't change the realities of children growing up without their dad at home except for visits. Worry about his well-being. The potential for another woman. Like my dad. Perhaps as Jan had gotten older, he'd settled down. Regardless, he was no longer the same 25-year-old navigator I'd once known. Nor was I that same naive young woman.

Acting upon my feelings, instead of trusting in Christ, I'd have missed out on countless days spent watching my sons play soccer and water polo with my husband coaching their teams. There wouldn't have been any writers' conferences or interactions with scientists. The struggles of trying to make financial ends meet that proved God's faithfulness to provide might have been eliminated. The living out of stories filled with meaning and purpose probably wouldn't have happened. I'd be a different person.

Even more important, I'd learned the world didn't revolve around me or my needs and/or wants. Choosing love for my husband and challenging coworkers had also taught me to choose love for those with differing worldviews, differing skin tones, and differing sexual preferences. It was the kind of love that encompassed a spirit of truth and kindness.

After more than two weeks of exploring new territory on my own, I was quite content to go home. So instead of trying something unfamiliar in Bergen's seafood market, I sought out a favorite— fish and chips with a glass of white wine at an outdoor café under a bright blue sky. It was a lovely afternoon.

After eating, I walked up the street to ride Bergen's funicular to the top of Mount Floyen. A spectacular view of the city and harbor greeted me. On the way back to the hotel, I ran into new friends from the ship and joined them for wine and an early evening snack. The entire trip marked the beginning of a new season of life, one where anything could happen including getting sick.

That night, I started coming down with a cold, but it didn't diminish the glorious train ride from Bergen to Oslo. Awe-inspiring scenery kept me glued to the window for the entire seven hours.

Upon arrival in Oslo, we toured the city and I remained fascinated, especially by the 212 Vigeland sculptures in Frogner Park. The nakedness of these bronze and granite human bodies seemed eerily chilling as babies and adults appeared to climb over each other in their attempt for supremacy. Though stunning, the sculpture seemed a godless portrayal of humankind's attempt to exert power over their fellow human beings, all the way from birth to old age. Far better to surrender to the Lord of life and treat one another as He intended—with love, honor, and dignity based on equality from conception to the grave.

Combined with not feeling well, after exploring the park, I was more than ready to return home. The home where I'd played as a child. The same place I once shared with two husbands, two sons, and for a moment in time with Jan. By God's amazing intervention, my home belonged to me. By His astonishing power, it had been rescued from its dysfunctional past and was in the process of being re-imagined.

That's where I belonged, at least for now. Because that's where life's wild ride would continue.

Chapter 22

Mysteries Resolved

Brutal reality set in quickly, guarding me against fantasy thinking. After 18 days of luxury, I traveled for about 26 hours with a vicious head cold. With apologies to the mom of the young boy who sat next to me on the flight from London, all I wanted was to be home snuggled in my own bed. Yet heavy rains delayed our flight from Europe making many of us miss our connections. Spending the night in the Dallas airport among strangers, who were probably as grumpy as I was, I cuddled up in a hard plastic chair where sleep eluded me. In the wee hours of the morning, airport workers came mercifully passing out blankets and small pillows. Looping my purse over my arm and my backpack under my legs so they wouldn't get stolen, I laid on the cool linoleum floor to rest and doze.

When the long overnight hours came to an end, I ate breakfast, then waited until noon for my flight home. Finally walking in my front door, there was no doubt the delay—as miserable as it was—had been for my good. Miranda, the young neighbor who watered my plants, told me that after she let Brian know I wouldn't return until the following day, he worked until midnight clearing a pathway so I could maneuver between the family room and bathroom. Every other room was a shambles.

Despite 105° heat, the air conditioning had been turned off. It could have been worse. While I was away, the electricians had worked through several days of 113°+ heat. Because I returned on Friday, they wouldn't be back for a couple of days. With a nearby fan offering an inadequate breeze, I tried to rest on a terribly uncomfortable couch.

The timing of my trip couldn't have been more strategic. Brian and his crew had moved all my furniture to the center of each room creating plastic-lined walkways around it. Day by day, they made progress. Within a week the obstacle course improved. Within a month, not only was the electrical finished, but new granite countertops also made me feel like I'd been transported to a palace.

Though it's been a few years since then, every morning I still wake up with a profound sense of gratitude. New upgraded linoleum looks like the travertine floors I'd long admired—yet it's far easier to maintain. The brilliance of recessed lighting brightens every room. A doorbell reveals who's there before I answer it. And, I finally replaced the old hand-me-down wicker bedroom furniture that was long past its prime.

So many unexpected changes transformed my home into a refuge—a place of beauty and peace. Another unanticipated development brought even greater satisfaction.

Long-Awaited Answers

Months after my trip, a little more than a year after my mother's memorial—on the morning of December 20, 2018—the phone rang. Janet rarely called so hearing her voice started my heart racing. Sitting down, I braced myself for bad news.

Her voice quivered as she spoke. "Diane, Suzie, and I just got off the phone with our friend from the DPAA. They know what happened to Daddy. His plane was shot down by Chinese soldiers as it flew alongside a Laotian supply road. DNA evidence disclosed that the entire crew died instantly."

This news poured over me like a bucket of iced water. Bursting into tears, I struggled to regain my composure. Shaken to the core, I wanted/needed to hear more, but the tears wouldn't stop streaming down my face. Janet waited patiently for my crying to subside, then explained how the DPAA surmised that bullets hit our dad's side of the plane first, then the pilot's. Their C-123 spiraled out of control before it nose-dived into the ground. No one could have survived.

For 47 years that had been my hope, that he'd died instantly without suffering. Yet, along with tremendous relief, the reality that my dad was dead and never coming back brought startling heart-wrenching grief—emotions long repressed by not knowing. Soon his remains, consisting only of a few bone fragments, could come home.

Of all the Air America crewmembers still missing, our dad's site was the first excavated. Diane and Janet's perseverance, plus a divine hand of grace, orchestrated that dig. These findings finally permitted my sisters and me to mourn our father's death.

Serendipity

Early in 2018 we had a Townley girls' sister/cousin lunch at the Cask & Cleaver. Gathered around our usual table in the warmth of the bar—Diane, Suzie, Janet, and Nancy voiced their excitement over booking a cruise around the Hawaiian Islands for March 2019. Finally, a getaway Janet could take Chuck on. I was thrilled for her. Taking care of her husband still involved extremely hard work every day, and he couldn't even say her name. This way he could enjoy being on the ship while she got to have some fun.

Yet, within a few weeks as harsh reality set in, Janet decided to cancel. Chuck's limitations were simply too severe. Once again, she was disappointed.

Months later at a government briefing about our dad—Janet, Diane, and Suzie learned specifics. Using mitochondrial DNA is the most effective way to make a positive identification. With DNA from my Aunt Eileen (his sister), Nancy (his niece), and her son, Steve, Daddy's ID was confirmed.

By now, the small bone fragments recovered from the excavation were located at Hickam Air Force base *in Hawaii*. Much like the timing of my trip to Norway, it "just happened" that Diane, Suzie, and Nancy had already booked a tour of Hickam for March 18, 2019. Determined not to miss out—Janet and Diane's daughter, Vicki, who also adored my dad, flew in to meet them and attend the hand-off. For years Vicki, too, had taken care of her husband who had suffered a traumatic brain injury, so being able to get away and share that time with Janet was a special gift.

None of us realized the extent of the respectful and dignified ceremony Hickam orchestrated to honor our family's sacrifice or Valerie and I might have gone too. Placed in a beautiful blue urn, Daddy's bone fragments were handed over to Janet to bring home.

The rest of the remains from the flight crew were so commingled that someday they may be buried in a joint grave. Although we'd hoped for Arlington, that didn't happen and the status for how to proceed remains unclear.

Sweet and Painful, Side by Side

On Easter Sunday 2019, the local newspaper ran a feature article on the front page of the newspaper honoring Roy F. Townley. It included my favorite photo of him in the pilot's seat. Another showed us, his very proud daughters, standing by his memorial tree in Upland. Janet held his blue urn as we laughed while telling the photographer how special our dad was.

That unforgettable night Josh's son, Caleb, my only grandson, was stillborn in the Philippines. Although that's another story, it conveys the dichotomies of living in the real world.

Occasionally someone contacts us to say they still have one of Daddy's MIA bracelets. Recently I spoke with Diane from Texas, who found his bracelet among her mother's things that had been put out for a yard sale. Googling my dad's name, she found the *Daily Bulletin's* story, then searched my name on Facebook. Her mother's friend, Carol, had worn the bracelet and prayed for my dad. A sweet quadriplegic, Carol had been injured in a motorcycle accident, much like my niece's husband, Kelley.

The reality is that regardless of circumstances, life goes on. Sometimes it's hard. Sometimes it's good. Occasionally the truth behind a mystery seems to take forever to arrive. Yet when it does, time can be erased in an instant. So can distance as our lives touch others far beyond our hometowns.

Sometimes the truth in our lives brings joy. Quite often it brings grief, pain, and suffering. If pain-filled challenges lead to denial, the problems multiply over time. Unfortunately, that's the way of life in a world marred by irresponsibility, challenging relationships, pandemics, power grabs, natural disasters, and sin. How much better when we learn to love others as ourselves. But we can't do that unless we learn how to love ourselves by staying in the truth, then treating ourselves with the gentle kindness and comfort of Christ.

Mysterious Justice

The year 2020 may go down in history as the year that changed everything. On Facebook, I watched COVID-19 exacerbate the political divide. As this wicked virus stole the lives of many, I saw friends follow the example of President Trump with arrogance and childish name calling sending mixed messages. Vicious rhetoric also stoked racial fires of injustice against African Americans and increased hate crimes among Asians. At the same time, Trump increased job and educational opportunities for Blacks and prevented the slaughter of many unborn babies made in the image of God. Many Republicans rallied around him as a result of his policies.

On the other hand, civil unrest intensified as the tragic deaths of a few African Americans, like George Floyd, at the hands of a few nefarious police officers dominated the nightly news. At the same time, numerous murders went unnoticed in cities like Chicago and many died at the hands of those in their own tribes.

The nightly news showed fires of destruction burning in cities like Portland and Seattle, yet Democrat politicians called the riots "peaceful protests" while choosing to ignore militants who destroyed police stations, tore down historical monuments, and assaulted those doing their best to maintain law and order. As a result, businesses were destroyed and people died.

Midway into 2021, there's concern that the backlash against conservatives may fuel additional atrocities as millions have been denounced and ignored by a liberal administration that seems to lump them together with domestic terrorists. Politicians and famous media stars contribute to the rhetoric threatening reeducation camps, deprogramming, and forced indoctrination into destructive agendas. Lawsuits and attacks on biblical principles may well escalate putting people like me at greater risk than COVID did.

Mysterious Marriage

Having failed at marriage twice, God's grace has continued showing me the value of a covenantal commitment within my own family. Both Janet and Vicki experienced the "worse" side of their vows as "in sickness" has meant continually caring for and loving men unable to take care of themselves. These courageous women insist that only God deserves the credit for getting them through the trials they've experienced.

Rather than going on trips that were not in her husband's best interests, Janet made difficult sacrifices to care for his needs. In that hard process, she came upon an inspiring solution. With her inheritance from our mom, she bought a truck and trailer that accommodates her husband's needs and delights his heart while they travel to places like the Colorado River with a fun bunch of people. Those outings have nourished and restored love between them.

Marriage is about so much more than sex. It's about the kind of love Janet has demonstrated for Chuck—and he for her. Although he still can't say her name, he shows it in the way he looks at her, laughs with her, and appreciates who she is. The same held true for Vicki until Kelley's death. As hard as her life became after his accident, she still misses him.

If Jan and I had known how to honor biblical principles perhaps we might have become mature enough for that kind of love. As it was, neither of us were ready for the kind of sacrifices marriage requires. Did our love last? That remains a mystery.

Mysterious Family

From California to Florida, from Canada to Mexico to the Philippines and beyond—I've built relationships with people I consider family. Some are family by birth, like my sisters, cousins, and sons or by marriage like my Filipina daughter-in-law, Clyde.

Many are family by blood, Christ's blood. We are children of the living God. Whether I'm sick or afraid or in financial need, my sisters and brothers in Christ are there for me. It's taken time, patience, and grace to build relationships, but over the years this family has brought me great joy and stirred me to do more with my life than I thought possible. They rejoice with me when things go right. And cry with me when things go wrong. Most important of all, they pray for me, and I can't wait to see all the ways those prayers were answered once I get to heaven. That's where I'll meet Diane from Texas and Carol, the woman who prayed for my dad. Maybe his being found was not only in answer to our prayers but also an answer to hers.

Mysterious Eternity

In August 2021, news headlines proclaimed that thousands were attempting to flee Kabul after the Taliban takeover in Afghanistan. My Facebook feed contains heart-wrenching pleas for prayer as my brothers and sisters in Christ are being hunted down and killed. Many, including women and children, are suffering unspeakable acts of evil.

After a 7.2 earthquake in Haiti left thousands injured, heavy rains from Tropical Storm Grace hampered rescue efforts. Until I received her email, I wondered if my sweet sister-in-Christ, a young physician's assistant who lives there providing medical aid for the poor, was still alive. Thankfully I received an email from her letting me know she's OK and asking for prayer.

At over 1,300 square miles, the monstrous Dixie fire is the second largest in California's history. It has ravaged many towns and lives including Sierra Bible Camp. The fire destroyed 21 buildings, some that had been used since the camp opened 67 years ago.

Hurricane Ida recently wreaked havoc on Louisiana and Mississippi and beyond. Rumor has it that power outages may persist for up to a month. As of yet, no one knows how many died.

Terror. Mayhem. Destruction and devastation. Death. There's no escape, not even for those committed to live for Jesus. Horrific tragedies are part of the world we live in.

The COVID-19 pandemic continues to claim victims from San Diego to New York City and around the world. For more than a year, some were so afraid, they didn't go outside for months at a time. Now, despite the vaccine, fear is starting to spread again with the new Delta variant. On the other hand, many are so afraid of the vaccine that if government mandates are enforced, they may lose their jobs rather than get it.

Fear often dictates our behaviors. Staying in the truth has alleviated many of my deepest concerns as I remain determined to apply the biblical admonition to walk in a spirit of power and love and discipline.

Because some fear can be healthy, only Christ can give me the wisdom I need in that process. Fear of fire or hurricanes has caused many people to evacuate and that action may have saved their lives. In Afghanistan many Christians have gone into hiding for good reason. Totalitarian terrorism thrives on the fear of evil men being in power. When men rule according to godless standards, injustice reigns.

Can it happen here? Maybe.

After his experience in China, Dr. Yeh thinks it can. I think so too. And, I doubt it will be the result of any particular political party. Rather a godless mindset by those who reject America's underlying foundation of biblical principles like "All men were created equal" will stimulate injustice. Without a moral standard, unjust men in power will oppress those under their authority. Without regard for truth, integrity, and accountability, our culture has become steeped in lies that refocus us on narcissistic behavior, cheap sex, and social justice, which has no viable foundation.

If America ever experiences the terror of oppression, I hope I'll be bold like my Afghani brothers and sisters in Christ. Facing death, they refuse to deny their faith in the Almighty God who alone is worthy of our allegiance.

Whether suffering atrocities in Afghanistan, deplorable conditions in Haiti, or COVID 19, my Christian family knows that eternity is real. And, that keeps many of us living without fear of death. Still, no one wants the process to be painful or prolonged. I don't want to be tortured nor do I want to suffer from dementia like my mother did.

At times I still miss her. And I'm grateful for the financial inheritance she left that God has used to provide more than I ever expected. If we were doing her memorial service today, I'd make sure to mention our fun shopping trips, what a great bridge player she was, her divinity, and how she always took special care buying and wrapping gifts like my Windblown Girl.

My greatest hope for my mom and everyone I love is that they experience Christ's kingdom where there is no time, no tears, and no sickness. Where there is no reason to be afraid. Rather it's where we will always be safe and secure. In that place, there will be more stunning colors than we can fathom. More music and singing. More laughter and more and more. There, I'll forever be with those who know Jesus—miles and misunderstandings will no longer separate me from people who mean the most to me. Hopefully Jan will be among them.

Unlimited Life

After letting go of my relationship with Jan and choosing to follow Christ, I decided to cultivate faithfulness, obedience to my Creator, and a high view of life—treating all people as created in God's image. Learning His ways has made me increasingly aware that this world does not revolve around me nor does it offer justice apart from Jesus Christ.

All the challenges, and there have been many, have taught me to trust an ever-present, all-powerful, all-knowing Savior. Even when I didn't understand the past or couldn't comprehend the future, Jesus has proved trustworthy, and His Holy Spirit gives me all the comfort and strength I need. Most of all, I've learned that my God is always good regardless of circumstances.

For many years, I thought of the Windblown Girl as standing on that rock looking across the sea waiting for the one she loved. But after losing my mom, returning from Norway, and learning about my dad, a fresh and irresistible insight made itself known. The Windblown Girl represents anyone (female/male, rich/poor, young/old) who stands on the Rock of Christ with the Bible clutched in their hands as they look toward eternity with its kaleidoscope of dazzling splendor—far more spectacular than anything I've seen from the beaches of the Caribbean to the Norwegian fjords. And, someday we'll live there forever with the One who wipes away every tear— the One who loves us most.

Questions for Reflection

PART I Escaping the Pain

1. In her attempt to escape the pain, Patti went on a Caribbean cruise, got involved with a Norwegian lover, drank too much, and tried to avoid thinking about her problems. What do you do to try to escape the pain in your life, and how does that work for you?

2. Patti's third cruise had similarities to the Titanic. All the glamour and romance yet heading for a hidden iceberg. What situation in your life is putting you on a similar collision course, and how do you need to change direction?

3. Why do you think Patti's physical relationship with Jan far exceeded her relationship with her husband? How could this awareness impact your marriage for good?

4. The influence of Patti's dad resulted in her fears of being abandoned or betrayed by someone she loved. What are some of your biggest fears in terms of romantic relationships?

5. What cultural lies did Patti start to accept when deciding to become physically involved with Jan, and how did they cause her tremendous pain? How do you think people try to do this today?

6. Many today try to separate their emotions from a physical relationship. How is that problematic?

7. Patti also wanted someone who made family a high priority and someone worthy of her trust. What characteristics do you long for in your dream guy or girl?

8. As reality set in, how did Patti's attempt to escape the pain work out?

PART II Embracing the Pain

9. After she came into a relationship with Jesus, Patti still struggled with old sinful ways of trying to avoid pain. Patti used the train imagery to get back on track and stay there. How could that imagery make a difference in the way you run your life?

10. Discuss or reflect on how dying to "self" and surrendering to Christ can change your life?

11. Many people call Jesus their Savior, but struggle to make Him the Lord of their lives. What position does He have in your life, and is that enough to give you peace and keep you secure? Why or why not?

12. Patti experienced the whisperings of the Holy Spirit on many occasions. How have you experienced the leading of the Holy Spirit and what difference has that made?

13. Identify some of the ways that Jesus convinced Patti over the years of His constant presence and care. In what ways have you seen Christ's care for you even if you didn't recognize it at the time?

14. What are the significance and benefit of the anchors in Patti's story?

15. Losing her marriage, her sons moving away, a failing business, and almost losing her home could have destroyed Patti. How did the imagery of the Windblown Girl figurine help her not turn to self-destructive habits in her pain and grief?

16. How does being created in the image of God impact your identity (self), your sexuality, and social issues (justice)?

17. Reflect on the imagery of the Windblown Girl figurine. How does it inspire you and give you hope?

Acknowledgments

The first requirement for writing a memoir is living it. Sometimes that's not easy, which was certainly true for me. Therefore, the people who deserve the most credit are those who helped me navigate life's stormy seas.

This book could never have happened without the mighty prayers of Lois Voorman and others who prayed for me over the years including: Geri Sullivan, Kristen Wiggenhorn, John Setser, and Willi Muro. Faithful friends, they prayed, not only for the writing and a multitude of other details, but also for God to help me meet life's challenging circumstances. By listening, encouraging, and reading lengthy email updates, Lois has walked alongside of me for more than two decades. Her unwavering belief in me has kept me heading in the right direction.

Wendy Wood and Lynda Young have also walked with me through the years. They laughed and cried with me and prayed. In addition, each of them played a crucial role in bringing this book to fruition. Though any mistakes are mine, Wendy brought her excellent editing skills into the process, while Lynda also offered critical insights that made the manuscript better.

Wayne and Elizabeth Morin have also been faithful friends who helped me think as we talked over coffee after church every Sunday until the pandemic. Together, we've solved many problems and celebrated many milestones.

With frequent phone calls and ongoing support my sister Valerie has helped me think through the past and encouraged me in a multitude of ways. Sharing our birthdays always brings a special celebration and so do all the ways she's made me a part of her family. Val just makes my life better as do our sisters Diane, Suzie, and Janet, and our cousin Nancy.

Every individual named, and many more who were not mentioned, contributed to this book in inestimable ways, but none more than my dear friend, Jonathan Price. Not only did he lend his award-winning graphic design talents to this project, but he also helped shoulder the load during some of life's most ferocious storms. His generosity, encouragement, prayers, and kindness over the years have made him family.

About the Author

For the past decade, Patti Townley-Covert has concentrated her research, writing, and speaking on justice issues, especially those underlying human trafficking. While engaged in the fight against modern-day slavery at the local level in Pomona, California, and also in Los Angeles County, she co-wrote *Do ONE Thing: Enlisting in the Battle Against Human Trafficking*, which can be found at EveryOneFree.org/guide.

Writing for national/international magazines and journals since 1986, Patti has brought clarity to issues involving family dynamics, apologetics, diversity, and the value of life. Her feature stories tend to grab hearts and have won several awards.

Patti also helps other writers bring their books to the marketplace of ideas. She co-wrote *Love, Money, Power: A Believer's Journey into Reality* with John Setser and has edited numerous books for NASA-level scientists in the areas of astronomy and biochemistry. Editing the books of a philosopher/theologian expanded her worldview thinking. So did her many years in Bible Study Fellowship. In addition, she's edited dozens of doctoral dissertations on organizational leadership.

About once a year Patti goes on an adventure. The most memorable have involved cruises to the Caribbean, New England, Mexico, and up the coast of Norway to the Arctic Circle. In 2022 she plans to spend about two weeks in Alaska including a visit to Denali National Park.

You can check out Patti's blog or subscribe to her e-newsletter at **PTCovert.com/** That's where over time, you'll also find *The Windblown Girl* questions for reflection or book clubs and other related materials. You can contact Patti at ***patti@ptcovert.com***

Author's Note

I want to thank the people in this book who made a significant difference in my life. At the same time, I'm aware that their memories of the events I've described may be quite different from my own. Regardless, I'm grateful for the way each individual helped shape me as a person and caused me to think deeper than I ever could have otherwise. They motivated me to tell my story because I'm convinced that people need to confront the lies our culture promotes. *The Windblown Girl: A Memoir about Self, Sexuality, and Social Issues* was not intended to hurt anyone in any way. Rather it's my hope and expectation that many will benefit from its message of exchanging cultural lies for absolute truth—truth that transcends the tests of time and circumstances.

Please note that some names were changed; however, the details and dialogue are consistent with my memories.

Recommended Reading

Self

Baxter, J. Sidlow. *Does God Still Guide?* (Grand Rapids: Kregel, 1968).

Cloud, Henry, and John Townsend. *Boundaries: When to Say YES, When to Say NO to Take Control of Your Life.* (Grand Rapids: Zondervan, 1999).

Crouch, Andy. *Culture Making: Recovering Our Creative Calling.* (Downers Grove, IL: InterVarsity Press, 2008).

Elliot, Elisabeth. *The Path of Loneliness: It May Seem A Wilderness, But It Can Lead You To God.* (Nashville: Thomas Nelson, Oliver-Nelson Books, 1988).

Peck, M. Scott. *People of the Lie: The Hope for Healing Human Evil.* 2nd ed. (New York: Touchstone, A Division of Simon & Schuster, Inc., 1998).

Smyth, Alan with Kristy Fox. *Prized Possession: A Father's Journey in Raising his Daughter.* (Bloomington, IN: AuthorHouse, 2013).

Stone, Bob, and Mick Ukleja. *The Ethics Challenge: Strengthening Your Integrity in a Greedy World.* (Garden City, NY: MorganJames, 2009).

Storr, Will. *Selfie: How We Became So Self-Obsessed and What It's Doing to Us.* (New York: The Overlook Press, Peter Mayer, 2018).

Twenge, Jean M. *Generation Me: Why Today's Young Americans Are More Confident, Assertive, Entitled—and More Miserable Than Ever Before.* (New York: Atria Paperback, a division of Simon & Schuster, 2014.

Ukleja, Mick, and Robert L. Lorber. *Who Are You? What Do You Want: Four Questions That Will Change Your Life.* (New York: Penguin Group, 2009).

VanAuken, Sheldon, with eighteen letters by C. S. Lewis. *Severe Mercy.* (New York: HarperCollins, 1980.)

White, Jerry. *Honesty Morality & Conscience.* Thirteenth printing (Colorado Springs: NavPress, 1987.)

Sexuality

Elliot, Elisabeth. *Passion and Purity.* (Grand Rapids, MI: Revell, a division of Baker Publishing Group, 1984, 2002) Repackaged edition published 2013.

Gregoire, Sheila Wray, Rebecca Gregoire Lindenbach, and Joanna Sawatsky. *The Great Sex Rescue: The Lies You've Been Taught and How to Recover What God Intended.* (Grand Rapids: Baker Books, 2021)

Orenstein, Peggy. *Girls and Sex: Navigating the Complicated New Landscape.* Reprint Edition. (New York: Harper Paperbacks, May 2017)

Pearcey, Nancy. *Love Thy Body: Answering Hard Questions about Life and Sexuality.* (Grand Rapids, Baker Books, 2018).

Roys, Julie. *Redeeming the Feminine Soul: God's Surprising Vision for Womanhood.* (Nashville, TN: Nelson Books, HarperCollins Christian Publishing, 2017).

Sales, Nancy Jo. "The Young and the Rentless." *Vanity Fair.* No. 672, August 2016, pp. 86-92.

Stepp, Laura Sessions. *Unhooked: How Young Women Pursue Sex, Delay Love and Lose at Both.* (New York: Riverhead Books, Penguin Group, 2007.)

Wax, Trevin. *This is Our Time.* (Nashville: B & H Publishing Group, 2017.)

Social Issues

Allen, Scott. *Why Social Justice is Not Biblical: An Urgent Appeal to Fellow Christians in a Time of Social Crisis.* (Grand Rapids: Credo House Publishers, 2020).

Cho, Eugene. *Overrated: Are We More in Love with the Idea of Changing the World Than Actually Changing the World?* (Colorado Springs: David C. Cook, 2014).

Keller, Timothy. *Generous Justice: How God's Grace Makes Us Just.* (NY: Riverhead Books, Penguin Group, 2010).

Singleton, Opal. *Seduced: The Grooming of America's Teenagers.* (Maitland, FL: Xulon Press, 2015).

Through God's Grace Ministry. *How You Can Fight Human Trafficking: Over 100 Ways To Make A Difference* (Irvine, CA: 2014).

Stevenson, Bryan. *Just Mercy: A Story of Justice and Redemption.* Paperback edition. (New York: Spiegel & Grau, an imprint of Random House, 2015).

Williams, Thaddeus J. *Confronting Injustice without Compromising Truth: 12 Questions Christians Should Ask About Social Justice* (Grand Rapids: Zondervan Academic, 2020).

Fiction with Themes Involving Self and Sex

Charlotte Bronte. *Jane Eyre.* (New York: Barnes & Noble Books, 2003).

McCullough, Colleen. *The Thorn Birds.* (New York: HarperCollins, 1977).

Waller, Robert James. *The Bridges of Madison County*. (New York: Warner Books, 1992).

ALSO AVAILABLE FROM
PATTI TOWNLEY-COVERT

If you found *The Windblown Girl* transformative and/or intriguing, you may also enjoy *Love. Money. Power. A Believer's Journey Into Reality* by John Setser with Patti Townley-Covert

If you are so inclined, please post honest reviews on Amazon and/or Goodreads. Reviews help books get noticed so authors greatly appreciate them.

If you'd like to chat with Patti and other memoir authors and readers, join the friendly fun Facebook group, **We Love Memoirs** at Facebook.com/groups/welovememoirs/

Available on **Amazon.com**

Made in the USA
Las Vegas, NV
21 September 2022

55737247R00154